MARCUSE – Dilemma and Liberation

MARCUSE –
Dilemma and Liberation
A Critical Analysis

by John Fry

HUMANITIES PRESS ● NEW JERSEY
THE HARVESTER PRESS ● SUSSEX

Reprinted in 1978 by Humanities Press in
the United States of America and by
Harvester Press in Great Britain by
arrangement with the author.

(U.S.A.) ISBN 0 391 00872 2
(England) ISBN 0 85527 297 X

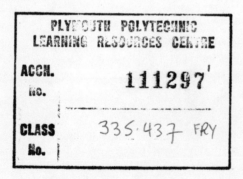
Printed in the United States of America

Contents

Introduction   7

Chapter One: **The Original Dilemma-Marcuse's Analysis**   11

Introduction   11

The end of inter-imperalist competition and rivalry   11

Arms spending as an effective long-term safety-valve   13

Technological advances and expanding affluence   13

The 'managed' economy   15

The effective containment of national liberation struggles in the Third
    World and their relatively insignificant impact on the stability of North
    American capitalism   16

The remaining fundamental contradiction in North American capitalism
    and potential crisis   17

Summary of economic propositions   19

The new working class: the impact of advanced technology on the struc-
    ture of the North American working class   20

Structural dislodgement and the basis and existence of working class
    consciousness in North America   22

Summary of propositions on alterations in working class structure and
    consciousness   25

The consequent theoretical and political dilemma   25

Chapter Two: **The ontological shift and its consequences**   28

Introduction   28

The ontological position before the shift   29

The dilemma overviewed   32

Idealism: its influence and return   34

The need for a new concept of essence   36

The necessity of a moral critique   38

The Freudian later instinct theory: the specifics of the concept of human
    essence   39

Summary of the nature and necessity of the ontological shift   42

From dilemma to vicious circle: the dilemma reinforced   44

The new method   48

Rethinking alienation   50

Rethinking of the realm of freedom and the realm of necessity   51

The notion of liberation   53

The new man   58

Students   60

Summary   65

Chapter Three: **Further Considerations of the Fundamental Economic Propositions and Implications**   68

Introduction   68

The freezing of inter-imperialist economic competition: further considerations   68

Arms spending, the unproblematic safety-valve: further considerations   86

The containment of the Third World and the economic insignificance of national liberation movements on North American economic stability and prosperity: further considerations   94

Effective national planning and the management of cyclical crises: further considerations   104

Summary: general crisis of North American capitalism   111

Chapter Four: **The Qritique of the Fundamental Social and Political Propositions and Implications**   116

Introduction   116

Unemployment and poverty: further considerations   116

The new working class and working class structure: further considerations   122

The basis and existence of working class consciousness: further considerations   134

The subjective and objective revolutionary potential of the North American student movement: further considerations   138

Chapter Five: **The New Ontology**   146

Conclusion   150

References   161

Bibliography   179

Introduction

> The mark of dialectical thinking is the ability to distinguish the essential
> from the apparent processes of reality and to grasp their relation. (1)
> (Herbert Marcuse, Reason and Revolution, p. 146).

Few contemporary thinkers have had as singular an impact on the theory,
analysis and praxis of the contemporary North American left as Herbert
Marcuse. Himself uncompromised through the witch-hunting of the fifties, he
has added a fresh and incisive perspective to the often dogmatic legacy of
North American pre-war Marxist thought. Most commonly referred to by the
establishment press as the 'prophet of the new left', his analysis of North
American society and his subsequent discussions of political praxis had far
reaching influence on the political analysis and praxis of the student movement
and counter-culture of the sixties and early seventies. His published works and
widespread lectures to student audiences have in significant measure provided
the analytical basis for and given theoretical coherence to the political protest
of these related movements.

One need only acquaint oneself with the debates pursued in these circles
concerning the problems of repression and social change in North America to
appreciate Marcuse's influence.

As for the academic 'new left', the significance of Marcuse's work is no less.
His socio-economic analysis and general views on the problems of repression
and liberation in America have focused upon numerous central issues and have
in many respects become reference points in the continuing analyses. On
theoretical grounds, his modification of Marxism through the introduction of
the Freudian later instinct theory in the fifties has become a point of central
controversy and influence in the ongoing debates in the North American left.

Marcuse's reception by these groups (left oriented students, members of the
'counter-culture', and the academic left), has by no means been totally favorable. But whether accepted in whole, in part, or totally rejected, his views on
tendencies in North American society, economy and culture have been consistantly provocative. Even with those who have 'transcended' Marcuse, the
imprint of his theoretical method and socio-economic analysis is frequently and
clearly detectable. However, the objective of this study is not a comprehensive
analysis of Marcuse's influence on the theory, analysis and political praxis of
the North American 'new left'. Rather, it is first an attempt to elaborate the
nature and implications of his own theory, socio-economic analysis and proposed general strategy for a liberating political praxis in North America.
Secondly, it is an effort to consider certain weaknesses of numerous key long

range social, economic and political tendencies which Marcuse attributes to contemporary North American society.

Perhaps it is inevitable when the often controversial theoretical and political views of a philosopher gain wide interest and currency, that misunderstandings and misinterpretations of their actual meaning and implications occur. One need only reflect on the reception and continuing debate regarding what Marx *really* meant. Indeed, in the heat of the social unrest in North America in the 60's and early 70's, the emergent popularity (and notoriety) of Marcuse's theoretical perspective and social analysis was accompanied by just such a diversity of interpretations. Within the academic left there remains substantial disagreement as to the meaning and implications of his theory and analysis.

Marcuse's particular style, as well as the novelty in North America of numerous of his concepts, appears to have only further aggravated the problem. Thus, one often finds certain aspects of Marcuse's analysis, his political proposals, or his theoretical points of departure, receiving favorable and/or unreserved reception by persons who in fact are in sharp disagreement with one or more of the often obscure, but necessarily attendent propositions and assumptions.

The fact that Marcuse has developed his analysis over a nearly two decade long period, a process marked by the adoption of series of propositions which were first formulated tentatively and only gradually worked intrinsically into the overall analysis and theoretical perspective, has further compounded the difficulty of appreciating the totality of his analysis and the full nature and implications of his theory. Thus, unclarities which often arise in the reading of, say, *An Essay on Liberation,* are due in large part to the necessity of being fully acquainted with the previous discussions and analyses Marcuse has pursued on related phenomena. More than most, his works have been continuing studies and rethinkings of some of the central issues in the general problems of repression and social change in North American society. At this point it should perhaps be added that neither Marcuse's influence nor his analyses have been confined to North America. However, it is there that his influence on the contemporary left has been most profound, and it is North American capitalism and society which (being in his view the most advanced) has been the primary focus of his analyses. Consequently, the critique of the main assumptions and propositions of his analyses of tendencies in advanced capitalist societies, will focus on the situation and apparent tendencies in North America. Only as they are obviously and immediately germane to such discussions in the context of Marcuse's analysis of social,e conomic and political tendencies in North America will developments outside this area be considered.

It is against the background of Marcuse's substantial influence upon the theoretical, social, economic and political discussions of the current North American left, and the substantial ambiguity of the meaning and implications of his ideas, that the objectives of this study should be defined.

8

Chapters one and two represent an attempt to sift through Marcuse's work of the past two decades or so and systematically elaborate what appear to be the fundamental tenets and conclusions in his analysis of the present realities and future long range tendencies in North American society and further, to consider the nature and implications of his subsequent revision of Marxism. It is largely on the basis of his socio-economic analysis that Marcuse arrives at the conclusion that a nearly insurmountable theoretical and political dilemma now faces Marxist theory and socialist revolutionary praxis.

According to Marcuse's analysis, the advances and achievements of technology, the end of inter-imperialist competition, the impact of sustained arms spending, and the effective cooperation between the state and big business in the planning and management of the economy, act and interact in such a way as to make probable the unforeseeably long range crisis-free stability of North American capitalism. Further, on this basis affluency, however 'counterfeit', has and will continue to rapidly spread to ever increasing proportions of the population within and even beyond North America. Consequently, the revolutionary potential of the North American working class has been effectively undercut as the long-range economic prognosis indicates the steady diminishment of the dimensions of economic insecurity and impoverishment—the traditiona *basis* of radical working class consciousness. What is more, the impact of the new technology in the factories of North America results in an unarrested long-range tendency towards the displacement of the traditional working class from the critical positions in the new productive apparatus, effecting a substantial undermining of their objective revolutionary potential. Thus, scientists, technicians and engineers, the indispensible candidates for these key positions in the nation's productive machinery, acquire a position of unprecedented objective revolutionary potential. However, sustained affluence undermines any subjective revolutionary potential in this group as well.

Marcuse is thereby confronted with the dilemma of on the one hand seeing the need and technological potential for a revolution (for he views the affluency and prosperity of North American society as counterfeit and perverted) while on the other hand being faced with an economic, social, political and psychological constellation so historically unique that it appears to ensure indefinite containment of the pregnant technological possibilities for liberation. Not only is traditional political strategy rendered largely inappropriate, but critical theory (Marxism) itself appears to emerge in this novel historical epoch as being conceptually inadequate for the tasks of analyzing this qualitatively new subject and subsequently of guiding further revolutionary praxis.

The problem therefore appears to be the necessity to revise critical theory so as to render it once again conceptually adequate to these tasks. The dilemma (the vicious circle) Marcuse has portrayed thereby acts as both the motivation and the justification for revising Marxism. At base this revision is achieved through the introduction of Freud's later instinct theory to act as the ontological point of departure for the new theory. This move appears designed to 're-vitalize' critical theory and entails a host of no so readily apparent theoretical consequences. Further, the introduction of libido (which he effects gradually, first in speculative and tentative terms, then later in an increasingly concrete and arbitrary manner), 'tightens' the initially perceived political dilemma, while at the same time offering a glimmer of hope for a break in the vicious circle. Students, the inevitable inheritors of the key positions in the new means of production, thus increasingly appear to manifest both objective revolutionary potential, and (according to Marcuse's psychoanalytic explanation of the roots of their rebellion) subjective revolutionary potential. Small wonder he has been so well received by them. It is always a compliment and a good source of support among a group to claim it to be the vital and indispensible center of the movement towards social change.

The second and related objective of this study is to assess the professed and implied universal validity of the long range tendencies he has foreseen and projected for North American economy and society. This task is pursued in turn in an attempt to evaluate Marcuse's self-declared justification for revising critical theory in an effort to render it conceptually more appropriate to the qualitatively new task at hand. In addition to evaluating his socio-economic justification for this rethinking and subsequent incorporation of the notion of libido into Marxism, an attempt will also be made to assess the epistemological status of this newly adopted ontological point of departure. This latter inquiry should consequently shed some light on the validity of the theoretical and political implications it has had for Marcuse's revised critical theory.

Given the very scope of the task involved in pursuing a further discussion of the main features of Marcuse's economic and social analysis as outlined above, it should be clear that no pretence to exhaustiveness shall or may be made. Further, it should be clear that inasmuch as this latter discussion is a consideration of possible and probable future tendencies, these considerations of Marcuse's positions are in large measure an attempt to indicate probable modifications or reversal of the tendencies he has depicted and which play such a central role in his entire study of repression and liberation. Nevertheless the arguments and data both presented and referred to should be adequate to demonstrate that there exist substantial grounds for questioning the universal validity of Marcuse's numerous long-range prognoses. Further, they should provide substantial grounds for a critical reconsideration of his insistence upon the vital necessity to revise critical theory in order to meet the analytical and political demands of a qualitatively new social, economic and political constellation in North America. In short, inasmuch as Marcuse's analysis makes the case for certain tendential developments, the discussions in chapters three and four of this study will attempt to point out significant tendencies not considered by Marcuse and which tend in varying degrees to detract from the strength of his overall argument for the necessity of revising critical theory.

Chapter One:

The Original Dilemma—Marcuse's Analysis

Introduction

> Confronted with the total character of the achievements of advanced industrial society, critical theory is left without the rational for transcending this society. (1)

Inasmuch as it is the political dilemma which Marcuse perceives in North America which represents the fundamental justification and motivation for his subsequent rethinking of critical theory (Marx), it seems appropriate to begin this study with an elaboration of the propositions central to that dilemma. Whether or not one subscribes to Marcuse's analysis, these key propositions may be seen to cover a range of problems of obvious relevance to the issues of repression and social change in advanced industrial societies. Either in whole or part, the views espoused by Marcuse enjoy wide currency among the North American left. Consequently their elaboration and consideration will hopefully have a certain value outside the immediate problem of the strength of Marcuse's justification for revising critical theory.

The end of inter-imperalist competition and rivalry

> As to the West: the former conflicts within society are modified and arbitrated under the double (and inter-related) impact of technical progress and international communism. Crass struggles are attenuated and 'imperalist contradictions' suspended before the threat from without. Mobilized against this threat, capitalist society shows an internal union and cohesion unknown at previous stages of industrial civilization . . ., mobilization against the enemy works as a mighty stimulus of production and employment, thus sustaining a high standard of living. (2)

Herein lie the key features of Marcuses analysis of North American capitalism. The pivotal argument in this analysis is his insistence that interimperalist competition and rivalry have been effectively superseded by a heretofore unknown, even unimaginable (3), degree of North American-dominated, non-competitive economic cohesion and integration. Contrary to Marx's steadfast insistance that the basis for 'long-term' inter-capitalist cooperation and consolidation could never emerge (4), Marcuse argues that such a basis could and did develop . . .

> . . . very gradually and with many regressions and breaks, under the impact of two world wars, atomic productivity and the growth of Communist Power. These events altered the structure of capitalism as defined by Marx and created the basis of a new economic and political organization of the Eastern World. From then on, the conflicting competitive interests among the Western nations were gradually integrated and superseded by the fundamental East-West Conflict, and an intercontinental political economy took shape . . . susceptible to a planned regulation of that 'blind anarchy' in which Marxism saw the root of capitalist contradictions. (5)

In Marcuse's view, the main factor influencing the subsiding of this inter-imperialist competition was the emergence and sustained power of the Soviet Union. The very presence on the world politico-economic scene of this 'enemy of all capitalism' (6), fostered an 'unprecedented' inter-imperialist cohesion transcending the normally characteristic competition. The common capitalist fear of being outstripped economically and militarily led both individual capitalists and formerly competing capitalist nations to put aside economic rivalry, reconciling any contradictions which might have the consequence of disrupting this 'united front' against the 'enemy'. Indeed, Marcuse argues that capitalism might long ago have succumbed to the 'normal' crisis and contraditions anticipated by Marx, had not this enemy emerged (or been invented). (7)

As to the Soviet Bloc, the dilemma was seen to be that on the one hand necessary preparedness against possible Western aggression (8) perpetuated the strengthening of politico-military power, while on the other, these very Soviet developments served to further reinforce the unity, cohesion and smooth functioning of the international capitalist economy inasmuch as they are publicly construed as further evidence of the strategic necessity for sustained Western cohesion and cooperation at all levels.

> But the continual strengthening of the Soviet political and military establishment in turn perpetuates the 'capitalist environment' and even promotes its intercontinental unification. (9)

As a result, the further development of socialism in the Soviet Bloc is deflected and delayed (perhaps even retarded) because its priority must necessarily remain the defense of its political-geographical integrity amid the surrounding hostile and potentially aggressive capitalist environment.

In this reciprocal reinforcement of North American dominated, inter-imperialist stability and progress and Soviet 'totalitarian' consolidation lies the root of Marcuse's dilemma. His proposals for liberation at this juncture (1953–1954) therefore focus largely on the need to undermine this intercontinental political economy by ending the arms race. (10)

Arms spending as an effective long-term safetyvalve

The emergence of the 'enemy' had resulted in the unique creation of a durable, cohesive and crisis-free capitalist political, military and economic front. The consequent transcendence of the characteristic intra- and inter-capitalist competition, rivalry and general and periodic crises had given the system a new and even unforeseeably long-term lease on life.

However, the cohesion and cooperation based on the fear of the 'enemy' is not the only source of capitalism's renewed vitality and longevity. Intrinsically related to this fear of communism is the emergence of a sustained and continually expanding defense economy. It is the merging of these vast expenditures with the initial fear of the enemy that further explains the long-range trend towards greater capitalist stability.

> 'world communism' has been the enemy who would have to be invented if he did not exist—the Enemy whose strength justified the 'defense economy' and the mobilization of the people in the national interest (11) ... Once justified and set in motion, this 'defense economy' develops a dynamic of its own. (12)

Indeed, related to the existence of the enemy, the rapidly expanding defense economy seems to further facilitate the transcedence of inter-imperialist competition and contradictions.

> The break is expected to come about through the reactivation of the 'inherent capitalist contradictions' in the 'imperialist camp'. They are frozen in the Western defense economy ... (13)

By providing an enormous self-renewing market (through rapid obsolescence and use), for a growing sector of the capital productive apparatus, the 'defense' requirements alleviated the major strains and stresses on an otherwise contradiction and crisis plagued economy. Capitalism's intrinsic need to expand in order to secure investment opportunities and markets for its growing capital and commodity surpluses was thus supplied with an effective and long-term safety-value—an economic regulator providing the maximum in flexibility and the minimum in problems.

As a result, Marcuse argues that complemented with the increases in the production of 'junk' (unnecessary products for private consumption) (14), the burgeoning arms race has perhaps supplied the final answer to capitalism's perpetual question of where and in what to invest. Consequently, he comes to view the arms economy as a general economic panacea and an effective cure-all for the characteristic economic strains and crisis of capitalism. (15)

Technological advances and expanding affluence

The self-perpetuating dialectic which emerges from the interaction between the sustained strength and subsequent fear of the 'enemy' on the one hand and the increasing defense expenditures on the other, gives sharp impetus to yet another stabilizing and reinforcing development. Both through direct and indirect military research the pace of technological advance is accelerated enormously. Spurred initially in the postdepression period by the military demands of World War II, the technological sophistication of the U.S. productive apparatus emerged at s superior level in the aftermath of the conflict.

This advanced level of technological sophistication combined with the other economic benefits accruing to North America as a result of the conflict lay the basis for her postwar world economic pre-eminence. Thus, the simultaneous emergence of the enemy and the sustained arms expenditures led not only to the West's immediate and acquiescent subjection to politico-economic dominance by North America, but these developments in turn led both directly and indirectly to technological advances which further increased the productivity of North American capitalism. The scientific and technological developments achieved through the quest for more effective weaponry systems frequently had both direct and indirect favorable consequences for the productive process at large. (16)

As the leader of the defense against the 'enemy' and with its enormously strengthened postwar economic position, North American capitalism was quite naturally the most heavily engaged in this hastened technological research and development and therefore the primary recipient of its benefits. The tendencial increase in the organic composition of capital was in turn spurred by the availability of technological advances and opportunities.

In Marcuse's view, the outcrop of these inter-related developments was the undisputed superiority of North American capitalism. This basic factor, plus the ensuent opportunities for international and domestic trade, complemented the unifying impact of the fear of the 'enemy', thus ensuring the continued expansion of North American economic, political and cultural dominance in the capitalist world. The development appeared to be only the beginning of an 'unforeseeably' long range trend towards increased capitalist stability and progress.

Resultingly, Marcuse argues that North American capitalism reveals a parallel long range capacity for delivering an increasing quantity and diversity of goods and services to a growing proportion of the domestic (and even external) (17) population (18). Indeed, he suggests that two of the most significant (and permanent) characteristics of the contemporary system are,

> (I) an abundant industrial and technical capacity which is to a great extent spent in the production and distribution of luxury goods, gadgets, waste, planned obsolescence, military and semimilitary equipment—in short, in what economists and sociologists used to call 'unproductive' goods and services; (2) a rising standard of living, which also extends to previously underprivileged parts of the population . . . (19)

Again, it should be emphasized that Marcuse perceives this tendency as an 'unforeseeably' long-range one (20). Intrinsically connected with the contradiction-transcending consequences of the 'enemy', sustained arms spending and unprecendented technological advances, this unparalleled affluency seems to testify to the system's progressiveness, and its ability to deliver the goods for an indefinitely long period of time. It should be mentioned in passing, however, that while Marcuse views this affluencey as more or less permanent, and expanding, he also sees it more as a coincidental by-product of, or complement to the system, more rather than its central goal.

> the satisfaction of needs is far more the by-product than the end of capitalist society. (21)

As a result of the conclusions of his analysis, Marcuse finds himself in the somewhat peculiar position of generally sharing the 'celebrationists' (22) depiction of developments in North American society, while at the same time rejecting the 'progressiveness' of the prevalent 'affluency'. It is seen rather as a perverted and restrictive form of affluency, which although making more pleasant man's subjugation to man, serves nevertheless to perpetuate it. (23)

The achievements of this society militare against the emergence of radical thought and action (24), since the abundant and readily available commodities of the productive apparatus sell not only themselves, but also the system which produces them. (25)

> But here, advanced industrial society confronts the critique with a situation which seems to deprive it of its very basis. Technical progress extended to a whole system of domination and coordination, creates forms of life (and of power) which appear to reconcile the forces opposing the system and to defeat or refute all protest in the name of the historical prospects for freedom from toil and domination. Contemporary society seems to be capable of containing social change—qualitative change which would establish essentially different institutions, a new direction of the productive process, new modes of human existence. This containment of social change is perhaps the most singular achievement of advanced industrial society. (26)

Thus:

> Productivity and prosperity in league with technology in the service of monopolistic politics seems to immunize advanced industrial society in its established structure. (27)

The 'managed' economy

Intrinsically related to the developments discussed above, Marcuse further argues that as a result of effective state and big business cooperation, planning and management, even the periodic cyclical crises which for so long were a salient characteristic of capitalist production and development, have been successfully controlled and avoided (28). Freed from these more or less regular disruptions. North American capitalism has been able to better ensure continued prosperity and stability. (29)

As the result of an unprecedented concentration of economic power and effective government interventions and cooperation in the management of the economy, disruptive discrepencies between supply and effective demand are being circumvented (30). In these developments lies yet another present and tendencial characteristic of contemporary North American capitalism.

> Traditional trouble spots are being cleaned out or isolated, disruptive elements taken in hand. The main trends are familiar: concentration of the economy on the needs of the big corporations, with the government as a stimulating, supporting, and sometimes even controlling force. (31)

Consequently, Marcuse feels certain that these tendencies towards increasing and effective state intervention and cooperation in economic management are merely the initial manifestations of an unforeseeably long-range trend which shall develop further as the 'dominant interests' perceive more clearly the necessity and benefits of adjusting the economy to the demands of the welfare state.

> Vastly increased government spending and direction, planning on a national and international scope, an enlarged foreign aid programme, comprehensive social security, public works on a grand scale, perhaps even partial nationalization belong to these requirements. (32)

The effective containment of national liberation struggles in the third World and their relatively insignificant impact on the stability of North American capitalism

Clearly Marcuse is aware of the exploitative relationship which exists between North America and Third World (33). In fact he stresses that the only truly revolutionary struggles now taking place against capitalism are those being fought in these areas (34). Further he points out the apparent relationships between these struggles and the radical political activity present and emerging in North America (35). Fundamentally, this latter argument lays stress on the impact which these struggles, and the general plight of the 'wretched of the earth', have upon the emergent revolutionary consciousness in North America by a sort of 'pricking' of the moral conscience of the 'new left' (the new revolutionary subject). The suffering and the struggle of peoples of the Third World, establish the essential example of solidarity and determination which the new left in North America may then emulate. (36)

Apart from this assessment of the character and consequences of Third World and the political developments therein, Marcuse's evaluation of their potential disruptive impact on the North American capitalist system is basically negative (37). He insists that the powers that be (U.S.A.) have had in the past and will continue to have in the future the military, political and economic resources; the resolution and determination, and the domestic public support, to effectively prevent any further revolutionary successes in these areas.

> The powers that be will not tolerate a repetition of the Cuban example. (38)

In consequence, he urges these Third World liberation struggles to recognize that they work only at 'preparation' (39) inasmuch as there can be no realistic hope for their success at this historical juncture.

> He insists that, the preconditions for the liberation and development of the Third World must emerge in the advanced capitalist countries. (40)

Therefore:

> All forces of opposition today are working at preparation and only at preparation ... for a possible crisis in the system. (41)

For the 'wretched of the earth', the dilemma is as follows:
Their struggle must continue and expand where possible (as preparatory work), while tempered by the necessary appreciation that there can be no hope for real success until American society and economy have been weakened by internal crisis and revolutionary struggle.

> Only the internal weakening of the superpower can finally stop the financing and equipping of surpression in the backward countires. (42)

Therefore:

> The chain of exploitation must be broken at its strongest link. (43)

Given his perception of the probable long-term future trends in North American capitalist stability and affluency, it follows that the necessary prior internal disruption and weakening of the super-power will be a very long time coming. Thus, those who labor, fight, and die in the geographically and tactically diverse struggles for national liberation in the Third World, may expect to continue to do so without real success for a correspondingly long time in the future.

The remaining fundamental contradiction in North American capitalism and potential crisis

Considering this historically unique capitalist constellation, Marcuse turns his attention to one specific potential contradition and source of crisis. He cautions, however, that it offers 'no more than a hope'. While identifying automation as an immeasurably beneficial development for advanced industrial society (44), he also recognizes in it the roots of perhaps *the* fundamental contradiction in advanced capitalism (45). Indeed, it appears to be the last hope for liberation.

Inspired by certain of Marx's tentative analyses and conditional long-range projections regarding the unstabilizing impact of unbridled automation in the capitalist productive process (46), Marcuse argues that at a certain point, the sheer quantity of these innovations places an almost unbearable strain on the 'old' productive and social relations—a strain which demands qualitative change. In other words, the new productive forces tend to break the bonds of private ownership.

> Advanced industrial society is approaching the stage where continued progress would demand the radical subversion of the prevailing direction and organization of progress. This stage would be reached when material production (including necessary services) becomes automated to the extent that all vital needs can be satisfied while necessary labor time is reduced to marginal time. From this point on, technical progress would transcend the realm of necessity, where it served as the instrument of domination and exploitation. (47)

Automation not only tends toward the reduction of necessary labor but in an inter-related maner, it alters the very nature of this labor. Consequently, automation leads to an increasing demand for a highly educated and highly skilled work force.

> The progressive reduction of physical labor power in the production process (the process of material production) and its replacement to an increasing degree by mental labor concentrate socially necessary labor in the class of technicians, scientists, engineers, etc. . . . . This suggests possible liberation from alienated labor. (48)

Unbridled automation tends to drive contemporary capitalism toward the untenable position of the near absolute abolition of socially necessary labor. Herein lies the final and basic manifestation of the systems 'irrational rationality' (49). Marcues argues that the possibilities for technological domination of nature and increasing full utilization of resources reveal potentially new and 'non-utopian' dimensions of human freedom and self-realization. Thus capitalism's necessary restraint or perversion of these possibilities make clear the fundamental irrationality of the system. Indeed, having attained this level of development, it is only the constraint and effective management of the system, largely through the perpetuation of waste (including arms spending), which enables it to continue as a smooth running system.

> Only the systematic increase in waste, destruction and management keeps the system going. (50)

18

The growing transparency of this contradiction between historically unprecedented possibilities for liberation on the one hand and the restraint and perversion of these potentialities by the powers that be on the other, suggests the possibility for the emergency of a widespread critical political consciousness. However, the managers of the prevailing system of domination are aware of this contingency and are prepared to defuse it.

> The more these technical capacities outgrow the framework of exploitation within which they continue to be defined and abused, the more they propel the drives and aspirations of men to a point at which the necessities of life cease to demand the aggressive performances of 'earning a living' . . . the managers and publicists of corporate capitalism are well aware of its meaning; they are prepared to 'contain' its dangerous consequencies. (51)

The progressive strides made in man's domination of nature provide at the same time vastly increased possibilities for the sustained and even extended domination of man by man (52). Techniques applicable in one area are, with certain 'imagination', employable in the other. Considering the absence of economic crisis and inter-imperalist competition and rivalry, it would appear that advanced capitalism's utilization of the available technological innovations is not pressed forward at the pace it might otherwise have been, had such competition and crisis persisted. Further, the expanding affluency continues to reinforce and testify to the 'truth' and viability of the system. The creation of 'unnatural' wants and needs through effective and continuous mass advertising binds the underlying population ever closer to the consumer society. Preoccupied with chrome, gadgets and sururban houses, the population manifests a corresponding decline in critical consciousness as

> The prevailing law of value is mirrored in the continually renewed conviction that everyone, left completely to himself, must earn a living in the general competitive struggle, if only in order to be able to continue to earn it in the future. (53)

Marcuse sees at once both the liberating possibilities of this contradiction and in his view, the more probable prospects for the total and 'pleasant' domination and repression of man. (54)

Summary of economic propositions

The image of contemporary North American capitalism which has emerged from the above elaboration, is perhaps best characterized as one manifesting a clear and almost unavoidable tendency towards long-term stability, coupled with and reinforced by increasingly widespread affluency and employment opportunities.

At base, this stability derives from the 'freezing' of inter-imperalist economic competition and rivalry, as a direct result of the existence and strengthening of the enemy (Communism). On this basis emerge:

(a) an expanding defense economy;
(b) a vastly accelerated rate of technological development and innovation;
(c) the effective politico-economic management of cyclical crisis;
(d) a continually expanding production of 'junk' commodities assuring a corresponding expansion of affluency for the underlying population; and
(e) an unwavering and effectively enforced determination to contain all struggles for national liberation in the Third World.

These appear to be the critical factors, which result in the ensurance of long-term future economic stability, progress, high employment rates and affluence in North America. The one fundamental contradiction (potentialities for unbridled automation vs restraint and perversion of these potentialities), is also viewed as being containable in the forseeable future. Thus, Marcuse concludes:

> The first tendency (capitalist containment of qualitative change in the forseeable future) is dominant, and whatever preconditions for a reversal may exist are being used to prevent it. Perhaps an accident may alter the situation, but unless the recognition of what is being done and what is being prevented subverts the consciousness and behaviour of man, not even a catastrophe will bring about a change. (56)

Opposition to the established system of domination is confronted by the sustained power of the system as it manifests an unshaken capacity to subject the underlying population to a comfortable repression through sustained affluence. (57)

> Under the condition of a rising standard of living, non-conformity with the system itself appears to be socially useless, and the more so when it entails tangible economic and political disadvantages and threatens the smooth operation of the whole. (58)

The new working class: the impact of advanced technology on the structure of the North American working class

> The long range process which in large areas of material production, tends to replace heavy physical labor by technological and mental energy, increases the social need for scientifically trained and intelligent workers. (59)

Based on the qualitative alteration in the nature of North American capitalism's productive apparatus, Marcuse argues that we are witnessing the beginning of yet another long range tendency towards an increasing demand for highly educated labor. It is the complexity and technological sophistication of the new productive machinery which creates this spiralling demand for highly educated and scientifically skilled workers—a work force capable of the further development, installation, operation and repair of the scientifically advanced and technologically sophisticated means of production.

> This tendency is strengthened by the changing composition of the working class. The declining proportions of blue collar workers, the increasing number and importance of white collar employees, technicians, engineers and specialists divide this class. (60)

Thus members of the traditional working class are increasingly frustrated in their aspirations of upward mobility in the work place.

> The chances for promotion decline as management prefers engineers and college graduates. (61)

The changing nature of the productive apparatus of advanced capitalism with its consequent growing demand for a highly educated and skilled work force, thus alters the traditional structure of the working class (62). A 'new working class' emerges (63). The strategic importance of this group develops as its members come to occupy the key positions in the new productive apparatus.

While due to its sheer numbers (64) the traditional working class continues to occupy its potential role as *the* historical revolutionary force (65), the new working class moves into an historically unique objective position. Because of its monopolization of necessary knowledge and expertise, this new working class enjoys a potential control over the productive process which places them in a historically unique objective revolutionary position.

> The intelligentsia obtains an increasingly decisive role in this process (productive process)—an instrumentalist intelligentsia, but intelligentsia nevertheless. This 'new working class' because of its position, could disrupt, reorganize, and redirect the mode and relationships of production. However, they have neither the interest nor the vital need to do so: they are well integrated and well rewarded. (66)

Owing to their key positions this group really seems to represent the nucleus of an objective revolutionary force. (67)

Thus, with the structural alterations in the working class, this 'new' group emerges as having the most objective revolutionary potential. The potential 'objective' revolutionary power of this group owing to its structural position in the productive apparatus is further reinforced as a result of the 'masses' increasingly close participation in this productive process in their role as frequent and satisfied consumers of its goods and services. With the extension and tightening of this bond, control over the new means of production leads also to immediate and effective control over the underlying population.

21

There are two dominant units; first, the giant production and distribution apparatus of modern industry, Having control over the apparatus or even its key positions, means having control over the masses in such a way, in fact, that this control seems to result automatically from the division of labor, to be its technical result, the rationale of the functioning apparatus that spans and maintains the whole society. (68)

Thus, both natural and scientific resources for liberation as well as the 'objectively' ideal revolutionary agent are present in advanced capitalist society. Marcuse hastens to stress, however, that those who occupy these objectively key positions are well rewarded and integrated into the prevailing politico-economic culture. Indeed, they are the 'favorite children' of the system (69). They work faithfully and diligently to accomplish its pre-established goals and strive unceasingly after the pre-established conception of personal, economic and social progress (70). Their political consciousness is moulded to the same extent and by the same processes as is the consciousness of those over whom they have control. Consequently, the apparatus they 'control' continues to work in the interest of the effective domination of men by men. In short, it continues to pervert possibilities for self-realization (71). Any optimism inspired by the unionization of this new working class is summarily dismissed.

The stepped-up drive to organize the growing white collar element in the industrial unions, if successful at all, may result in a growth of trade union consciousness of these groups, but hardly in their political radicalization. (72)

Finally, it should be noted that Marcuse's discussion of the impact of automation offers no consideration of its possible decimating impact on what he terms the 'higher forms of mental labor'. Indeed, the inference is clear that these functions, due to their complex nature, are more or less exempted from the labor trivializing forward sweep of technological innovation (73). It is this latter implicit assumption, as well as certain other unconsidered aspects of his discussion of the long range impact of technology on the structure of the working class which shall be considered in a section of chapter four.

Structural dislodgement and the basis and existence of working class consciousness in North America

Those social groups which dialectical theory identified as the forces of negation are either defeated or reconciled with the established system. Before the power of the given facts, the power of negative thinking stands condemned. (74)

Due to its dislocation from the key positions in the productive process, Marcuse notes a marked diminishment in the objective revolutionary potential of the traditional North American working class (75). Therefore, the central position which this 'living negation' of capitalism had justifiably held in critical theory has apparently been undermined by actual social and economic developments. The emergence of these qualitatively altered socio-economic realities demands a corresponding alteration in the focus and conceptual structure of critical theory in order to facilitate the further analysis of these historically unprecedented developments. It should be re-emphasized however that the traditional working class as yet remains an indispensable force in socialist revolutionary praxis. But in light of apparently long term tendencies, regarding their objective position in the new means of production, they no longer represent the 'vital center' of an objective revolutionary force—the essential catalyst. (76)

Under the impact of sustained and expanding affluency, the most significant characteristic of the North American working class (both 'old' and 'new'), has become their total and acquiescent integration into the established system. Radical class consciousness does not and will not emerge. It is effectively stifled (77) as the 'goods' and 'services' roll in an ever increasing variety and quantity to an increasing proportion of the population.

> The distinction between true and false consciousness, real and immediate interest is still meaningful. But this distinction itself must be validated. Men must come to see it and to find their way from false to true consciousness, from their immediate to their real interest. They can do so only if they live in need of changing their way of life, or denying the positive, of refusing. It is precisely this need which the established society manages to repress to the degree to which it is capable of 'delivering the goods' on an increasingly large scale. (78)

Thus, among the working classes in the most advanced areas of capitalism (North America in particular), there exists an overwhelming interest in the preservation and improvement of the status quo (79). Formerly antagonistic classes in capitalist society have united (80) under the impact of sustained affluency. In North America at least, the working class no longer appears to be the 'subjective' agent of revolutionary change. (81)

Indeed, Marcuse further reinforces this conclusion with his instance that quite apart from the politically stifling incluence of sustained affluence, the 'work experience' has been fundamentally altered under the impact of technology (and rendered more 'acceptable' even enjoyable). He refers here not simply to the shift from physical to mental labor but rather to the ensuent mechanistic and 'drugging' rhythm of the new work pace and operations.

> Now the ever more complete mechanization of labor in advanced capitalism, while sustaining exploitation, modified the attitude and the status of the exploited. (82)

Consequently,

> ... the organized worker in advanced areas of technological society lives
> this denial less conspicuously ... some sort of technological community
> seems to integrate the human atoms at work. (83)

Complimenting the politically stifling impact of sustained affluence, these new 'rhythmic' work operations and work pace highten satisfaction with the system in general and lead to an even greater degree of 'happy' and numb aquiescence. Under such conditions the working class no longer appears 'subjectively' to represent the 'living contradiction' of capitalist society. (84)

To the extent that work place frustration is absent from the experience of the working class, the ability to recognize the 'class enemy' has been blurred—all as result of the altered nature of the productive process, and the new techniques of mental manipulation.

> Hatred and frustration are deprived of their specific target, and the
> technological veil conceals the reproduction of inequality and enslave-
> ment. (85)

This 'cooling-out' of the North American working class is strengthened and further assured (indeed, this appears to be in a certain sense the critical factor), by the existence of the 'enemy' (communism). Would-be contradictions and class conflicts (a notion rendered almost ludicrous in light of Marcuse's analysis discussed thus far), are suspended—a development which gives rise to sustained inter-class cohesion and solidarity in the face of the larger 'enemy' which looms ever present from without—(and within).

> Class struggles are attenuated ... before the threat from without.
> Mobilized against this threat capitalist society shows an internal union
> and cohesion unknown at previous stages of industrial civilization. (86)

The net result of these dialectically related forces is therefore a complete und 'unforeseeably' long-term stifling of radical working class consciousness in North America. Under the combined and interrelated impact of the 'enemy' and expanding affluence, aided and reinforced by effective mental integration through sophisticated manipulative techniques, the smooth functioning, 'goods-delivering' society seems to refute all criticism. Thus, it effectively undercuts the traditional basis (improverishment, debilitating and unpleasant work experiences, and occupational insecurity) for radical working class consiousness.

'Positive thinking' is enforced not by terror, but rather and more effectively by the sheer achievements of the system (87). Consequently opposition to and denial of the 'goodness' and 'progressiveness' of the established system appears both futile and irrational.

> If the individuals are satisfied with the goods and services handed down
> to them by the administration, why should they insist on different

institutions for a different production of different goods and services? (88)

Therefore:

... in the contemporary period, the technological controls appear to be the very embodiment of reason for the benefit of all social groups and interests—to such an extent that all contradiction seems irrational and all counteraction impossible. (89)

Summary of propositions on alterations in working class structure and consciousness

The image of the North American working class which emerges from Marcuse's analysis is characterized by:

(a) the structural dislodgement of the traditional working class from the key positions in the new productive process and their replacement by a new working class of scientists, technicians and engineers;
(b) the complete, complementary and 'unforseeably' long-range integration of both 'old' and 'new' working classes into the established system of values and goals.

While the 'new' working class—the indispensable instrumentalist intelligentsia—have come to occupy and historically unique, position in the productive process, rendering them a key objective revolutionary potential to this apparatus, they along with the traditional working class, are totally lacking in 'subjective' revolutionary potential. The combined and interrelated impact of the 'enemy', sustained (even expanding) affluence, sophisticated and effective mental manipulation, and the new pacifying and drugging work rhythm, seems to assure the preservation, even the expansion, of this total integration and resultant political apathy (90) for an unforseeably long time into the future.

Consequently, Marcuse concludes that:

The modifications in the structure of capitalism alter the basis for the development and organization of potential revolutionary forces. (91)

Therefore:

In the absence of demonstrable agents and agencies of social change, the critique is thus thrown back to a high level of abstraction. There is no ground on which theory and practice, thought and action meet. (92)

The consequent theoretical and political dilemma

The critical theory of society possesses no concepts which could bridge this gap between the present and its future; holding no promise and showing no success, it remains negative. Thus it wants to remain loyal to those who, without hope, have given and give their lives to the Great Refusal. (93)

The foregoing discussions of Marcuse's analysis of realities and tendencies in North American economy and society have sketched out what may be viewed as the first draft of the theoretical and political dilemma he perceives. The initial hints of this political pessimism may be found as early as 1934 (94), but are most clearly manifest in embryo form in 'Soviet Marxism' (95) and 'Eros and Civilization' (96) and given further clarity in 'One Dimensional Man' (97). It is never an easy (or perhaps completely possible) task to locate precisely the key turning points in the development and consolidation of an individual's perspective on a given set of phenomena. Nevertheless, it is clear that the premonition or first conceptualizations of Marcuse's subsequently concretized pessimistic analysis of the present and future socialist revolutionary potential in North American society, were first manifest in the work of the early fifties. The twenty ensuing years have seen the full development of these first somewhat tentatively couched ideas and propositions. During this period, both the analysis and the consequent new conception of an new approach to liberation, have become at once less cautious and vague, while at the same time more explicit and uncompromising.

This political and therefore theoretical dilemma is, as we have seen, the result of an analysis of North American society which manifests the following characteristics and tendencies:

(a) a smooth functioning economy resulting from effective joint state and business planning and management, extended arms spending, increasing production of 'junk', an advanced technological base, transcended inter-imperalist competition and rivalry, and effective 'containment' of national liberation struggles and sympathies in Third World areas; and

(b) an increasingly fully employed well paid, consuming, effectively indoctrinated and so, political contented and apathetic working class. These two sets of factors—economic and political—mutually reinforce each other, thereby ensuring long term future developments along these same lines. The prospects for revolutionary praxis in the face of this 'progressive', stable, and expanding affluence are stifled at every turn. There appears no hope, no possible grounds upon which radical class consciousness could develop.

> The power and efficiency of the system, the thorough assimilation of mind with fact, of thought with required behavior, of aspirations with reality, militate against the emergence of a new subject. (98)

All protest against the smooth functioning whole lies bare and defenseless to the counter-charge of irrationality. The power of positive thinking prevails, sustained and 'proven' by the overwhelming power of the given facts—even though these 'facts' abuse and brutalize the 'truth'.

> Validated by the accomplishments of science and technology, justified by its growing productivity, the status quo defies all transcedence ... Operationalism, in theory and practice, become the theory and practice of containment. Underneath its obvious dynamics, this society is a thoroughly static system of life: Self propelling in its oppresive productivity and in its beneficial coordination. Containment of technical progress goes hand in hand with its growth in the established direction. (99)

It is this all pervasive and oppressive dilemma which Marcuse perceives as the result of the present reality and perhaps the inescapable long-term future tendencies in North American Society. Confronted by these developments, the traditionally conceptualized objective basis of an emergent radical working class consciousness appears to have been permanently and effectively undercut. A situation from which Marcuse sees no issue. Both at the level of critical thought and of socialist revolutionary praxis, the 'soil', the objective justification for refusal appears to have been denied by the very accomplishments of the system.

> On theoretical as well as empirical grounds, the dialectical concept pronounces its own hopelessness. (100)

It is this dilemma, this no-issue political straight-jacket, which appears to be the central factor motivating the subsequent shift in ontological perspective and its consequent far reaching theoretical and political implications. The discussions in chapters three and four will attempt to look more closely at the several proposed basic long range economic, social and political tendencies which give rise to Marcuse's perception of this dilemma. They will be endeavours to 'balanceout' certain aspects of his socio-economic analysis by taking into consideration a variety of developments and apparent tendencies singularly unanticipated and/or unconsidered by Marcuse. Before that however, closer consideration should be given to the full consequences and implications this apparent dilemma has held for Marcuse's subsequent work.

Chapter Two:

The ontological* shift and its consequences

Introduction

This chapter will focus further on the factors which appear to have motivated Marcuse's shift in perspective regarding the essence of man. Also, it will be a discussion of the particular nature of the 'new' ontology and of the theoretical, analytical and political consequences its adoption has effected in Marcuse's work. At base, and in general terms, this shift is best characterized by a move from Marx to Freud (the latter as represented by his later theory of instincts).

The analysis of often subtle modifications and shifts in intellectual perspectives is an undertaking to be pursued with some caution. It is not always possible, given the dialectical nature of intellectual development, to identify a particular point in time as the precise moment of modification. Consequently, while a clear shift has taken place in Marcuse's ontological perspective, it must be viewed in the dialectical manner by which it has become manifest.

The first indications of this shift were seen, in 'Eros and Civilization', conceived and written during the period from 1950–1954. In this work, many of the novel and radical socio-political implications of Marcuse's version of the later Freudian instinct theory were given first airing. The numerous provocative insights contained in this study were still frequently couched in speculative and tentative terms. The full radical theoretical, social and political implications of many of these insights became (through the ongoing intellectual dialectic with his previous and continuing socio-economic analysis) only gradually more explicit and concretized.

Early mention has been made of the fact that at least the germ of most of Marcuse's analysis of North American society was present at and even before this period. Indeed, a central premise of this study is that it was in large measure the prior perception of these apparent socio-economic realities and tendencies (including the ensuent political-cum-theoretical dilemma), which was the main justification and motivation for effecting the ontological shift. It also seems clear that as Marcuse's socio-economic analysis proceeded to develop through

* In the following discussions, the term 'ontological' is used in the particular sense of referring to the essence of man. That is, to man's fundamental and universal nature, prior to and initially exclusive of biographical and historical modifications. At times the two terms 'essence' and 'ontology' are used interchangeably.

the fifties and sixties, the impact of this ontological shift on his theoretical position became increasingly pronounced and dinstinctive. As this new point of departure became more firmly rooted in his basic intellectual outlook, his theory, concrete analyses and subsequent proposals for liberation increasingly revealed the undeniable and integral mark of Eros.

While the initial motivation for the incorporation of Freud's later instinct theory stemmed largely from the perceived present and emergent dilemma facing revolutionary praxis in North America, the radical implications of the new ontology effected both a reinforcement of this dilemma as well as the possibility for an exit from the situation.

The ontological position before the shift

> Reality, where essence is concerned, is the totality of the relations of production. (2)

Prior to the perception and impact of the dilemma, Marcuse's ontological position (perhaps it would be fairer to Marx to say his concept of human essence), appears to be fundamentally orthodox Marxist. The later Freudian theory of instincts with its emphasis on a constant (yet interchangeable) and creative/destructive reservoir of psychic energy manifesting through the imagination (Art) the fundamental and universal essence of man, had as yet no concrete or even implicit influence on either Marcuse's theory or praxis. While he was certainly aware of Freud's ideas through his association with the Frankfurt school, and although his early writings show a unique concern for problems closely related to notions of ontology, in the classic Marxis tradition, he unwaveringly conceived the essence of man as being historically developed in the process of man's interaction with his environment. Reference to an 'inner source of creative and/or destructive energy was completely absent from his pre-fifty works. (3)

It may be objected that there is in facto no particular concept of essence inherent in Marxist theory. Thinking in terms of universal dispositions, instincts, etc., that is certainly true. But the very notion that man's essence is always historically peculiar, itself implies a certain notion of human essence, though of a somewhat different order. In short, the plasticity, and variability of man seems to be the necessary ontological point of departure for an approach which stresses the historically particular nature of human essence. Essence develops through the confrontation of human intellect and the historically particular environment.

> The materialist concept of essence is an historical concept. Essence is conceived only as the essence of a particular 'appearance', whose factual form is viewed with regard to what it is in itself and what it could be (but is not in fact). This relation, however, originates in history and changes in history. (4)

29

No reference was made nor any resort taken to 'basic instinctual drives', *a priori* impulses, or 'Demands of the Life Instincts'. Rather, stressing his materialist position, Marcuse stated during that period,

> Its claim differs completely from those put forward by all other philosophical theories, for it rejects the adequacy of *a prior* logical or epistemological validation. (5)

Directly related to this ontological point of departure, his general assessment of the political nature of art was precisely the opposite of what it has become since the 'shift'. In 1937 he wrote:

> By exhibiting the beautiful as present, art pacifies rebellious desire. (6)

At this point artistic creation is not seen as the manifestation of man's universal essence. In marked contrast, in 1972, he writes,

> Art as Form means not the beautification of the given but the construction of an entirely different and opposed reality. The aesthetic view is part of the revolution. (7)
>
> Art is perhaps the most visible 'return of the repressed', not only on the individual but also on the generic-historical level. The artistic imagination shapes the 'unconscious memory' of the liberation that failed, or the promise that was betrayed. (7 a)

Under the influence of Freud, art has moved from a politically pacifying cultural manifestation to the very token of Truth (the unsublimated manifestation of Eros). In short it represents the unmodified manifestation of those dispositions and inclinations which are universal (but repressed) in all men at all times. Art thus becomes, as will be seen later, the essential even indispensible guide to authentic revolutionary praxis. (8)

A further manifestation of this contrast between the 'old' and the 'new' ontology may be seen in Marcuse's discussions regarding the emergence of a 'new man' characterized in one aspect by 'new needs'. Under the influence of the 'old' Marxist ontological point of departure he argues that

> When the imperative has been fulfilled, when practice has created man's new social organizations, the new essence of man appears in reality. (9)

And further

> When all present subjective and objective potentialities of development have been unbound, the needs and wants themselves will change. (10)

While the development of a new man with new needs is clearly a dialectical process occurring in relation to changing existential experiences, the ultimate priority is seen at this stage of Marcuse's thinking to rest finally in the emergence of altered socio-economic relationships. Contrary to this view and again under the impact of the new ontology, Marcuse has now come to hold the position that 'new men' with 'new needs' must exist *prior* to successful and authentic revolutionary praxis.

> But the construction of such a society *presupposes** a type of man with a different sensitivity as well as consciousness: men who would speak a different language, have different gestures, follow different impulses: men who would have developed an instinctual barrier against cruelty, brutality and ugliness. (11)
> In short, the economic, political and cultural features of classless society must have become the basic needs of those who fight for them. (12)

Parallels no doubt exist between the Marxian and Freudian (*cum Marcusean*) notion of human essence. For Marcuse the most striking appears to be the similarity between Marx's stress on historical and biographical influences in the forming of the particular emergent essence, and Freud's reference to the dual ontogenetic and phylogenetic processes of psychic modification of the fundamental 'instinctual' essence of man. The crucial distinction, however, is *that in Marx there is never any discussion of an a priori* and universally existing instinctual structure or set of dispositions subseqently modified under the impact of interaction with the social environment. Nevertheless, Marcuse seeks to uncover the Freudian intent in Marx's position. With reference to a *single* passage in Marx's work, he writes:

> The aesthetic vision is part of the revolution; it is a vision of Marx: 'the animal constructs (formient) only according to need; man forms also in accordance with the laws of beauty'. (13)

The implication is clear. Marcuse would have us see this 'vision of Marx' as the first glimmering perception of the as yet not fully comprehended nature of Eros. It seems that Marx is not only surpassed by the ontological shift, but is made also to testify to his own relative demise.

While the similarities are apparent, the two ontological notions remain of a qualitatively different order: Marx stressing man's interaction with his environment as the fundamental formative process of an always historically particular human essence; Freud (Marcuse) stressing in addition to this interaction (and even this represents a qualitatively different conception than Marx's), the influence of a constant and fundamental reservoir of physic energy as the basis

---

* Emphasis added.

of thought and activity. This new ontological perspective is no mere extension of Marx—of that which Marcuse implies was in fact latent in Marx's thinking—rather, it represents a qualitative leap. Nevertheless, it is this apparent similarity, which under the initial motivation and justification of the perceived theoretical and political dilemma appears to give further impetus and, more importantly, specific direction to the subsequently altered ontological perspective—the resultant move from Marx to Freud.

The Freudian later instinct theory appeared to both complement Marx's discussions of human essence and to harmonize rather well with certain older idealist notions of human essence with which Marcuse was long familiar and partially symphathetic to. So, Libido seemed to provide the material basis 'under the material basis', and afforded Marcuse the way to have his idealist cake and eat it too. This point will be more fully discussed in a subeequent section of this chapter.

Of more importance, however, in motivating the shift to Freud, was the dilemma confronting critical theory according to Marcuse's socio-economic and political analysis. Unlike the Marxist ontological point of departure, Libido injected a new 'independent' dynamic into the political dilemma. It seems this latter fact of best explains the basic motivation for the shift.

The dilemma overviewed

> Now it precisely this new consciousness, this 'space within', the space for transcending the historical practice, which is being barred by a society in which subjects as well as objects constitute instrumentalities in a whole that has it *raison d'être* in the accomplishments of its over-powering productivity. Its supreme promise is an ever-more comfortable life for an ever-growing number of people who, in a strict sense, cannot imagine a qualitatively different universe of discourse and action. (14)

Previous elaboration of the nature and origins of the (Marcuse's) »dilemma» have been given. In sum, the North American working class (indeed the society at large) has become completely one dimensional at all levels of social existence and endeavour. Under the combined and related impact of sustained affluency, the absence of both frustration and readily perceivable alienating existential experiences at work and in broader social environment, and the ever present enemy, radical working class consciousness and critical thinking find no roots—no fertile soil in which to grow. These developments, Marcuse projects, are only the beginning of long-range tendencies. Therefore, given the "old" Marxist ontological perspective stressing the dialectical development of particular forms of consciousness as being based in the socio-economic experiences; and further, given the stress which this ontological point of departure places on the emergence of radical class consciousness as a basic result of obvious deprivation and exploitation (whether relative or absolute); how may necessary radical working class consciousness be realistically expected to develop in the midst and on the basis of fear of the 'enemy' as well as sustained and expanding affluence and evermore widespread 'happiness' and 'satisfaction' with the system.

Herein lies the crux of Marcuse's problem. The final and central motivation for the ontological shift from Marx to Freud. Eros, the inner force, provides the glimmer of hope, the basis for a potential break in the otherwise unbreakable continuum of repression.

The new ontology allows a more dynamic essence. The *mere* interplay between man and his environment no longer adequately depicts the nature and origin of human essence. The consciousness of man now becomes subject to an additional 'inner' and previously unappreciated influence—the essential Demands of the Life Instincts (the ultimate expression of Truth and Form).

The recognition of the ability of Eros, this undeniable universal essence, to influence thought and praxis opens whole new and even qualitatively different prospects for liberation. Within and this side of the sustained 'happy' oppressiveness of the system, the new ontology contains within it the potential basis for an emergent radical consciousness. Psychic energy in the form of Eros becomes the potential 'motor force', the roots for denial and refusal which had been undercut and transcended by the achievements of the system.

Indeed and on the basis of the new ontological perspective, consciousness appears to become something other than it had been (in the Marxist frame of reference) up to this point. No longer does it represent *the* process and manifestation of human cognition; rather it becomes just one, and perhaps even then, the least 'true' and 'authentic' aspect of man's total cognitive processes (15). Thus, its adoption apparently motivated and justified by the theoretical and political dilemma, the new ontology promises to lend the necessary 'dynamic' for a potential break with this same circle of oppressive affluence. In a very real sense, the move to Freud marks the resurrection of a voluntarism completely absent from Marx.

> Freud's psychology reaches into a dimension of the mental apparatus where the individual is still genus ... The primary instincts pertain to life and death—that is to say, to organic matter as such. And they link organic matter back with inorganic matter, and forward with its higher mental manifestations. In other words, Freud's theory contains certain assumptions on the structure of being: It contains ontological assumptions. (16)

And in consequence

> The artistic images* have preserved the determinate negation of the established reality—ultimate freedom. (17)

* In Marcuse's Freudian frame of reference, this refers to the unsublimated manifestations of Eros—expressions of the authentic essence of man.

Idealism: its influence and return

> We have suggested certain nodal points in the development of Western philosophy which reveal the limitations of its system of reason—and the effort to surpass this system. The struggle appears in the antagonism between becoming and being ... In its most advanced position, Freud's theory partakes of this philosophical dynamic. His metapsychology attempting to define the essence of being, defines it as Eros. (18)

Stress has been placed upon Marcuse's orthodox Marxist ontological position prior to the fifties. Here it should be emphasized, however, that Western idealist philosophy from Plato through Hegel (and on) also significantly influenced Marcuse's theoretical formulations (19). While the influence of Marx was unmistakenly dominant, his familiarity with and unconcealed attraction to numerous provocative notions and incisive perspectives of Western idealist philosophy, had a striking impact upon both his further motivation towards, as well as the specific direction of the subsequent ontological shift. Most noteworthy in this respect were certain insights and proposals of Plato, Kant, Hegel and Schiller (20). His clear appreciation of their discussions of ontology and closely related phenomena foreshadow his subsequent adoption and interpretation of the Freudian later instinct theory. Indeed, in retrospect he seems to view these early idealist ontological and related discussions not only as precursors to the 'discovery' of libido, but even as manifestations of its influence (however repressed) on the evolving structure and content of Western idealist philosophy, in much the same manner as he tends to read Freud into Marx.

> The history of ontology reflects the reality principle which governs the world ever more exclusively. (21)

In the thirties Marcuse argued that the central concern of idealist philosophy from Plato on, was with the essence of being and the tension between this essence and existence. (22)

This tension came to find its parallel in Freud's (Marcuse's) notion of the constant tension between the Pleasure principle (reflecting the true essence of man) and the Reality principle (reflecting the historically specific demands and restrictions of the social environment). Thus the validation of Freud becomes the validation of certain central features of Western idealist philosophy.

With Marcuse's acceptance and novel incorporation of Freud's later instinct theory into his basic theoretical perspective, Plato's 'Idea' (23) (The Form), Hegel's 'World Spirit' (24), as well as his related notion of a 'basic impulse to freedom' (24), Kants' notion of 'productive senses' (25) and the related notion 'transcendental consciousness' (26), and Schiller's conception of an 'Aesthetic state' (27), all found realization and epistemological verification Eros (libido) lent 'final' legitimacy to a whole train of key notions in idealist philosophy.

In a particular sense, Marcuse appears to have come full circle: from his sympathetic discussion of the Hegelian ontology in his doctoral dissertation, through Marx to Freud. The return to idealism appears to be vindicated by the proving of idealism—by the discovery of Eros, the material basis for a universal concept of essence. In chapter five an attempt will be made to determine if Marcuse's 'reinforced' or 'materially based' idealism remains open to the same criticism Marx, and indeed Marcuse too, had earlier leveled at it. In short, that discussion will focus on the epistemological status of Libido.

In 1934 the dilemma for idealism is set

> Unless, the idealists declared, the general concepts that claimed such necessity and universality could be shown *to be more than the product of the imagination,** could be shown to draw their validity neither from experience nor from individual psychology, unless, in other words, they were shown applicable to experience without arising from experience, reason would have to bow to the dictates of empirical teaching. And if cognition by reason, that is, by concepts that are not derived from experience, means metaphysics, then the attack upon metaphysics was at the same time an attack upon the conditions of human freedom, for the right of reason to guide experience was a proper part of these conditions. (28)

The theoretical political dilemma perceived by Marcuse in the 'fifties' added particular urgency to the transcendence of this central problem of idealist philosophy. This feat was made potentially realizable through the instrumentality of the ontological shift. Marcuse, drawing essential support from Freud, submitted the 'final' argument for the beleaguered idealists and their inheritors on the left. He writes:

> Freud's metapsychology here restors *imagination* to its rights. As a fundamental, independent mental process, phantasy has a truth value of its own, which corresponds to an experience of its own, namely, the surmounting of an antagonistic human reality. Imagination envisions the reconciliation of the individual with the whole, of desire with realization, of happiness with reason. (29)

Beginning from the idealists' concern to have their 'necessary' universal concepts firmly rooted', and not *merely products of the imagination,* Marcuse with the help of Freud and Eros discover this very *imagination* to be in fact, the ultimate truth of human essence (and consequently of form, rationality, and

* Emphasis added.

sensitivity). Thus, without even departing from the original point of consterna-
tion, Marcuse supplies Western idealism with its own ultimate 'proof', the truth
of its own universal concepts of essence—indeed, with its very *raison d'être*. In
certain fundamental respects, idealism was thereby absolved from the most
basic and serious critiques of the radical empiricists, operationalists, and
logical positivitsts, as its greatest accused weakness its fundamental reliance on
notions which appeared to be nothing more than products of the *'imagination'*—become at a stroke of the psychoanalytic sword its ultimate and undeniable strength. The right of pure reason to deny the given facts was thus
re-established. The point to be considered, however, is this: does this development represent the discovery of a fundamental truth or merely the
redefinition of a concept; the proof idealism or simply the return to idealism
via the psychoanalytic back-door? The discussions in chapter five will hopefully throw some light on these questions.

The need for a new concept of essence

> The Doctrine of Essence seeks to liberate knowledge from the worship
> of 'observable facts' and from the scientific sense that imposes this
> worship. (30)

Commenting on Hegel's explanation of the importance of a notion of 'Essence', Marcuse previews the issue which was to become the pivotal point of
much of his later discussions on repression and liberation. An immediate and
fundamental consequence of his perception of the political dilemma was an
increasing dissatisfaction with the conseptual adequacy of Marxist ontology*
(and theory) to supply an explanation, critique and a 'break' from the novel
developments in North American economy and society.

> Confronted by the total character of the achievements of advanced
> industrial society, critical theory is left without the rational for trans-
> cending this society. (31)

The benevolance, power and pleasure of the status-quo denied the necessity
and militated against the rationality for going beyond the given state of
power and affluence in an qualitative sense. Reinforced and perpetuated
further by the heirs to early British positivism (32), the dominant modes of
thought (radical empiricism, operationalism and logical positivism), appeared
to grant absolution to the established system through the instrumentality of
the philosophical denial of the relevance or even existence of a whole array of
problems.

* Or Marx's notion of human essence.

36

The new mode of thought* is today the predominant tendency in philosophy, psychology, sociology and other fields. Many of the most seriously troublesome concepts are being 'eliminated' by showing that no adequate account of them in terms of operations and behaviour can be given. The radical empiricist onslaught . . . thus provides the methodolical justification for the debunking of the mind by the intellectuals—a positivism which, in its denial of the transcending elements of Reason, forms the academic counterpart of the socially required behaviour. Outside the academic establishment, the 'far reaching change in all our habits of thought' is more serious. It serves to coordinate ideas and goals with those exacted by the prevailing system, and to repel those which are irreconcilable with the system. (33)

Given its successes, Marcuse argues that capitalism has the right to demand that those who work for the overthrow of the system, justify their actions (34). However, he has already concluded that traditional Marxism is conceptually inadequate to supply such justification. Thus, the problem which confronts him is as follows: How may one argue for, and indeed insist upon, the abolition of a poverty which does not exist; on what grounds may one demand the replacement of debilitating work which has already been surpassed, and; why should one insist on the establishment of an efficient, stabile, affluent and 'satisfying' society, if such conditions already prevail.

Granted that the 'happiness' is not authentic, and the affluence is perverted (35), the object however is to reveal and make undeniably obvious this perversion and inauthenticity. It must be demonstrated to the underlying population that while 'the whole is truth, the whole is false' (36). How may there be grounds for refusing? How can outmoded critical theory hope to give concrete expression and guidance to this refusal? Once again the answer lies rooted in Eros (libido), the 'newly discovered' authentic essence of man. With the incorporation of Freud into critical theory. Eros put the lie to the repressive and restrictive affluence of the status quo. Against the measure of Eros and the Demands of the Life Instincts, its happiness, affluence, harmony and progress are unveiled as counterfeit. Thus, this new universal 'material' base *under* the material base, provides negative thinking with the warrant to deny the 'authenticity' and the 'truth' of the established facts. On the firm footing of Eros, 'rejuvinated' critical theory may now effectively confront operationalism's pretended monopoly on truth.

What more solid basis could be given the Great Refusal than the true universal essence of man. A Critique of the status quo which is based on an accurate perception of man's authentic essence, and which is developed in harmony with its ongoing manifestations and demands—a critique which lays bare the fundamental violation of the universal human essence by the

* Marcuse's is referring specifically to operationalism here.

37

conditions and objectives of the status quo—is a critique which represents the ultimate and undeniable condemnation of the given state of affairs and their tendencial future developments. No quantitative increase in affluence and 'happiness' (37), nor in the prevailing social harmony, can escape the negative judgement of Eros.

The necessity of a moral critique

> If you only operate within the framework of technical rationality and from the start exclude historically transcendent concepts ... then you continually find yourself in the situation of being asked, and not being able to answer the question, what is really so terrible about this system, which continually expands social wealth so that the strata of the population that previously lived in greatest poverty and misery today have automobiles, television sets and one-family houses?—
>
> What is bad about this system that we have to take the tremendous risk of preaching its overthrow? It you content yourself with material arguments and exclude all other arguments you will not get anywhere. *We must finally relearn what we forgot during the fascist period, ...:** that humanitarian and moral arguments are not merely deceitful ideology. If we exclude them from our argumentation at the start, we impoverish ourselves and disarm ourselves in the face of the strongest arguments of the defenders of the status quo. (38)

This position represents a decided shift (as Marcuse himself makes explicit above), in his assessment of the nature, value and political utlity of moral argumentation. It is a further manifestation of his attempt to bring critical theory into line with his perception of a qualitatively altered social reality.

In 1938 he had strongly criticized the reliance of critical politics on Judeo-Christian derived moral arguments and precepts. He had argued that through its subjection to a universal law of reason, such morality had tolerated, indeed encouraged, both the isolation and the practical limitation of the individual (39), thus posing a formidable obstacle to effective political praxis. Instead, he urged the development of a socialist morality, a morality developing in dialectical relationship to man's ongoing liberating (and liberated) political praxis. (40)

However, confronted by the overwhelming achievements of advanced capitalist society even the latter 'socialist' morality proved increasingly an inadequate basis upon which to meet the challenge of repressive affluence. In the flood of prosperity such moral appeals had an increasingly hollow ring. Indeed, it seemed apparent that man's historically developing essence was being complemented and its further progressive development facilitated, well within the framework and under the 'healthy' stimulation and influence of

* Emphasis added.

unforeseen capitalist stability and progress. Thus, the critique of the quality of this progress and consequently of what man under advanced capitalism was 'in fact' becoming, was effectively frustrated. (41)

The concealed tension between man's essence and his existence under the conditions of advanced capitalism found only weak expression and argumentation on the basis of the 'old' (traditional Marxist) notion of essence and the consequent concepts of social morality. With the ontological shift, this tension finally received clear expression and concretization in a fundamental moral indictment of the smooth functioning, comfortable and affluent conditions of the status quo. This indictment was however based neither on the Judeo-Christian morality, nor on the orthodox 'developing' socialist morality. The 'new morality' was a manifestation of the Demands of the Life Instincts, of Eros (based in the last analysis on the notion of Libido) and the conflict between this essential nature of man and the prevailing societal forms, roles, and interrelated notions of progress, pleasure and rationality.

Being based upon and derived from the very instinctual, even 'biological' structure and essence of man, this 'new morality' was *de facto* the 'final word' in moral judgements. If in the midst of affluence and progress, there appeared no other grounds for 'Refusing'—for demanding the overthrow of the system—there existed at least (and importantly) instinctually and 'biologically' rooted morals grounds for its rejection. Indeed, as a consequence this argumentation has come to occupy the dominant position in Marcuse's ongoing analysis and attack on the status quo of advanced capitalist society.

> The aesthetic morality is the opposite of puritanism ... it insists on freedom as a biological necessity: being physically incapable of tolerating repression other than that required for the protection and amelioration of life. (42)

The Freudian later instinct theory:
the specifics of the new concept of human essence

This brief discussion will be confined to Marcuse's view of Freud's later instinct theory. While Marcuse clearly views himself as an orthodox Freudian, particularly regarding discussions in the realm of the later instinct theory, the question of Freudian 'orthodoxy' is not of immediate concern here. We shall leave the point with Marcuse's statement on the matter.

> In contrast to the revisionists, I believe that Freud's theory is in its very substance 'sociological', and that no cultural or sociological orientation is needed to reveal this substance. (43)

The central (and indispensible) assumption of Freud's later instinct theory is the notion of a constant source of psychic energy-'libido'. This concept supplies the motor force and basic point of departure for the subsequently (or prior) developed idea of the dual instinctual nature of man. This universally manifested reservoir of 'psychic' energy finds release and expression through two instinct channels; the Life Instincts, represented by Eros, and the Death Instincts, represented by Thanatos. The fundamental proposition that libido, the initial reservoir of 'neutral*' psychic energy is of a constant quantity, leads logically to the further proposition that any increase (due in general to socio-historic or biographical conditioning) in the proportional quantity of 'neutral' psychic energy appropriated by either of the two basic groups of instincts, results in a simultaneous and proportionally corresponding decrease in the amount of this psychic energy available for appropriation by the other set of instincts (and vice versa) (44). Consequently Marcuse argues that the activity and conflict between these two groups of instincts represents not only the instrumentality through which the organism develops, but also it belongs to the 'inherent essence of the development of civilization.' (45)

In regard to the more specific characteristics of the two sets of instincts it should be noted that the Life Instincts strive for binding living substance into ever larger and more permanent units. The Death Instincts on the other hand desire and strive for regression to a condition before birth, free from needs and free from pain. These latter instincts are the aggressive and destructive instincts. (46)

Historically the Life Instincts have prevailed and dominated over the Death Instincts to the extent that the aggressiviness of the latter has been deflected away from the organism and toward the fundamentally hostile environment (47). Thus, by finding expression in socially useful forms of aggression, the Death Instincts have served and indirectly complemented the Life Instincts by assisting in the struggle for life and the preservation of organism.

> Out of the common nature of instinctual life develop two antagonistic instincts. The life instincts (Eros) gain ascendency over the death instincts. They continually counteract and delay the 'descent towards death'. (48).

These two categories of instincts are confronted by an environment both too poor and too hostile to permit the immediate satisfaction of the demands of the Life Instincts under Eros. Thus, the existence of external hostility and (ananke) prevents the organism from living in accordance with the dictates of the Pleasure Principle (49) (the sum of the demands of the Life Instincts). Consequently, the Reality Principle** becomes the general guideline along

---

* neutral in this sense meaning as yet neither appropriated by the Life nor the Death instincts.
** This term refers to the degree and nature of restraint imposed upon the free satisfaction of the Life Instincts by social necessity. In conjunction with this term Marcuse introduces the novel notion of the 'Performance Principle', representing the historically particular form of the 'Reality Principle'. See Eros and Civilization, p. 32.

which the organism develops and preserves itself in the face of the restraining environment. This instinctual repression implies the delayed, inhibited, and vicarious gratification of the Demands of the Life Instincts (50). The acceptance by the organism of the dominance of the Reality principle (performance principle) results in secure, socially useful, and relatively lasting gratification as well as in the passive (even satisfying) acceptance of 'non-libidinal' work. (51)

> The energy won from sexuality and sublimated, constantly increases the psychic 'investment fund' for the increasing productivity of labor. (52)

Inasmuch as conflict persists between the dictates of the Pleasure Principle and those of the Reality Principle, it is often minimized or alleviated by a process which Marcuse terms 'repressive desublimation'. Through this process, the Demands of the Life Instincts originally characterized by polymorphous perverse, sexuality, are 'permitted' expression and gratification in 'safe' (even useful) forms of activity. Normally non-or-anti-erotic objects are erotocized (i.e. clothes, cars, boats, houses, gadgets etc.). Further, the narrower and limited forms of erotic activity (genital sexuality) meet with fewer taboos and less socially enforced restraints. Thus, initially polymorphous perverse, sexuality is repressed and 'perverted' into more limited and less socially explosive (even socially reinforcing) genital sexuality −53), while erotic impulses in general transcend their natural object (or are denied them), finding forms of expression and reciprocal objects which still further curb the potentially socially disruptive content of these impulses. Thereby they are channeled in ways which are instead, socially useful. (54)

To return to the characteristics of the basic instinctual structure, it should be noted that modifications in this structure (or sublimation of the authentic instinctual impulses) takes place at two separate yet interrelated levels. At the *ontogenetic* level, the initial instinctual structure is modified (or sublimated) as a consequence of the influence of the immediate biographical experiences gained from the organism's interaction with the social environment.* Thereby, the realities and restraints imposed by family, school, community, economy and polity, effect a sublimation of the instinctual structure—a deflection in varying degrees from the organism's original and authentic instinctual 'demands'.

On the *phylogenetic* level, the instinctual structure is sublimated under the impact of biologically (genetically) transferred restraints arising from the experiences of generations in civilization's archaic past.

The conclusion Marcuse apparently wishes to draw is that different social environments are either more or less conducive to the expression, and so the disproportional development and strength, of one or the other of the two basic groups of instincts. Thus, in a milieu of minimal scarcity and consequently,

---

* 'Social' environment is used here in the broadest sense of the term.

minimal social hostility to relatively unsublimated expressions of Eros, the Life Instincts gain ascendency and their increasing strength gives rise to a dynamic of its own as ever greater proportions of the constant reservoir of neutral psychic energy (libido) are appropriated by the dominant Life Instincts. Developments in the opposite direction may also be visualized.

To this extent then, the organism's instinctual structure may be viewed as possessing a high degree of plasticity and maleability (55). The sublimated manifestations of these basic instincts are a consequence of their original authentic impulses plus the sum impact and interplay of the ontogenetic and phylogenetic processes of sublimation.

Finally, (and this is of utmost importance not only to Marcuse's present theoretical posture, but also his ongoing socio-cultural analysis and his subsequent notion of and program for achieving 'authentic' liberation) consideration should be given to the potential for unsublimated or desublimated (not repressively) expressions of Eros. Such manifestations of the authentic Demands of the Life Instincts—they very token of the Truth regarding the essence of man—are indeed, exceptional. However, even in the 'one dimensionality' of the established culture they do exist.

Freud perceives one form of mental activity as being free from all forms of sublimation (both ontogenetic and phylogenetic) and so unperverted expressions of the true inner essence of man. That mental activity is *phantasy* (art, dreams imagination). (56)

Insofar as these expressions are manifestations of the authentic essence of man, they possess a truth value far beyond and above the 'truth' and rationality derived from the exigencies and experiences of the external world of (ananke) scarcity and socially unnecessary repression. This unsublimated expression of the authentic nature of man and so of the Truth lies at the very core of Marcuse's later theory, social analysis, and, specific discussions of liberation. So inextricable has libido—Eros—become, that it is logically impossible to subscribe to Marcuse's present theory analysis and proposed praxis without at the same time accepting some of the most provocative and speculative notions of psychoanalysis. Underpinning his theory, the initial and indispensible postulate of libido—the constant and universal reservoir of psychic energy (57) has become the vital centre of his thinking, the cornerstone without which the edifice would collapse.

> Phantasy plays a most decisive function in the total mental structure: it links the unconsciousness with the highest products of consciousness (art), the dream with reality; it preserves ... the tabooed images of freedom. (57)

Summary of the nature and necessity of the ontological shift

The factors discussed above appear to be in varying degrees responsible for not only the disaffection with the traditional Marxist concept of essence, but also for the particular attraction and adoption of the later Freudian instinct theory as the appropriate substitute. Most importantly it was suggested that given the unforeseeably long-term stability, affluency and peculiar 'progressivesness' of advanced capitalist society, it became increasingly difficult, if not impossible, to either logically or practically conceptualize the emergence of a radical and militant working class consciousness. Maintaining the basic Marxist ontological point of departure, with its consequent and interrelated conception of the relationship between existence and consciousness, the sustained affluence seemed to ensure the perpetuation of endless political apathy and acquiscence among the North American working class.

In the midst of this political-cum-theoretical dilemma, Freud's later instinct theory with its fundamental emphasis on a modifiable but nevertheless constant and *independent internal* psychic dynamic—a reservoir of 'psychic energy' (in a certain sense a quite voluntaristic conception of psychic processes)—provided the 'material basis' for the rational denial of the status quo, and the potential or motor foce for radical political activity. In short, it provided the 'material basis under the material basis' for the rejection of a society whose prevalent socio-economic and political conditions resulted in neither the frustration nor the undeniably obvious and intolerable conditions which in the traditional Marxist sense could inspire widespread social discontent, thus supplying a base for the potential emergence of a radically negative political consciousness.

It might perhaps be re-emphasized at this juncture that Marcuse views his incorporation of Freud into critical theory not so much as a rejection of Marxist ontology and theory, but rather as a logical refinement and extension of the traditional Marxist perspective, on the sound basis of certain radical and apparently complementary insights of psychoanalytic theory. This revision of the traditional Marxist notion of human essence had, as a result of Marcuse's socio-economic analysis, become increasingly necessary due to the fundamented qualitative changes in the nature of capitalism and advanced capitalist society. Nevertheless, the new ontology appears to be more then a mere logical extention of ideas inherent of 'sensed' in Marx's formulations. No matter how forced the similarities, the ontological re-orientation seems to represent a qualitative alteration in the nature of critical theory.

The adoption of the 'new' Freudian perspective has had a profound impact upon Marcuse's theory, analysis and proposed political praxis. Both the rigor and logical consistancy of his arguments as well as the basis and magnitude of his apparent errors may be appreciated only with an initial clear understanding of the nature and impact of this new ontological point of departure. It has in fact, become the indispensible pivot of all his subsequent thinking related to the problems of repression and of liberation.

The following discussions will focus on what appear to be the most salient theoretical, analytical and political consequences of this altered ontological stance.

From dilemma to vicious circle:
The dilemma reinforced

> With the conquest of the erotic danger zone by the state, the public control of individual needs would be completed. Effective barriers would have been erected in the very instincts of man against his liberation. (58)

Ample discussion has been devoted to the theoretical and political dilemma Marcuse began to perceive during the early fifties. The purpose of this section is rather to indicate the extent to which the altered ontological perspective strengthened, deepened, and reinforced his conception of this dilemma.Indeed, the incorporation of Eros (libido) seems to have resulted in a qualitative change in the perception of the dilemma.

After the 'shift', Marcuse's discussions of repression and containment no longer operated merely at the level of considerations of false consciousness. The introduction of libido to his theoretical outlook is paralleled by a subtle but crucial differentiation between false consciousness on the one hand and long-term instinctual repression on the other (59). In this formulation, manipulation and control of the mental process at the latter level implies a fundamental 'biological'—'organic'—modifcation of man's basic nature.

> ... the malleability of 'human nature' reaches into the depth of man's instinctual structure, changes in morality may 'sink down' into the 'biological' dimension and modify organic behavior. (61)

The qualitative difference between this 'new' conception and Marx's notion of the basis and nature of false consciousness is striking. Nevertheless, Marcuse would have us view this new and more extensive mental manipulation as a logical and consequent development in the continuum of the repression of the psyche. Thus, he seems to suggest that it represents not a divergency from, but rather a refinement of Marx's discussions.

The new and more effective techniques for the further domination of both man and nature results in the increasing subjection of underlying population to the manipulative power of the perpetrators and guardians of the status quo (62). The free and potentially liberating demands of the Life Instincts come ever more effectively under the sway of the powers and instrumentalities of repression (sublimation). (63)

While on the one hand the development of the productive forces makes continually more realizable the satisfaction of basic needs with a minimum of socially necessary alienated labor, on the other hand, social control is further facilitated as the focus of the oedipal complex continues to shift from the traditional to the institutional fathers under the impact of the monopolization and technification of the means of productions (64). Thus is effected a shrinkage of the Ego (65) over and against the Super-Ego (66). The emergent

44

possibilities for a radical abolition of the long history of the socially necessitated repression of the Demands of the Life Instincts demand that the guardians of the status quo be both diligent and effective in their continual regression of these increasingly 'reasonable' demands of Eros (67). With the substitution of the institutional for the traditional fathers in the Oedipal situation, this task is immeasurably aided.

The surplus repression thus necessitated for the perpetuation of advanced capitalist society (68) strengthens and broadens the sway of the Death Instincts and results in the increase of aggressiveness at all levels of social experience. A central problem for the powers that be, therefore, is to find an appropriate harmless (even useful) object(s) for these strengthened aggresive impulses to focus on. The 'enemy' (Communism), already effective in deterring the radical politicization of the working class by 'reasonably' demanding a cessation of class conflict in face of the 'threat from without' supplies the ready made recipient for these increasing aggressive tendencies (69). This 'enemy' becomes the focal object of a perverted and growing instinctual (even biological) need in man. Further, this particular 'object' has the added economic benefit of further intensifying, indeed of rooting in the very biological structure of man, the fundamental disposition to support the economically essential and self-beneficial arms economy. As late as 1960, Marcuse had seen only one possible way out of the dilemma:

> The most promising way of utlizing the capitalist crisis is to undermine the ground of the 'defense economy' on which the relative stability of capitalism still rests. (70)

However, as the full implications of the new ontological positions were drawn out, even this possibility appears more remote and unattainable. How may the ground of the defense economy be undermined when they have in fact become a part of the very instinctual and biological structure of the population? Thus, to return to our original point, the unity of objectively opposing classes (already placated at the level of consciousness), is further reinforced at the instinctual/biological level. Both political apathy and economic prosperity are further ensured in a single stroke.

Under these conditions, the very notion of an emergent radical class consciousness appears as the ultimate in utopian speculation. Once set in motion, a dialectic ensues as the strengthened Death Instincts lead to steadily intensifying anti-enemy sentiments and actions, which in its turn result in a still further increase in the strength of Thanatos (and on, and on). An increasing proportion of the neutral 'investment fund' of psychic energy is thus appropriated by the Death Instincts as the Life Instincts consequently become progressively and proportionally weaker. At the socio-political level this instinctual/political/economic dialectic results in a subsequent strengthening of the inter-class and inter-imperialist harmony already prevalent and supported by widespread affluence, stability and false consciousness.

By means of these same manipulative techniques for the creation of false needs in the underlying population (72), the system not only makes palatable (even pleasant) its abuses and contradictions (73) but in doing so it also creates and perpetuates 'needs' designed to facilitate and complement the necessary further expansion of the capitalist production and marketing of weapons of war and other commodities. (74)

> The people recognize themselves in their commodities; they find their soul in their automobile, hi-fi set, split-level home, kitchen equipment. The very mechanization which ties the individual to his society has changed, and societal control is anchored in the new needs which it has produced. (75)

Insofar as the needs of the system have become their own, not merely at the level of consciousness, but more significantly and permanently at the instinctual and biological level, the point is reached when the quantity and quality of domination leads to a condition where the people cannot reject the system without rejecting themselves. It would appear therefore that such developments imply the necessity of a revolution, as Marcuse puts it:

> ... against the will and against the prevailing interests of the great majority of the people. (76)

The political consequences of his 'reinforced' dilemma are hinted at in a reference Marcuse makes regarding the initial causes of domination.

> These causes are economic, political, but since they have shaped the very instincts of men, *no economic and political changes will bring this historical continuum to a stop unless they are carried through by men who are physiologically and psychologically able to experience things and each other, outside the context of violence and exploitation.* (77)

This little statement contains the fundamental politico-psychological rational and justification for Marcuse's shifted theoretical, methodological and political posture. In brief, it reflects the basic motivation and justification for his novel major emphasis on subjective factors. When control and repression have gone beyond the stage of *mere* false consciousness, when the 'commands' of the powers that be have become firmly established in the very biological structure of men, then, under these circumstances:

> ... impoverishment does not necessarily provide the soil for revolution. (78)

* Emphasis added.

46

Consequently, insofar as the need for freedom has been repressed in the individual psyche—and insofar as the masters and their commands have been introjected into the biological structure of man, the struggle for liberation then must operate increasingly at the individual and subjective levels, *prior to* the struggle at the socio-economic and political levels. At this historical juncture a unique situation has emerged with the total manipulation and perversion of man's instinctual structure and biological characteristics: a situation which *demands* the *prior* development of radically 'new needs,—'new' men and women—in short, a new historical subject as an essential and indispensable precondition for 'authentic' socialist revolutionary struggle.

> In the advanced capitalist countries, the radicalization of the working classes is counteracted by a socially engineered arrest of consciousness, and by the development and satisfaction of new needs which perpetuate the servitude of the exploited. A vested interest in the system is thus fostered in the instinctual structure of the exploited, and the rupture in the continuum of repression—a necessary precondition for liberation—does not occur. It follows that the radical change which is to transform existing society must reach into a dimension of human existence hardly considered in Marxist theory—the 'biological' dimension in which the vital needs and satisfactions of man assert themselves. Inasmuch as these needs and satisfactions reproduce a life in servitude, liberation presupposes changes in this biological dimension . . . (79)

Under the impact of the mass media (80) coupled with sustained and expanding affluence, the powers that be have developed a level of 'happy' control and 'self-imposed' repression which was previously not only unforeseen, but even unimaginable. Correspondingly unique is the resultant dilemma for 'would be' revolutionary praxis. Such praxis must now deal not only with the socio-economic factors but also, and of more immediate importance, it must now overcome the strengthening 'Psychic Thermidor' (the return of the repressed due to the instinctually even biologically introjected and 'rooted' commands of the previous masters). (81)

The success of the struggle for liberation thus depends on the necessarily prior individual struggle for the re-ascendence of Eros in the psyches of those who will and must guide the revolution. (82)

However:

> . . . for new, revolutionary needs to develop, the mechanisms that produce the old needs must be abolished. In order for the mechanisms to be abolished, there must first be a need to abolish them. That is the circle in which we are placed and I do not know how to get out of it. (83)

The original socio-economic based political dilemma has now become a re-enforced political, psychological, even instinctual/biological dilemma.

The new method

> ... the capitalist development reaches a new stage to which the traditional Marxian categories no longer apply. A new historical period begins, characterized by a change in the basic class relations. Then Marxism is faced with the task of redefining the conception of the transition to socialism and the strategy in this period. (84)

It should be clear that any alteration in the fundamental ontological premises of a theory, demands subsequent and logically appropriate adjustments to the 'superstructure' of the theory. Thus, Marcuse's move from Marx to Freud at the ontological level increasingly finds its parallel at the broader theoretical level by a shift which may perhaps best be characterized as a move from Marx to Fourier. (85)

The ontological shift, initially motivated by the first perceptions of the socio-economic based political and theoretical 'dilemma', effected in turn Marcuse's further socio-economic and political analysis so as to reinforce the originally perceived 'dilemma' in the manner discussed above. Thus, the ongoing analysis was made to further testify to the validity of the prior ontological shift, an approach which contains perhaps more than a hint of circular reasoning.

Be that as it may, the new theoretical cornerstone—'psychic energy'—and the bleak liberation prospects portrayed by Marcuse in his 'reinforced' dilemma, have logically lead him to place increasing emphasis on subjective factors as the most significant basis of continued repression (86), and, consequently, also the primary objective of revolutionary praxis. In this manner, both the image of a psychic thermidor threatening to 'undo' any movement towards liberation (87), and the inter-related notion of the instinctual-biological integration of the underlying population into the dominant system of values and beliefs, point to the necessity for a prior concern with subjective factors.

> Under these circumstances, radical change in consciousness is the beginning, the first step in changing social existence: emergence of the new Subject. Historically, it is again the period of the englightenment prior to material change. (89)

In light of these developments, the primary emergence of a new Subject, individuals manifesting relatively unsublimated Life Instincts, becomes the initial focus of liberating political praxis, (90) while activity focussing upon more or less direct changes at the level of economic and also socio-political institutions must now await this necessarily prior development.

> The translation of economic into radical political struggle would be the consequence rather than the cause of change. (91)

This is not meant to imply, *in the final analysis,* a diminished evaluation of the importance of radical change in the sphere of social, economic and political institutions. Rather, it reflects a fundamental re-ordering of priorites for revolutionary political praxis. As the incorporation of Eros gradually effects a subtle but distinct *reversal* of the Marxian notion of the relationship between existence and consciousness, considerations of socio-economic and political revolution remain essential, but again, *only in the last analysis.*

While the techno-economic potentialities for liberation are largely present in the contemporary capitalist productive forces, according to Marcuse's analysis it is only the lack of the 'vital need' and the dominance of perverted self-enslaving biologically rooted needs (in short the absence of the indispensible revolutionary Subject), which restrains and retards these potential liberating forces.

Under such conditions the applicability and thus utility of traditional Marxist theory seems surpassed. It is outdated as its central concepts appear to apply to an era and 'type' of capitalism and capitalist society which has been qualitatively transcended by current and unforseeably long-range tendencies in North America (92). Thus, on these grounds Marcuse argues that his revision of Marxism is necessitated and validated by the actual present and tendencial historical developments of advanced capitalism. (93)

The ensuent revitalized 'enlightenment' with its central focus on subjective factors and the individual, is clearly intended to be applied to any further analysis of tendencies and developments in advanced capitalist society. Inextricably bound up with his proposals for liberation, Marcuse's ongoing analysis is logically obliged to lend primary consideration to the *new base*—subjective factors. Inasmuch as these factors in an historically unique development have become the basic and effective cause of further socio-economic developments and stability (in a dialectical manner *of course*), they have become *de facto* the *base,* while in a particular sense, the traditionally conceived base, economic factors and social relations, have become the superstructure. As noted above, the relationship between existence and consciousness as perceived by Marx, appears to have been subtly reversed. It is now the historically unprecedented era of consciousness determining (in both the short and long run) existence. This reversal is explained by the before mentioned apparent novel differentiation between instinctual repression and false consciousness (between the conscious and the unconscious mental processes). Thus, it is not exactly consciousness which determines existence in this new era, but rather, existence is determined by the repressed and 'falsified' instinctual structure which has 'sunk down' and become firmly rooted in the biological structure of man. Thus, at a certain juncture of sustained and effective instinctual repression, these perverted instinctual demands—'productive needs'—become so deep-rooted and so thoroughly entrenched in the organism, that not even a sustained radical alteration in man's existential experience can counter-act the development of the psychic thermidor which has taken place.

This is the point at which subjective factors become dominant and *basic*. It is this development which most urgently demands a new and appropriate theoretical orientation which recognizes are makes theoretical, analytical and political allowance for the novem primary and dominant position of subjective factors. Only such an approach can fully grasp the structure, dynamic and possible (however remote) weakenesses of the new situation. (94)

With this socially justified theoretical and political turn to the primacy of subjective factors, and the corresponding central emphasis on the individual, Marcuse proceeds to point out the increasingly indispensible role to be played by psychoanalytic therapy in revolutionary praxis. It may help, he suggests, achieve the initial and necessary task of restoring the individual to himself—of re-strengthening the ego—of creating once again (or perhaps for the first time) the individual's own ego-ideal, while at the same time releasing him from the domination of the collective ideal imposed by the institutional fathers of monopoly capitalism. In short, psychoanalytic therapy may enable the individual to live in refusal and opposition to the establishment (95). The opposition must therefore re-examine the prospects and preconditions for, as well as the very concept of socialism. It must critically re-examine Marxism. (96)

> An attempt to recapture the critical intent of these categories, and to understand how the intent was cancelled by social reality, appears from the outset to be regression from a theory joined with historical practice to abstract, speculative thought: from the critique of political economy to philosphy. (97)

Driven by the conclusions of his socio-economic and political analysis of contemporary North American society, and further warranted and directed by the reality and implications of libido, Marcuse appears to have succeeded in standing Marx on his head. The new Marcusean critical theory now appears to see eye-to-eye with Hegel. With the 'sinking down' of the values and goals of the status-quo to the instinctual, even biological structure of man, the most abstract manifestations of the traditionally conceived superstructure have become the Base, while the former base has, in a very real sense become the Superstructure.

Rethinking alienation

Once again the mark of Eros is clear. In the present dilemma the champions of the status quo point defiantly to the 'real' harmony which prevails between man's wants and desires on the other hand, and the goals and rewards of the established system on the other. This is no illusory harmony, no mere false consciousness, rather it is a very real harmony prevailing between the biologically rooted needs of the underlying population and the demands and available life style of the system. The differentiation between false consciousness and the expression of the repressed instincts is again apparent.

No matter how real this harmony is, however much it appears and is construed as the ultimate progressive social achievement in human history, Marcuse—firmly grounded in Eros (as usual)—argues, indeed insists, that this state of affairs is not a harmony which involves or is in any way related to man's *authentic* essence (Eros). Rather while being real, this is nevertheless a harmony between the dominant social realities on the one hand and a perverted and totally sublimated instinctual structure (a false essence) on the other.

Therefore, while in the traditional sense developments in North American society appear to have transcended alienation, a new and perhaps the most extensive form or level of alienation has come to prevail: the alienation of man from his 'authentic' essence. The developments of this epoch have resulted at once in a 'real' and non-alienated relationship between the present instinctual and biological nature of man and his existence, while at the same time this *current* instinctual/biological nature remains a fundamental perversion and denial of man's 'true' and 'authentic' essence.—that which becomes manifest only under conditions allowing for the full and unsublimated expression of the Demands of the Life Instincts. Once more, the basis for Marcuse's insistence on the recognition of the theoretical and political priority and predominance of the individual and subjective factors is apparent.

In such manner, the arguments of the apologists and champions of the status quo are completely undercut. What defense can be offered? No matter how great the achievements, no matter how real the harmony; Marcuse's reply is simply that by the measure of Eros (man's authentic essence), they are counterfeit—they are a lie against Humanity.

On this basis, the subsequent discussions of alienation lay decreasing stress on man's relationship to his political, economic and social existence, and increasingly emphasize this 'inner' alienation of man: The false and enslaving dualism that has developed under the impact of the conditions, rewards and manipulative techniques of advanced capitalist society has resulted in the alienation of his authentic from his historically particular (sublimated) essence. The concept focuses on the fact that under the impact of present and ongoing socio-economic, political and psychological developments, man has ceased to be a subject-object of pleasure and instead become a subject-object of work. The more or less total overcoming of the Pleasure Principle by the Reality (Performance) principle is thus the key to understanding man's present and growing alienation from nature and from his own essence. (99)

Such a conception of alienation seems a qualitative modification from Marx's conception.

Rethinking of the realm of freedom and the realm of necessity

The later Marxian concept implies the continual separation between the realm of necessity and the realm of freedom—not only in time, but also in

such a manner that the same subject lives a different life in two realms . . .
However, the development of the productive forces beyond their
capitalist organization suggests the possibility of freedom *within* the
realm of necessity. (100)

Perhaps more than any other concept, the impact of the new ontology is most
clearly evident in Marcuse's altered notion of the relationship between freedom and necessity. Marx had argued, and prior to the shift Marcuse had
agreed, that the realm of freedom could never exist within and this side of the
realm of necessity. Necessary labor would forever remain *unfree* labor. The
most that could be achieved in this respect would be the maximum shortening
of the working day and the most rational organization of this necessary labor.
(101)

In the wake of his shift to Freud, Marcuse has come to re-assess this view as
absolete. He now argues that scientific and technological advances have made
it possible (even though social relations make it as yet unrealizable) to shorten
the work day to the extent that leisure time becomes dominant time (102). On
this basis Marcuse further argues that the possibilities exist for 'libidinal' work
(103), thus building upon Freud's suggestion that sexual as well sublimated love
is connected with communal labor and that the work which has contributed to
man's development from animal is originally 'libidinal'. (104)

It is revealing to note here the continuing influence of certain concepts and
notions drawn from Western idealist philosophy. Referring to the letters 'on the
Aesthetic Education of Man', Marcuse points out that Schiller had developed
the idea of transferring labor into the free play of human faculties, as the
'authentic' goal of human existence (105). Plato too is cited as one of the
'forerunners' of this notion of freedom within necessity. (106)

The central notion entails the ideas of labor becoming play (play=imagina-
tion=phantasy=Art=Truth=the unsublimated expression of Eros); becoming it were, the free expression of the Demands of the Life Insticts. (107)

Thus it is the purpose and not the content of work which marks the
activity as play or work . . . For example, if work, were accompanied by
the reactivation of pregenital polymorphous eroticism, it would tend to
become gratifying in itself without losing its work content. (108)

Not only is it theoretically possible at both the level of technology and the
level of human essence, that socially necessary work could become play, but
it may also be expected that the emergence of a non-repressive Reality Principle would give free reign to Eros in the creation 'new and durable work
relations' (109). This latter proposition may be a viewed as the definitive
counterargument to the widely held view that without a certain degree of
repression and apprehension for his continued (comfortable) existence, men
would become dull, lethargic and unwilling to work at all. Marcuse insists, on
the contrary, that precisely to the degree that work relations are developed

under the influence of and in harmony with a non-repressive Reality Principle—in harmony that is with their authentic essence—men and women will
enthusiastically engage in 'work' (play). Inasmuch as the new work and work
relations will be in harmony with the Demands of the Life Instincts (110) the
instinctual need to resist will no longer prevail. Thus, in a certain sense Marcuse is positing what may be viewed as a 'work' instinct. A proposition which
would seem to imply that the proponements of the idea of man as a basically
lethargic being, are mentally trapped, operating within the truth-restraining
confines of a conceptual frame of reference corresponding to the politico-
economic restrictions of the dominant repressive social order.

The notion of liberation

> The basic trend of such liberation . . . would be the recovery of a large
> part of the instinctual energy diverted to alienated labor, and its release
> for the fulfillment of the autonomously developing needs of the individ-
> ual . . . The result would be not a reversion to the prehistory of civiliza-
> tion but rather a fundamental change in the content and goal of civiliza-
> tion, in the principle of progress. (111)

Here, the very image of the future, the object of the struggle is at stake. This
is Marcuse's necessary new concept of and new route to, socialism-
(liberation). While the particulars of the future society are not fully laid out, the
departure from Marx's caution and hesitancy to speculate is noteworthy.
Indeed, Marcuse argues that on the grounds of present scientific and technological potentialies, the time has come for utopian thinking (112) in the realm of
human liberation. (113)

What was once utopian in the sense of its scientific and technological
inconceivability is now (with the sweeping advances in scientific knowledge
and technical innovation) justifiable and proper projection. The continued
denial of these possibilities is only a consequence of the prevailing structure of
power, relations of production, and the prevailing conception of progress.

Liberation and progress ('progressive' progress) are still contingent upon the
full utilization and development of the productive forces. However, in the
advanced areas of capitalism, the time has long since passed when the *prior*
need was to develop the scientific and technological basis for liberation.
Indeed, Marcuse insists,

> That development has reached a level where it actually demands new
> vital needs in order to to justice to its own potentialities. (114)

With the introduction of Eros and the simultaneous comprehension of man's
authentic nature, the concept of progress and liberation become more clearly

53

definable. Authentic liberation can only be the creation of a life in harmony with the unfolding Demands of the Life Instincts. Thus, progress is only progress, if it aims at and leads to the creation of a social environment which is conducive to the full and unsublimated expression of Eros while being structuraly responsive to the ongoing expression and development of these Life Instincts. (115)

> Order is freedom only if it is founded on and sustained by the free gratification of the individuals. (116)

Once accepted, the point, of course, is to realize through appropriate and effective praxis, this concept of liberation. On the basis of the previous discussion regarding the level of instinctual repression and integration, praxis must clearly focus initially and essentially on subjective factors, attempting to restore the individual to himself. The need for free existence must be created (or allowed to develop)*prior* to the revolution at the socio-economic level (117). Unless this need informs and guides revolutionary, praxis 'authentic' liberation will not be achieved. (118)

> ... radical change in consciousness is the beginning, the first step in changing social existence: emergence of a new Subject. (119)

Thus, as has been pointed out earlier, radical social change implies prior 'cultural subversion' (120). The initial struggle must therefore concern itself with the creation of the necessary 'mental space' for refusal (121)—space in which the individual may regain the privacy of his peron (122) and escape the 'massification' of the mind perpetuated by the powers that be through their insidious techniques of mental subversion. Consequently, at this stage of advanced capitalist society, the potential break with the administered consciousness and needs, increasingly becomes the 'Archimedian' point for a larger emancipation. (123)

> The imagination, unifying sensibility and reason, becomes 'productive' as it becomes practical;a guiding force in the reconstruction of reality—reconstruction with the help of a *gaya scienza,* a science and technology released from their service to destruction and exploitation, and thus free for the liberating exingencies of the imagination. The rational transformation of the world could then lead to a society formed by the aesthetic sensibility of man. (124)

If freedom is identified as the unsublimated or unmutilated expression of 'Form' as manifest by the Demands of the Life Instincts through the medium of the 'productive imagination', then it appears to be essential that the revolution be inspired and guided by the type of man who has already achieved an historically unique degree of instinctual freedom—the type of men and women, 'who *must* have revolution because otherwise they will fall apart'. (125)

> In short, the economic, political and cultural features of a classless society must have become the basic needs of those who fight for it. (126)

The discussion of the precise characteristics of these new men will be taken up in proceeding section. However, it should be noted here that given the absolute necessity for the prior emergence of these new men (127), and further considering Marcuse's depiction of the 'one dimensionality' of the society, it appears more than a little incongruous to expect that such a radical cultural, instinctual and biological transformation could be achieved prior to the destruction of the instrumentalities which created and sustain this repression (128). Indeed, Marcuse, as noted above, is quite conscious of this problem. If conceivable at all, it certainly would not be on a broad scale. It is this situation which impresses Marcuse to conclude, as noted above, that the revolution in North America, itself an indispensible precondition for liberation in the Third World areas, must of necessity be against the will and wishes of the vast majority of the North American population. (129)

> In the last analysis, the question of what are true and false needs must be answered by the individuals themselves, *but only in the last analysis, that is:* if and when they are free to give their own answer. (130)*

If the masses must be 'forced to be free' (131), then the immediate, theoretical and political consequence must be the acceptance of the unavoidable necessity of a revolutionary 'vanguard' of a very particular type. It must be a vanguard comprised of men and women who have, in the midst of affluence 'happiness', and generally unlimited social and economic opportunity, successfully and absolutely abstracted themselves from the influence and values of the 'massified' culture and the technological manipulation of instinctss to become the living embodiment of Eros. Only such men and women thus able to perceive the 'Form' of freedom and the nature of 'authentic' progress, may guide the revolution if the struggle is not to fall prey (as have all past revolutions) (132) to the destructive and 'undoing' effects of the Psychic Thermidor.

What then is to be done? Once again, the enduring influence of idealism appears to permeate Marcuse's subsequent response. Motivated by the dilemma he has perceived, and once more justified by Eros, he answers:

---

* Emphasis added.

> From Plato to Rousseau, the only honest answer is the idea of an educational dictatorship, exercised by those who are supposed to have acquired knowledge of the real Good. (133)*

If it were only a matter of choosing between dictatorship and democracy the problem would not exist. Democracy, however, does not exist, and inasmuch as the record of the prevailing elite of businessmen, generals and non-intellectual politicians has proven anything but promising;

> the political prerogatives for the intelligentsia may not necessarily be worse for society as a whole. (134)

Thus, under the guidance of the 'Erotic elite', and with the brute power of (for some unfathourable reason) the revolting masses (no pun intended), the struggle for liberation would be assured of overcoming both the socio-histocical and the psychic Thermidors, thereby achieving authentic liberation.

> Such a world could (in a literal sense!) embody, incorporate, the human faculties and desires to such an extent that they appear as part of the objective determination of nature. (135)

Before turning to a discussion of the more specific characteristics of the new man, some consideration should be given to Marcuse's view of correct political praxis in this novel and unique epoch. In a previous section an overview was given of Marcuse's perception of the central potential capitalist contradictions and sources of crisis. In short, he had suggested that as the organic composition of capital increased to a point near total automation, they resulting parallel increases in the degree and extent of affluency, the shortening of the working day and the radically altered nature of the remaining socially necessary labor (136) would combine and interact in such a manner as to make crystal clear the irrationality of the system (137). Nevertheless, he argued that the new science and technology also made possible the more effective domination of man by man. Thus the prospects for the emergence of new needs and radical political consciousness appear to be near totally undercut. The perpetuation of false needs reinforces the system at two interrelated levels. On the one hand i leads to the creation of an inauthentic but nevertheless 'real' harmony between the values, beliefs, and objectives of the status quo, while on the other hand, the satisfaction of these false (but real) needs provides an indispensable and constantly expanding market for the mass produced 'junk' commodities (including armaments). Therefore, the strength and scope of domination expands while the system's efficiency and rationality—its 'pro-

* Here, the connection between Marcuse's Freudian 'authorized' solution and the formulations of Western idealist philosophy regarding the same and similar problems is almost too glaring to trouble pointing out. Indeed, it is a clear return, to espousing the central 'lesson' in Plato's allegory of the cave.

gressiveness'—is continually testified to and proven by its own 'obscene' accomplishments. (138)

Perhaps *the* key factor in the perpetuation of this vicious circle has become the manipulative impact of television and the allied media. As the central contradiction becomes mere obvious, the powers that be rely more and more on the media to effect the necessary sublimation of the liberating impulses of the instincts and the subversion of the resulting radical political consciousness. The unceasing message penetrates to and molds the very biological nature of man. It thus enforces the acceptance of the surplus repression demanded by the system while at the same time deflecting and denying the unprecedented liberating potentialities inherent in that system. Thereby the media accomplished and sustains the shift in the focus of the oedipal complex from the traditional to the institutional fathers (139) while correspondingly restricting (even eliminating) the mediating role of the Ego through the establishment of a more or less direct relationship between the new Super Ego (represented by the institutional fathers) and the demands of Eros and Thanatos. The reduced or abolished role of the Ego implies the restriction of the individual's private mental space, thus rendering him—a relatively unmediated recipiant of the restraining and controlling influence of institutional fathers—the embodiment of the new super ego. These developments are an historically unique and singularly insidious form of domination of man by man. Therein, the creation (or recreation) of this private mental space becomes, as noted above, the first objective of authentic revolutionary praxis.

Given these developments, Marcuse suggests that one glimmer of hope for liberating praxis would be to effect the non-functioning of television and the allied media. Through this instrumentality, the impact of the institutional fathers—the super-ego—would be alleviated allowing 'space' for the re-emergence of the private individual and a consequent system-shattering crisis.

> To take an (unfortunately fantastic* example: the mere absense of all advertising and of all indoctrination media of information and entertainment would plunge the individual into a traumatic void where he would have the chance to wonder and to think, to know himself (or rather the negation of himself) and his society. (140)

Such a situation would in the first instance institute an economic crisis brought on by the consequent underconsumption of 'junk' (141), and the related withdrawal of necessary political support for the sustained massive arms expenditures. Thus, the non-functioning of the media could effectively undercut the two most essential (even indispensible) areas of capitalist production. Further, this removal of the 'unceasing message' would lead to a

---

* Fantastic in the sense that he does not know how to effect a non-functioning television and the allied media.

marked undermining and weakening of the dominance of the super-ego with the result that in the historically unique absence (or extreme weakness) of the mediating ego, Eros would then achieve unprecedented scope for unsublimated expression (142). The resultant more direct and unmediated relation between consciousness and praxis on the one hand and the Demands of the Life Instincts on the other, would allow Eros to become the dominant and guiding force of liberating praxis—the unrestrained authentic 'architect' of new and complementary human relationships at all levels of interaction. (143)

Thus, the non-functioning of the media (particularly television and radio), appears to be a primary objective of revolutionary praxis.

> The non-functioning of television and the allied media might thus begin to achieve what the inherent contradictions of capitalism did not achieve—the disintegration of the system. The creation of repressive needs has long since become part of socially necessary labor—necessary in the sense that without it, the established mode of production could not be sustained. (144)

In harmony with both Marcuse's ontological point of departure and his socio-economic and political analysis, the following statement on correct praxis is perhaps the most specific and telling of all.

> The radical social content of aesthetic needs becomes evident as the demand for their most elemental satisfaction is translated into group action on an enlarged scale. From the harmless drive for better zoning regulations and a modicum of protection from noise and dirt to the pressure for closing whole city areas to automobiles, prohibition of transistor radios in public places, decommercialization of nature, total urban reconstruction, control of the birth rate—such action would become increasingly subversive of the institutions of capitalism and their morality. The quantity of such reforms could turn into the quality of radical change to a degree to which they would critically weaken the economic, political, and cultural pressure and power groups which have a vested interest in preserving the environment and ecology of profitable merchandizing. (145)

The new man

> ... society would be rational and free to the extent to which it was organized, sustained, and reproduced by an essentially new historical subject. (146)

While sufficient consideration has been given to Marcuse's rationale for insisting on the emergence of a new Subject prior to revolutionary struggle, some brief discussion should be offered regarding the more specific characteristics of these new men. In short, the new man is one whose total being, whose complete manner and mode of existence, is a manifestation of 'new needs', a 'new sensibility', a 'new rationality'. Everything is new. The key ingredient in each of these historically new and politically indispensible characteristics is Eros, and at a more fundamental level, libido—the notion of psychic energy. Eros is manifest and expressed through the creative—productive imagination—through Art in the broadest sense of the term and spelled with a capital Freudian 'A' (148). Once more the influence of and similarities with certain philosophical concepts from Western idealism are apparent. (149)

The 'new' needs refer to those universal human needs which become unambiguously manifest once the demands of the life instincts are allowed to reach consciousness unsublimated. They are the undeniably 'authentic' needs of the true essence of the human organism. Indeed, they *are* the essence of man (150). They express the accomplished dominance of the Life over the Death Instincts. Consequently, the existence of these new needs entails an instinctually/biologically based rejection of previously tolerated social miseries and injustices (151). To the extent that these needs become a political factor (152) (an indispensible prerequisite for 'authentic' revolutionary praxis), they will assist in the further shaping of the 'standard of living' (153) and the overcoming of the restrictive socially perpetuated feelings of guilt. (154)

Related to this, the emergence of a new rationality becomes an equally indispensible factor in counter-acting the prevailing mentally stifling influence of the 'irrational-rationality'. The liberating potentialities of the capitalist forces of production are restrained not only by the prevailing relations of production, but also (and correspondingly) by a regressive rationality which expresses the union between current and developing scientific-technological potentialities on the one hand and the values and goals of the reality principle (performance principle) on the other. As such, this 'irrational rationality' facilitates the closing of thought to the consideration of the present and impending potentialities for 'authentic' liberation. The imposition of this instinctually, even biologically, rooted conceptual straight-jacket on the 'object' population, further accentuates the necessity for the preparatory creation of a 'new' rationality. This new rationality would have as its basis the interplay between the unsublimated Demands of the Life Instincts and the prevalent and impending scientific-technological knowledge and potentialities for liberation.

Beyond the limits (and beyond the power) of repressive reason appears the prospect for a new relationship between sensibility and reason, namely the harmony between sensibility and a radical consciousness: rational faculties capable of projecting and defining the objective (material) conditions of freedom, its real limits and chances. But instead of being shaped and permeated by the rationality of domination, the

59

sensibility would be guided by the imagination, mediating between the rational faculties and the sensuous needs. (155)

Further, the 'new' morality characteristic of these new men indicates the transcendence of the Judeo-Christian (even traditional socialist) morality by one based upon Eros (156). Thus, the moral determination of right and wrong good and bad, is based on the developing relationship between the material potentialities and the 'authentic' needs of man as manifest by the Demands of the Life Instincts. Therefore, it becomes an instinctually/biologically based measure of moral value. Social relations and progress are evaluated on the basis of man's authentic nature. With the advent of this new morality the urgent necessity for a fundamental moral judgement of the real but nevertheless unauthentic harmony of North American society becomes realizable. Indeed, it is clear that Marcuse's present rejection of the 'benefits', 'progress' and 'harmony' of this society is now based in the first instance on such a *moral* condemnation.

Finally, the association of these new men in strengthened by a 'new solidarity', in instinctual/biological solidarity manifesting itself in praxis and underpinned by a common appreciation of, and the common influence of, the truth of Eros (157). This new solidarity provides the indestructible cohesion of thought and action indespensible for the success of this revolutionary vanguard.

The inextricable connection binding and mediating between these various *'new'* characteristics is their common relationship to Eros—the Demands of the Life Instincts—and in the last analysis to the original 'investment fund' of psychic energy. In short, Eros becomes manifest in every faculty and in every project of the new man. It is for this reason that given the political dilemma Marcuse perceives, the emergence of these new men and women is not merely a useful or a valuable, but in fact an *indispensible prerequisite* for 'authentic' liberating praxis.

Students

They are not professional martyrs: they prefer not to be beaten, not to go to jail. But for them, this is not a question of choice; the protest and refusals are parts of their metabolism. (158)

Having demonstrated both the necessity and the nature of the new man, it remains only for Marcuse to locate him in North American society—no mean task considering his analysis of the prevalent realities and tendencies he has depicted. Nevertheless, with appropriately discrete caution he succeeds. In the North American student movement he discovers the potential *avante guarde* (159). It perhaps should be restated that while Marcuse views these new men as the essential vanguard of an 'authentic' revolutionary struggle, he also maintains that the struggle will not succeed without the support of the traditional working class.

It is possible to regard the student opposition as the nucleus of a revolution, but if we only have a nucleus, then we don't have a revolution. (160)

A certain paradox appears to exist between this position and his parallel conclusion that the revolution must be made against the wishes and the will of the vast majority of the population. It may be explained in part by the role which Marcuse assigns to the traditional working class. While it is essential that they engage in political activity which rejects certain aspects of the status quo, due to their total instinctual/biological integration into that system, their political activity (if forthcoming at all) will therefore be not of a type which would take them beyond the confines of the general socio-economic and psychological frame of reference. To the extent that praxis is restricted by this 'psychic thermidor', it is essential that the new Subject guide and inspire the struggle for liberation, thus taking it beyond the confines of the vicious circle of repression. It is in this sense that the revolution will be against the will of the majority.

In the discussions which follow, dealing with the subjective nature and objective position of the students in North American society, this apparent paradox is further 'overcome' as the nature and extent of potential control that this vanguard has over the underlying population becomes clearer.

Marcuse's selection of the student group—the radical intelligentsia (a phrase which incidently leaves room for himself)—as *the* revolutionary nucleus (the catalyst), have the main basis: 1) Subjective factors and 2) objective factors.

The subjective basis lies in the total character of the student revolt. He argues that this is a rebellion in and against North American society's 'false and immoral comforts, its cruel affluence' (161). In the midst of sustained and expanding affluence, with unprecedented opportunity for participation in an enjoyment of this prosperity and the most sublime manifestations of bourgeois culture (162), this group has chosen to reject—indeed it is instinctually and biologically driven to reject—these 'blessings' in their totality. (163)

... very real are the young who have no more patience, who have, with their own bodies and minds experienced the horrors and oppressive comforts of the given reality. (164)

This young radical intelligentsia, exposed to the enlightening and radicalizing education of the universities (165), has turned against the abundant opportunities and diverse comforts of bourgeois society; they have, in the very face of the 'oppressive comforts' and unprecedented opportunities, become instinctually and biologically immune (166) to and repulsed by the obscenities, instinctually and biologically immune (166) to and repulsed by the obscenity, of its rewards.

61

The point of wonder is, how and why, under professed conditions of such unprecedented affluency, comfort and opportunity, does such a uniquely deep rooted opposition arise? What has been the basis and motivation for this total opposition to the ever expanding blessings of North American bourgeois culture and society?

Its basis explains at the same time its depth. The answer Marcuse gives is as follows: Precisely because of this sustained and widespread affluence and general socio-economic security, the period of adolescence for North American youth has been uniquely prolonged. Freed from the necessity to immediately become productive atoms in society, students have simultaneously been freed from the obligations and responsibilities which such roles entail. In light of this development and given the parallel and related shifted focus of the oedipal complex from the traditional to the institutional fathers under the impact of the extreme monopolization of the economy, politics and culture, the present generation of students is the first to have avoided to an historically unprecedented degree, the repression of their original and authentic instinctual impulses and demands. This repression had formerly been effected by the now displaced traditional father—the moulder of the super ego (167). These interacting developments have been further complemented by the novel (beginning in the postwar years) and widespread permissive child rearing practices in North America. As a consequence, youth now reach maturity having suffered a significantly lower degree of instinctual repression, and correspondingly have enjoyed proportionally much more experience and opportunity for the unsublimated expression and satisfaction of the Demands of the Life Instincts. (168)

As noted above, the replacement of the traditional by the institutional fathers in the oedipal situation has also had the effect of strengthening and expanding the domain of the super-ego. Inasmuch as the ego had previously been developed through its work in its mediating role between the id and the super-ego (shaped by the repression imposed by the traditional fathers), the broadening dominan of the institutional fathers combined with the effectiveness of the new technological means of mental manipulation resulted in a more immediate repression of Eros by the new and all encompassing super-ego. This development we recall was accompanied by a consequent shrinkage of the power and influence of the formerly mediating ego (or in Marcuse's present terminology, by a loss of the individual's private 'mental space'.).

As a result of these developments, the opportunity now appears to exist for either the unprecedented repression or the unsublimated expression of the Demands of the Life Instincts. (Eros). However, inasmuch as the full impact of the institutional fathers (the new and directly repressive super-ego) is not fully experienced until the individual enters the system as a producer-consumer, the dominant tendency during the prolonged period of adolescence is towards substantialy less instinctual repression (169). Thus escaping both the impact of the 'old' and the 'new' super-ego (the traditional as well as the institutional fathers), Eros is able to achieve a previously unknown degree of unsublimated expression.

The combination of these developments with increasingly widespread and prolonged university attendance (the university in Marcuse's view being the main radicalizing agency in bourgeois society) (170) has culminated in the emergence of the student group as the main source of 'new men and women' —the most 'authentically' subjectively suitable revolutionary individuals in prosperous and stable North America. Their praxis is guided and inspired by the Demands of the Life Instincts (171). Certainly this does not imply a complete escape from instinctual repression, but it does signify a long and historically unprecedented stride in this direction.

> ... in the rebellion of the young intelligentsia, the right and the truth of the imagination become the demands of political action. (172)

Or:

> In a word: they have taken the idea of revolution out of the continuum of repression and placed it into its authentic dimension: that of liberation. (173)

It was these increasingly widespread manifestations of Eros which lead Marcuse to identify the North American middle-class students (to be sure, the 'radical intelligentsia' among them), as subjectively the most suitable (even ideal) Subject to guide and inspire the struggle for liberation and lead the way to the transcendence of both the Psychic and the Socio-Historic Thermidors.

To appreciate Marcuse's perception of the 'objective' basis of the radical intelligentsia's revolutionary potential, it is necessary to briefly recall his conclusions regarding the changing structure of the North American working class. In short, the long range impact of advanced technology was seen to be the placing a steadily increasing emphasis on the functional importance of the 'new working class' of engineers, scientists and technicians. Given the nature of the new means of production, this 'new working class' inevitably comes to occupy the key positions in the productive apparatus of advanced capitalism. Indeed,

> Owing to their key positions, this group really seems to represent the nucleus of an objective revolutionary force, but at the same time it is the favorite child of the system, which also shapes the consciousness of this group. (174)

Further, considering the nature of the new means of production and the instinctual/biological bond which ties the underlying population to this apparatus, as well as the consequent professed separation of effecive control between the owners and the managers of the apparatus, the cumulative effect of these conditions and developments appears to give these managers—this 'new working class'—potential and effectively complete control over not only the means of production of advanced capitalist society, but consequently and at the same time, potentially complete and effective control over the underlying population. Inasmuch as this population (the consumers) is instinctually/biologically bound to and controlled by the new means of production, so are they controlled by the managers of that apparatus.

> The separation from the means of production . . . turns into the subjection of the whole to its calculating managers. (175)

Herein lies the thinly veiled key to Marcuse's attribution of 'objective' revolutionary potential to the North American student group—the radical intelligentsia. The old working class is gradually ousted from its former key structural position, thereby undercutting its objective revolutionary potential. As noted earlier

> The chances for promotion decline as management prefers engineers and college graduates. (176)

This increasing demand for a highly skilled and highly educated work force by the captains of industry and commerce puts a perpetual premium on the student population.

> The role of the students today as the intelligentsia out of which, as you know, the executives and leaders of even existing society are recruited, is historically more important than it perhaps was in the past. (177)

Consequently, the student group, this major source of *new* men and women, is in the politically novel and opportune position of also being the indispensible supply source of the managers, leaders and executives of industry in the present and future generations. They will of necessity become 'the calculating managers' of the new means of production, distribution and administration. Inasmuch as the altered nature of the means of production has lead to subsequent and fundamental alterations in the structure of the working class, these students—the *new* men—are the most probable (even the unavoidable) inheritors of the command positions in the new productive apparatus. Further, given the socio-political and psychological developments in North American society, the also stand to gain at the same time effective (event absolute) control over the underlying population (178). This further explains the apparent paradox noted earlier regarding exactly how the underlying population would be *made to be free* while at the same time being an essential source of power for the revolutionary struggle. Under the 'guidance' of the radical intelligentsia through the control of their productive apparatus to which the underlying population has become instinctually/biologically bound, the praxis of the masses may be effectively manipulated in the interest and toward the goal of 'authentic' liberation. Thus,

> The student rebellion hits this society at a vulnerable point; accordingly the reaction is venemous and violent. (179)

Here may be seen the emergent conjunction of 'ideal' subjective and objective factors. The student group is not only *the* authentically radical group (the very embodiment of Eros—the true essence of man—but also its members are increasingly and unavoidably coming to occupy the supreme positions of power and control in the new productive apparatus. Positions which, given the nature of the previously discussed socio-economic political and psychological developments in North America, provide them at the same time potential effective instinctually/biologically based control over the underlying population.

This is indeed an historically unique 'nucleus'.

Having at once both unprecedented subjective and objective revolutionary potential, the North American student group—the radical intelligentsia—appear to answer the question posed by Marcuse at the peak of his political pessimism

> How is it even thinkable that the vicious circle may be broken? (180)

Summary

This discussion of the development, characteristics and consequences of Marcuse's notion of liberation has come full circle. His caution and even his pessimism is often a healthy antidote for the overly glib confidence of numerous prophets of capitalist crisis, collapse and social revolution, while his emphasis on certain subjective and superstructural phenomena and developments is a facit of critical social analysis frequently overlooked. Nevertheless, caution and pessimism for their own sake is neither a political nor an analytical virtue. The unnecessary rejection of theories or the underestimation or incorrect location of revolutionary potentialities is just as damaging to further analysis and revolutionary political praxis as is unwarranted or misplaced confidence. It is in this context that Marcuse's analysis should be assessed.

It has been argued that Marcuse's analysis of North American society and his subsequent projection of certain long range future tendencies were key factors in motivating his 'rethinking' of Marxism. The political dilemma confronting revolutionary socialist praxis appeared to be brought about by fundamental changes in the nature of advanced capitalist economy and society.

The effective long term management of the economy, sustained growth and expanding stability and affluence appeared to give rise to the effective long term repression of radical political consciousness and praxis. Indeed, both structurally and psychologically, the revolutionary potential of the working class was seen to have been effectively undermined as a result of fundamental changes in the means of production, technologically assisted psychological repression and expanding and sustained affluence.

Under such conditions, it appeared to Marcuse that traditional critical theory, Marxism, was rendered conceptually inadequate to analyze this qualitatively new socio-economic political and psychological constellation.

Even the need for socialist revolution appeared to be in question. Both as a tool of further analysis and as a guide to revolutionary political praxis, critical theory appeared to have been transcended by these newly emerging and unanticipated developments. It seems that Marcuse was initially prompted by this political-cum-theoretical dilemma to rethink Marxism. His previous acquaintance with Freudian thought and its apparent frequent affinity to certain of the idealist notions and concepts of Hegel, Kant, and Plato with which he was in partial sympathy, seemed to encourage him to 'solve' the dilemma through the interjection of Freud's later instinct theory, into critical theory. By this means it seemed possible on the one hand to justify the call for revolutionary political praxis in the face of sustained affluence and apparent social contentment, while on the other hand indicating the remaining 'glimmers of hope' for and strategies to achieve liberation. Further, the union of Marx and Freud seemed to vindicate some of the most controversial and provocative concepts and notions of idealist philosophy. The challenge of positivism and the overwhelming power of the given facts were once again able to be confronted by 'negative' thinking and arguments of both the *possible* and the *desirable*. Placing Eros the centre of the *new* theoretical structure, appeared to lay an indisputable material basis 'under the material basis'. This revision of critical theory carried with it far reaching and fundamental changes in the approach and focus of future socio-economic analysis as well as in strategy proposals for liberation. While the incorporation of Freud into critical theory seemed to reinforce the political dilemma which Marcuse had perceived, it nevertheless appeared to solve the theoretical dilemma and offer at least a 'glimmer of hope' for liberation where none had existed before.

In chapters three and four, the central propositions in Marcuse's social and economic analysis will be critically considered in the light of now apparent short and long-range tendencies in North American society and economy. The objectives of these discussions will be to determine if there exist reasonable grounds for doubting the universal validity of Marcuse's analysis, and consequently, of the need for reconsidering his instance on the necessity to revise Marxism. Chapter five will give some brief consideration to the epistemological status of the notion of libido which lies at the basis of Freud's later instinct theory. A discussion which by implication should shed some light on the validity of the specific and extensive theoretical and political consequences the ontological shift has had in Marcuse's work. In the stifling one dimensionality of sustained affluence and stability, the inner dynamic of Libido appears to have given 'material basis' and dynamic to a new voluntarism which promises a break in the vicious circle. Not only is a new basis for radical political consciousness discovered but at the same stroke revised critical theory is provided with the unassailable basis—the perception of authentic universal human essence—for the rational and moral transcendence of the prevailing good society.

Thus, the questions to be considered in the chapters which follow are:

(1) On Marcuse's own grounds, was this revision necessary—is critical theory the better for it? and
(2) does the epistemological status of libido—the cornerstone of the revised critical theory—justify the theoretical, social and political conclusions and implications drawn from it?

Chapter Three:

Further Considerations of the Fundamental Economic Propositions and Implications

Introduction

In this chapter an attempt will be made to consider certain possible limitations to the long range economic tendencies projected by Marcuse. Inasmuch as these tendencies appear to provide the basic justification for his revision of critical theory, the discussions which follow aim to cast some light on the validity of this economic warrant.

It should be immediately stressed that the further discussions of the various economic propositions central to Marcuse's analysis make no pretence at being exhaustive. Indeed they are not pro-con analyses, for Marcuse has already argued the case *for* the tendencies and developments he depicts. Instead they represent an effort to balance out Marcuse's discussions by indicating certain unconsidered factors and tendencies. Further, given the scope of the phenomena to be discussed and the limitations of space, an attempt has been made to synthesize the main arguments and developments which appear to indicate tendencies partially or wholly at odds with those projected by Marcuse. For this same reason extensive use has been made of references to sources of data and further argumentation. The primary objective of this chapter then is to determine is significant factors and tendencies exist which detract from the universal validity of Marcuse's analysis, and which consequently undermine his economic justification for revising critical theory. In the final analysis it is this latter point which is of central concern.

The freezing of inter-imperialist economic competition—
further considerations

> ...the conflicting competitive interest among the Western nations were gradually integrated, ... and superseded by the fundamental East-West conflict, and an intercontinental political economy took shape ... susceptible to a planned regulation of that 'blind anarchy' in which Marxism saw the root of capitalist contradictions. (1)
> ... imperialist contradictions [are]* suspended before the threat from without. (2)

Marcuse's notion of inter-imperialist competition refers to the economic competition between the several advanced capitalist nations for larger shares of

* My insertion.

the international market, investment opportunities and raw material supplies. His insistence that a planned intercontinental political economy has come into being reflects a view that beginning in the early postwar period the leading capitalist nations, under the threat of international communism, 'voluntarily' united behind North American economic leadership to form a cohesive and single purposed international economic unit. This conclusion while formulated on the basis of developments in the early postwar period (roughly up to 1954), lead Marcuse to make, indeed to insist upon, long range tendencies in this direction. It is clear from his subsequent work that he both implicitly and explicitly continues to affirm these views.

In this section the discussion will focus on Marcuse's explanation of the basis and extent of inter-imperialist economic unity and co-operative planning. Particularly in the past decade, certain apparent counter-tendencies have begun to emerge. It is these unconsidered developments and tendencies which shall be discussed here in an attempt to 'balance out' as it were, the implied exclusiveness of Marcuse's projections. While not pretending themselves to exhaustiveness, the factors discussed here may facilitate a fairer evaluation of Marcuse's analysis and thus give a partial indication of the validity of his insistence on the necessity for revising critial theory. First to Marcuse's explanation of the cause of the 'freezing' of inter-imperialist economic competition.

It seems that the inter-imperialist unity which emerged in the immediate aftermath of the Second World War may be better understood if one perceives its basis not so much in the common fear of the 'enemy' as does Marcuse, but rather as the result of the near complete crippling and destruction of all the major competitors of North American capitalism. Two world wars had lain Germany, Italy, France, Japan and Great Britain prostrate—stripped of practically all autonomous economic and military power (3). In Britain there had been practically no net investment in industry during the entire wartime period, while on the continent near total devastation and exhaustion of the nations' productive apparatuses was the consequence of the conflict. (4)

Largely through the instrumentality of the Marshall Plan, North America attemted to shore up the faltering Western European societies and thereby prevent their conversion to socialism as a result of substantial early post-war left wing sympathies in these areas (5). This system of grants to industrialized and potentially wealthy European nations totalled roughly thirteen billion dollars (6), but was at that, a relatively small price to pay for the preservation and revitalization of the capitalist system. On the global level, the weakened (and in the case of the latter destroyed) economic and military position of Western Europe and Japan confronted with the rising movements for national independence in the colonial areas, resulted in the forced granting of political independence to the bulk of these colonies by the 'old' imperialis powers and their partial simultaneous incorporation into a North American dominated and policed economic imperialist system. (7)

North America emerged from the Second World War as the undisputed economic and military leader of the capitalist world. Bolstered both by the profits accumulated during the war (8) and the weakened military-economic position of her former rivals, she was able to dominate the capitalist world for the next twenty years. In the early postwar period, North American capitalism overshadowed the international capitalist markets and investment fields while Western Europe and Japan generally produced for and invested in their domestic markets (especially until around the early and mid-fifties). The combination of depleted money-capital resources and the need for vast domestic reconstruction in the aftermath of the conflict significantly circumscribed the scope of early postwar economic operations for the weakened imperialist nations to primarily domestic arenas.

Thus the need for the global reconstruction, re-euipment and extension of capitalism in this period, complemented the general backlog of consumer demand to create unprecedented economic expansion room for capitalism. A host of new productive techniques and products deriving in large part from the technological breakthroughs achieved by the intense arms research of the wartime period gave added scope to these abundant economic opportunities. Problems arising from surplus productive capacity and surplus money-capital accumulation were significantly absent.

Rather than a common fear of communism, it would seem that the early postwar lull in inter-imperialist economic competition was far more the result of the practical inability of the 'old' imperialist powers to seriously compete with North American capitalism, as well as the unusually abundant investment, marketing and raw material acquisition opportunities. This is not meant to dismiss the impact of the 'enemy' in giving rise to a political and military, even economic, unity in the capitalist camp. However, to insist on the exclusiveness of the factor, as Marcuse does, seems to overlook other and perhaps more important critical factors. Indeed, the military unity itself, while certainly inspired by the presence of the Soviet Bloc, appeared to owe much of its cohesion to the weakened economic and military position of Western Europe (and Japan) and their consequent inability to defend their territorial integrity.

It should be noted however that the achievement of a political and military unity even among the Western European nations has been far from successful. The customs Union (E.E.C.) finally achieved in 1957 was by far the most significant move toward any form of unification.

Of particular instructive value in the question of the apparent *basis* of the early postwar lull in inter-imperialist competition is the history of the rise and fall of the Western embargo policy imposed on the 'enemy' in the immediate aftermath of the war.

Along with the decision to re-establish Western European and Japanese capitalism, the U.S. introduced the 'Foreign Assistance Act' of 1948. This was the first in a series of legislation designed to connect aid with trade. Under the threat of this legislation which culminated in the so-called 'Battle Act' of 1951,

70

the U.S. obliged all aid recipients to impose embargoes on trade with the Soviet Bloc countries (and later China) (9). Primarily under U.S. direction, lists of 'strategic' materials were drawn up. Trade violations of these lists were restrained not only by mutual agreement on the requirements of international capitalist security, but also, and in many ways more decisively, by the omnipresent fear of U.S. retaliatory aid restrictions aimed at the offending countries. (10)

The Western European perspective on this embargo policy was essentially less harsh than that of their North American senior partner. While they found little difficulty in accepting an embargo policy aimed at what were traditionally considered to be 'strategic' goods, the list imposed by the Americans under the threat of aid restrictions went far beyond that traditional conception. It cut into numerous areas of 'peaceful' trade and it was on the issue of these materials and commodities that there was reluctance to cooperate (11). Inasmuch as North American trade with the now restricted countries had always been minimal, the imposition of an extensive embargo policy represented no serious alteration of its traditional trade and investment patterns. Western Europe on the other hand had traditionally enjoyed substantial trading ties with Eastern Europe and the Soviet Union. Thus, this same embargo policy deprived it of a vital trading partner (12) and obliged it to turn to North America instead. As reluctant as it was, during the early postwar yers, the weakened economic condition of Western Europe, its economic indebtedness to America and, perhaps of most importance, the more substantial income it accrued in these early postwar years from American aid than from East-West European trade (13), weighed heavily in favor of the wisdom of adhering to the inflated embargo lists and joining in a broader common front against the 'enemy'.

The factors which led to the disintegration of this embargo policy and the voluntary economic unity it supposedly reflected reveal just how critical and enduring a factor the fear of the 'enemy' in fact was in the perpetuation of this common imperialist front. As Western European economies began to regain strength in the early and mid-fifties, the relative significance of American aid began to diminish. With the drawing to close of the initial postwar reconstruction boom, Western European capitalism began to achieve productive capacities in surplus of effective domestic demand, and pressure began to build for the re-acquisition of a more substantial share of international trade. With Eastern Europe and the Soviet Union as traditional trading partners, these pressures were initially aimed at the re-establishment of broader trade ties with these areas. The death of Stalin, the slight easing of East-West tension, and a serious recession in 1953–1954, complemented the increasing strength of Western European capitalism to mark 1953 as the beginning of the long period of European withdrawal from its cooperation in the embargo policy (14). The combination and conjunction of these factors appeared to motivate a gradual 'reconsideration' of the wisdom of these trade restrictions. In 1954 and against American wishes the Concom lists (those embargo lists applying to

Eastern Europe and the Soviet Union) were revised. At the same time British and Western European pressure began to build for a parallel revision of the Chincom lists (those applying to China). This latter move was strongly opposed by the U.S. but was finally effected unilaterally by the British, who were quickly followed by Western Europe. (15)

While the U.S. continued to unilaterally enforce a far more 'comprehensive' embargo and attempted usually unsuccessfully (now that the aid withdrawal threat was not so effective), to bring its Western European allies into line by exerting pressure through such international organization as NATO, after 1958 the whole embargo policy began to rapidly disintegrate (16). Thus it seems reasonably clear that the changing Western European definition of 'strategic' commodities and materials was far more a reflection of its growing economic strength (17) and problems, than an indication of a declining fear of the 'enemy'. While fear was undoubtedly a factor in the emergence of this aspect of the common economic front against the 'enemy', it appears that it was at least as much due to a fear of the senior partner (U.S.A., through aid restrictions), as it was to fear of the external 'enemy'—(international communism). Indeed, following Marcuse's argumentation, it is extremely problematic that this aspect of the common imperialist front (the embargo policy) should have disintegrated precisely at a time when the 'enemy' appeared to be stronger than ever before, not only in Eastern Europe; the Soviet Union, and China, but also in South-East Asia, Africa, and Latin America. In *this* sense, the economic base of Western European capitalist countries showed its strength compared to the political and ideological superstructure.

Granted this is but one aspect of the supposed inter-imperialist unity and cooperation, but inasmuch as it is related so immediately to the phenomena (the 'enemy') which is the supposed critical factor underpinning the 'freezing' of competition and the emergence of a united imperialist front, it seems particularly instructive regarding the comprehensiveness of Marcuse's long range projection. Indeed, the further aggravation of those economic factors (increasing productive capacity, raw material needs, and accumulating money capital), which appear to have been critical in undermining the embargo policy, seem also responsible for the broader undermining of the professed inter-imperialist economic planning and 'non-competitive cooperation' of the early postwar years. It is to these broader developments and tendencies that the discussion now turns.

It is interesting to note that in a particular sense it seems to have been precisely this fear of the enemy which hastened the reemergence of inter-imperialist competition after the early postwar lull. The North American sponsored postwar economic reconstruction which was undoubtedly partially motivated by a substantial fear of the enemy, resulted in a definite economic unity and cooperation during the early period. However, this economic assistance at the same time hastened the laying of the basis for European independence and a subsequent re-emergence of economic competition be-

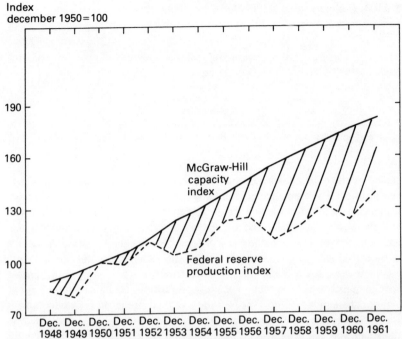

Index
december 1950=100

Fig. 1. *Source:* Hearings before the subcommittee on Economic statistics of the joint Economic committee of the U.S. Eighty-seventh congress, U.S. Government printing office, Washington, 1962, p. 13.

tween the partner capitalist nations (18). In Japan this process of reconstruction began as early as 1946. (19)

With the saturation of the North American domestic monopoly market and the consequent accumulation of surplus money capital at the end of the first postwar economic cycle, American private capital began to flow into Western Europe. (20)

Indeed it has been suggested by some analysts such as Charles Kindleberger (21), that U.S. monopoly capitalists actively promoted the idea of a Common European Market, because they calculated that *they* would conquer the Market before European firms had been able to build up enterprises corresponding to this 150-million-people market. U.S. productive units on the other hand were experiencing serious under utilization of productive capacity, and in size were ready made for such a market. (See fig. 1 and table 1.)

This area, unlike the relatively limited and less secure marketing and investment opportunities of the Third World (22), offered investment opportunities, markets, skilled manpower, and political stability suitable to the dimensions and requirements of North American productive and moneycapital surpluses and capacities. This massive transfusion of first state then private money capital into both Western Europe and Japan was generall accom-

73

Table 1. *Capacity utlization in Manufacturing (percent)*

1960	80.6	1967		85.3
1961	78.5	1968		84.5
1962	82.1	1969	(4th quarter)	81.7
1963	83.3	1970	(1st quarter)	79.8
1964	85.7		(2nd quarter)	78.0
1965	88.5		(3tf quarter)	76.2
1966	90.5		(4th quarter)	72.3

Source: The Dynamies of U.S. Capitalism, P. Sweezy and H. Magdoff, p. 49.

panied by the most advanced productive techniques and technology America had to offer. The tremendous technological lead gained by North American capitalism during the war and its resulting favorable production differential was thereby substantially undermined by this early burst of moneycapital/technology export. Just as the entry of Japan, Russia and Italy into the family of industrial nations in the last quarter of the 19th century did not see their complete duplication of the industrial countries that went before them (23), so with the postwar reconstruction of Western Europe and Japan did they adopt and duplicate only the most modern parts of their predecessors—benefactors —(in the latter case North America's) productive apparatus. Inasmuch as their factories and capital goods had been either devastated or significantly worn out by the end of the war, the 'old' imperialist nations were obliged to largely rebuild from the bottom-up. A situation which while having obvious and enormous short term disadvantages, entailed nevertheless certain very tangible long range advantages. Either by purchase or by imitation the ensuing reconstruction extensively utilized the superior North American technology and capital goods (24). Thus, at the very outset of the postwar reconstruction, the basis was laid for a narrowing of the technological gap and a subsequent reduction of the productivity differential enjoyed by North American capitalism (25). These developments in turn hastened re-emergence of Japanese and Western European capitalism to strengths and technological sophistications enabling, indeed obliging, them to once again seriously challenge and compete with their 'benefactor' for bigger slices of the available international markets, investment opportunities and raw material supplies.

While Western Europe and Japan were still of a much smaller scale and continuing to trail technologically in most areas of production, by the mid-fifties the *basis* had been laid for the re-emergence of serious competition between North America and her until recently, prostrate competitors. The early postwar lull in this competition arising from both the industrial inability (due to wartime devastation and exhaustion), of the 'old' imperialist rivals, and the more than adequate markets and investment opportunities of this period soon began to show the first signs of strain. The productive capacities and profits of the revitalized and modernized industrial apparatuses of Western

Europe and Japan began to outstrip the domestic demands for money capital and consumer and capital goods. With the end of the first postwar expansion and reconstruction boom leading to a growing money capital surplus due to the lack of adequately profitable investment opportunities in this already saturated market, capitalists in these areas once again began to seriously eye the international market and investment field. Thus, it appears that by the mid- and late fifties, the 'old' imperialist centers, while still relatively much weaker than North American imperialism, were increasingly pressed by rising surpluses of productive capacity, production and money capital to attempt to 'unfreeze' inter-imperialist competition, in an effort to maintain the high rates of investment necessary to continued and expanding prosperity. The technological push given them only a few years earlier by their North American 'partners' facilitated in no mean way the Western European and Japanese re-emergence as small but increasingly effective competitors on the international market.

While suffering from the competitive disadvantage resulting from the superior production scale of their American rivals, Japanese and Western European capitalists nevertheless enjoyed certain advantages in other areas. Although they had lost most of their colonial holdings during and in the immediate aftermath of the war (largely to the subsequent indirect control of the rising American empire), the 'old' imperialist nations were at the same time released from the taxing economic, political and military burdens of keeping these areas 'free' for private investment and exploitation in the face of swelling national liberation movements and sympathies. The ready American acceptance of the role of world capitalist policeman (a role entailing substantial disadvantages as well as obvious advantages), enabled Western European and Japanese capitalism to share the benefits (though not without significant U.S. restraints) of a world kept 'free' largely by means of American dollars and efforts (26). This applied not only to the Third World areas but to the 'defense' of the 'old' capitalist nations themselves. On this latter point it is interesting to note that the worsening economic situation in North America in the past years has brought U.S. threats to withdraw from paying this policing bill. The most recent move in this direction was a hard line public statement by Nixon threatening to let Western Europe go it alone on their defense costs and requirements unless American efforts in this area are met with unspecified sympathetic economic reciprocation (27). Indeed, as Secretary of the Treasury John Connally had stated in 1971, the cost of defending the Third World, Western Europe and Japan has, for the last decade, been a major cause of the chronic balance of payments in the U.S. (28)

Obvious advantages accrue from the enormous military expenditures, but as the costs continue to rise and Japan and Western Europe compete more effectively on the world (including the U.S. domestic) market, the scales appear to be tipping in favor of the disadvantages, as arms spending induced inflation persists in North America and foreign military aid and involvement lead to worsening balance of payment situations. It may not be long before the cracks that are beginning to show in the economic unity of the 'common front' of the capitalist nations become manifest at the level of military unity as well.

Indeed, the somewhat estranged position of France vis-a-vis NATO already manifests signs of disintegration. While NATO appears still a strong alliance, it is clear from recent murmurs of various member countries that the alliance is not as unproblematic as it once was. The sometimes conflicting immediate economic interests of the individual states seem to place an increasing strain on the alliance. The political and military considerations, as well as economic considerations (28) arising from U.S. postwar excess productive capacity, which influenced North American support for E.E.C. at its early stages, soon began to be counterbalanced by soley economic considerations. The E.E.C. was showing itself increasingly capable of not only capturing (or recapturing) the European market, but of cutting into other U.S. markets, including the North American domestic one. The consequent aggravation of U.S. surplus productive capacity strongly influenced a shifted positive to negative U.S. stance on the E.E.C.

Further, with the closing of the technological gap between North America and her aspiring competitors and with the steady increases in the sixties of the scale of European and Japanese productive units effected by the concentration of capital in these areas, the labor cost factor appears to become increasingly critical in achieving competitive advantage in the international market place. In the early postwar period, North American superiority of scale and technological sophistication appeared to more than compensate for the much higher wages of its working class, thus enabling American capitalism to realize a lower labor cost per unit output. However, while the U.S. is still generally superior in scale, the growing sizes of the Western European and Japanese productive units and the narrowing (30) (and in some cases the elimination) of the North American technological lead, seems to be steadily pushing the wage cost factor to the forefront in determining which of imperialist centers enjoys the lowest overall cost per unit output and consequently the competitive edge.

First detectable in labor intensive industries such as shoes and textiles (31), the substantially lower salaries and wages of the Japanese and Western European working classes (32) appear to be an increasingly decisive factor in their effective competitive ability with the North American giant.

In the early 60's the approximate industrial wage ratio between Western Europe and North America was $\frac{1}{2}/1$ and between Japan and North America was 1/5 (33). While industrial wage costs rose in Japan and Western Europe at between 4 and 5 times the rate of increase in North America between 1960–1968 (34), this disproportional rate of increase has diminished substantially since 1967 (35), and the lower wages and salaries of the Western European and Japanese working classes remain a key factor in the competitive struggle for shares of the international market and in determining average profit rates for the several imperialist centers. Further, it seems unlikely that

76

in a tightening and toughening world market and investment field, Japan and Western Europe are likely to easily surrender one of the most significant competitive advantages they enjoy. Consequently, the coming decade will in all probability witness a tougher line taken by capitalism in these areas in response to working class demands for wage and salary increases.

As for the wage struggle in North America (aspects of which will be more fully discussed in chapter three), the institutionally generated expectations, and to some extent the precedent of working class 'affluency', would appear to promise even more intense and aggravated wage struggles as the socially fostered rising expectations become more unattainable. (36)

It seems unlikely that American capitalism will be able to afford to continue to pay their working class the accustomed 2 to 5 times higher wages than their Japanese and European counterparts (37). Thus it may well be that as North American capitalism's alternate competitive advantages are diminished (though certainly not eliminated) (38), their own working class, so long a *relatively* privileged sector at the direct and indirect expense of their brother in the Third World and the other capitalist centers, will tend to become the object of more intense exploitation (39) as the struggle for competitive advantage in the international market becomes more severe.

The previously mentioned American advantage of larger production scale, while generally still intact, is also being undermined as a result of capital concentration in both Western Europe (under the political auspices of the E.E.C.) and in Japan. In many areas such as the oil, steel, ship building, electrical appliance and chemical industries, this size differential has been practically eliminated (40). While differences of scale still favor North American capitalism in the computer and car industries, here too the concentration of capital in Western Europe and Japan appears to be steadily eroding the indisputed American lead. (41) (see tables 2–4).

Thus, in terms of favorable wage costs, comparable modernity of capital goods and technology, expanding scales of production and all round productive capacity and efficiency, Western European and Japanese capitalism appear to be increasingly capable of effective competition with their 'relatively' superior North American counterpart. The growing surpluses of money capital, productive capacity and production arising from the disproportionally high industrial growth rates (42), of the 'old' imperialist powers during the long postwar boom have not only made it possible for Western Europe and Japan to challenge American economic hegemony, but more importantly these developments coupled with the end of this postwar reconstruction boom make it absolutely necessary that they do so. The high rates of investments underpinning the long postwar prosperity can no longer be realized by picking up the left-overs after North American capitalism. The international market and investment field have become the only substantial alternative to counteract tendencial falling sales, investment rates and so, general economie property. To the extent that American capitalism has attained a monopoly in the international market due to

Table 2. *Car production (in millions)*

	1937	1950	1955	1966	1967
U.S.A.	3.9	6.7	7.9	8.6	7.4
The Six	0.5	0.6	1.5	6.1	5.7
Britain	0.4	0.5	0.9	1.6	1.5
Japan[a]	0.1	–	0.1	2.2	3.1

[a] The figures for Japan include trucks, the figures for the other countries do not.
[b] 1956.
Source: E. Mandel, Europe vs America, New York, Monthly Review Press 1970, p. 14.

the early postwar industrial incapacity of her former rivals, moves by Europe and Japan to re-establish themselves in the arena of international trade and investment seem to imply an emergent competition and conflict of immediate economic interests.

Ever since the conflict between Adenauer and Kennedy, the contradictions appear to have been increasing. The gold-dollar issue between U.S. and its major European trading partners reflects the present acuteness of the contradictions.

The increasing U.S. trade deficit, while deriving in large part from foreign military expenditures, also stems significantly from this emerging economic competition—competition which has even moved into the previously exclusively U.S. dominated domestic market.

The tables 5 and 6 give some indication of the disproportional postwar growth rates favoring the 'old' imperialist centers.

This disproportional growth rate is perhaps most acute in the chemical industry where, between 1967 and 1970, Japanese and Western European firms experienced rates of growth ranging from 2 to 8 times that of their rival companies in North America (43). Nevertheless, while the postwar sprint of Japan and Western Europe has been impressive, the opportunities for further 'catching-up' to the leader by means of rapid (and relatively inexpensive)

Table 3. *Production of plastics (in thousands of tons*

	1955	1965
U.S.A.	1 744.2	5 217.8
West Germany	355.2	1 953.2
The Six	595.5	3 893.0
Britain	323.4	973.0
Japan	101	1 603.0

Table 4. *Production of crude iron (in millions of tons)*

	1929	1946	1953	1966	1967
U.S.A.	57.3	61	101.3	124.7	118
The Six	35.6	11.8	39.7	85	90
Britain	9.8	12.9	17.9	24.7	24.2
Japan	3.8	2.0	9.8	47.4	62.1

Source: Ernst Mandel, Europe vs. American, New York, Monthly Review Press, 1970, p. 15.

technological progress will probably diminish as America's rivals will increasingly have to rely upon their own research rather than copying or purchasing North American advances (44). The narrower the technological gap the less there is to copy and innovate from, and, the stiffer the competition, the more covetous North American firms are likely to become of the technological advantages they still retain. Thus it would seem that not only the 'policing' bill of world capitalism as mentioned above, but also the research bill for its impressive scientific and technological advances, will probably fall more heavily upon the emergent rivals who for long have been enjoying a relatively inexpensive ride at the cost of American capitalism.

The advantages are clearly no longer all on one side, and while North American capitalism is still, in relative terms, the strongest of the imperialist centers, it has been unable to prevent the erosion of the absolute economic superiority it enjoyed in the early postwar period (45). The apparently axiomatic American economic dominance and the consequent 'cohesion' of the imperialist powers reflected in the economic constellation prevalent in the immediate aftermath of the Second World War, has now become once more problematic. Western Europe and Japan are beginning to feel the necessity, as well as experience the ability, to effectively compete with American capitalism on the international market place (46). It seems that the time is rapidly passing when one could, as Marcuse continues to do, simply consider all non-

Table 5. *Rates of growth of industrial production (per cent a year)*

	1960–65	1965–70	1971
U.S.	5.7	4.0	−1.5
Japan	11.4	16.7	5.5
U.K.	3.2	2.2	1.0
France	5.3	6.4	4.0
Germany	5.3	6.3	1.9
Italy	5.9	7.2	−3.3

Source: A. Glyn & R. B. Sutcliffe, British Capitalism, Workers and the Profit Squeeze, Middlesex, Penguin, 1972, p. 95.

Table 6. *Growth rates of Gross National product – International comparisons, selected periods 1913–1969*

Period	United States[a] Total	Per capita	Canada Total	Per capita	France Total	Per capita	Germany, Fed. Re.[b] Total	Per capita	Italy Total	Per capita	United Kingdom Total	Per capita	Japan Total	Per capita
1913–1929	3.1	1.7	2.4	0.7	1.7	1.8	0.4	-0.1	1.8	1.2	0.8	0.3	3.9	(NA)
1929–1950	2.9	1.8	3.2	1.8	–	-0.1	1.9	0.7	1.0	0.3	1.6	1.2	0.6	(NA)
1929–1969	3.3	2.0	3.8[c]	2.0[a]	2.5	2.0	4.2	2.9	3.2	2.4	2.2	1.7	4.9	(NA)
1950–1960	3.2	1.4	4.0	1.3	4.9	3.9	8.6	7.1	5.6[a]	4.8[d]	2.7	2.3	8.2[c]	7.0[e]
1950–1969	3.9	2.3	4.5[a]	5.3	4.3	6.8	5.4	5.6[d]	4.8[d]	2.7	2.2	9.7[e]	8.6[e]	
1960–1969	4.5	3.2	5.2[c]	3.3[c]	5.8	4.7	4.7	3.7	2.8	2.1	11.1	9.9		

[a] To make rates comparable with those of other countries shown, official series shown in table 510 has been adjusted by addition of military retirement and mustering out payments, research transfers, depreciation on Government buildings, and certain personal taxes and by subtraction of net interest originating in households and institutions.

– Represents zero.

NA Not available.

[b] Beginning 1960, includes Saar and West Berlin.

[c] Final year, 1968.

[d] Initial year, 1951.

[e] Initial year, 1952.

Source: Statistical Abstracts of U.S., 1972, p. 313.

American capitalism as mere contented voluntary appendages of the American giant under the impact of the threat from without—the 'enemy'.

The apparent re-emergence of serious competition for export markets between the several imperialist centers seems to give rise to a broadening of this competition. The accumulation of money capital in the various metropoles find restricted investment opportunities in their domestic economies to the extent that productive capacities of existing facilities are already adequate to meet aggregate demand on a monopoly market. Thus the surplus pool of money capital accumulated from both domestic and existing foreign investments and sales places pressure on capitalists to extend the export of money capital as well as commodities. This growing necessity to increase both money capital and commodity exports demands and facilitates an enlarged scale of production in both the exporting and recipient countries (47). Recent struggles between North America and Japan have revealed improved money capital export opportunities to Japan to be a major concession sought (and won) by the Americans (48). On this same line, the recent devaluation of the American dollar, while contributing to an improved competitive position for American commodity exports on the world market, has also resulted in a worsening of the conditions for North American money capital exports as the costs in U.S. dollars of establishing factories, etc. abroad has risen sharply (49). Thus the increased competition for world markets and investment opportunities appears to be self-intensifying as profits realized in foreign investment eventually return to add to the pool of surplus investment capital, while the increasing productive capacity and efficiency of the productive apparatuses spurred on by the need to gain a competitive edge, results in a further hastening of the growth of surplus productive capacity. Taken together these developments appear to steadily renew and intensify the pressure in the several capitalist metropoles towards further and increased exports of both commodities and money capital on their individual efforts to counteract tendencies towards economic stagnation. It seems that the development of the capitalist world's productive and investment capacities are outstripping the requirements and capacities of the 'effective' markets available to this free world. Indeed, it seems reasonable to conclude that it is precisely these surpluses which appear to contribute most significantly to the decreased fear of the *enemy,* as the natural resources, markets, and opportunities for capital investment in the domain of this 'enemy' become a more attractive (and stable) outlet for intensifying pressures for capitalist expansion arising from growing surpluses—(better a long term if lower, guaranteed profit or market from 'iron curtain' investment and sales, than unused money capital and productive capacity). When the chips are down, capitalism seems to be far less biased about its customers than many politicians and sociologists, including Marcuse, had supposed in the heyday of the fifties. Thus, the recent political about faces by the leading capitalist nations in regard to their posture toward the enemy, should be seen as rooted less in a basic liberalization of Western (and Eastern) political attitudes, and far more in the chronic economic problems of capitalism due to growing money capital, production and productive capacity surpluses.

The tendencial increase in economic competition between the major capitalist centers is by no means restricted to marketing and investment in the advanced industrial countries. Indeed, inasmuch as raw materials form the basis of industrial production and prosperity, (a point cogently demonstrated by the recent price increases and delivery restrictions of oil from the Arab world), the Third World should be viewed as major and inter-related arena for the tendencial growth of inter-imperialist competition (50). The re-emergence of Western Europe and Japan has witnessed an increased drive on their part to gain (or regain) either control or at least a foothold in the major raw material resource areas of the Third World (51). Along with the role of world policeman went definite advantages in the control and aquisition of Third World sources of raw materials. Indeed, the monopolization of the major sources of basic industrial raw materials is one of the most effective means of 'beating-out' competition from other imperialist centers. (52) It is this factor which must be appreciated in understanding the North American drive to gain monopoly control of even those resources for which they have an adequate and economical alternate and/or domestic supply. (53)

Attempts to undermine the American advantage in this area have been seen not only in the case of Western European capitalism (54) but also with Japan (a country which at any given time has only enough industrial raw materials on hands for 20 days continued production as opposed to 60 days for its major rivals) (55). Particularly Japan, though in many respects this also applies to Western Europe, is faced with the prospect of continuing its dependence upon U.S. domestic and controlled foreign sources of basic industrial raw materials, or developing alternative 'independent' sources. In a climate of apparent increasing economic competition between the major imperialist centers, and in the wake of even the first manifestations of North American determination to undermine wherever possible the competitive advantages of its emergent rivals. (56), it appears probable that Japan will in future make concerted efforts to establish 'independent' raw material sources in the Third World (and in the domain of the 'enemy' as well). Only in this way may Japan deprive American capitalism of one of its major trump cards in the competitive struggle. Indeed, indications of the Japanese moves in this direction may be seen in the foreign investment guarantee plan formulated by the Japanese government in 1970. This plan was designed to guarantee up to 90% of investment losses incurred due to political or credit problems (57). While this program is applicable to investment in the advanced industrial countries as well as the Third World, it seems clear that the primary intent is to secure investment against such problems in the Third World, inasmuch as they are most acute and threatening in these latter regions. This program, parallel in form and intent to the one sponsored by the U.S. government, appears necessary in light of the rising investment uncertainty in major areas of the raw material rich Third World.

Further, the 70's have also witness significant moves by Japan to enter joint and long term raw material development projects with the Soviet Union ('the enemy') in Siberia (58). It should be noted here that Japan is not alone in increasing trade and investment with the Soviet Union. Recent years have seen significant moves by North America and Western Europan capitalism to take advantage of the long latent investment, raw material and trade options in this area (59). The vast resources of this area provide perhaps the most substantial single opportunity for Japanese capitalism to develop sources of basic industrial raw materials independent of American control. It should also be noted here that these Japanese/Soviet resource development negotiations and projects are intrinsically tied to political agreements (60). Thus, at least in this respect, it seems that the resource price and scarcity problems facing Japan, and due in large measure to American capitalism's efforts to dull the competitive edge of Japanese capitalism, are giving rise to a certain diminishment of Japan's fear of the 'enemy'.

Rooted in the steady increases in production, productive capacity, and money capital which are confronted by markets and investment opportunities growing at a much slower rate, the apparent rise in inter-imperialist competition (61) seems to restrict even monopoly capitalism's ability to increase prices in response to rising costs per se. Thus it represents a major threat to the maintenance of the average rate of profit (62). The closing technological gap between the several imperialist centers, along with the gradually increasing scale of industrial production in Western Europe and Japan, seems to push the wage cost factor to an increasingly critical position in the determination of competitive ability. If America's economic dominance and competitive superiority (and so the firmness of the common economic front against the 'enemy') was previously axiomatic, now it seems safe at least to say that those same propositions have, especially since the mid-sixties, become problematic. (63)

In the wake of the re-emergence of inter-imperialist competition, structural unemployment in North America has been aggravated to reach serious proportions (64). Further, international monetary crises, largely absent during the entire postwar period, have begun to re-emerge. Since 1969 their continual ups-and-downs have once again reflected emergent serious inter-imperialist economic competition and raised the threat of international trade wars in the capitalist world (65), a prospect which has loomed larger since the further intensification of these crises in 1971 (66). The re-emergence of competition among the several capitalist centers under the impact of rising productive capacities, capital surpluses and raw material needs, and the simultaneous and related relative shrinking of international markets, investment opportunities and cheap raw material supplies, was, along with U.S. foreign military expenditures in the sixties (primarily in Indo-China), the major factor contributing to the re-emergence of international monetary crises (67). Further, the very monetary crises, to which it had significantly given rise, seemed to threaten a further aggravation of this fundamental instability and competition emerging in the capitalist world. (68)

While the monetary crises have continued to ebb and flood during the past half decade, the substantial shattering of the 1944 Bretton Woods agreement by the dynamics of the very capitalist world it was designed to accommodate has apparently yet to see the development of a lasting and commonly acceptable alternative. The unabated frequency of these monetary crises since they first emerged in the late sixties seems indicative of the fact that, while their effects are in many respects commonly disturbing to the economic affairs of the several capitalist centers, the divergency between immediate and long term economic interests and priorities has placed a major obstacle in the way of a commonly acceptable solution. Unlike the situation in 1944 at the adoption of the Bretton Woods agreement, the necessities and priorites of foreign trade and investment have re-attained a position of more vital interest for *all* the capitalist 'partners'. The loss by North America of absolute economic superiority (69) with re-emergence of Western European and Japanese capitalism has substantially altered the constellation of power in internation capitalism—an alteration not reflected or able to be accommodated under the terms of the 1944 Bretton Woods agreement. The increasing productivity, productive capacity and capital investment funds in the 'old' imperialist centers naturally creates increasing pressure for large shares of the international market. Foreign trade and investment now assumes a position of decisive importance for all the major capitalist nations as each tries to achieve a favorable balance of payments and individual corporations seek expanding markets and investment opportunities to match their increasing productive capacities and growing money capital suppluses.

As the absolute productive and competitive superiority of the North American productive apparatus is called more and more into question with the strengthening competitive ability of Japanese and Western European capitalism, so too is the absolute superiority of the dollar among international currencies. Thus the pivot of the Bretton Woods agreement is gradually undermined and America, unlike as was the case in 1944, is less able to unilaterally dictate the terms of a new agreement.

While there exists an obvious and often over-riding interest on the part of the leading capitalist nations to achieve a commonly acceptable solution and agreement (not only do international financial transactions become difficult in the face of continued monetary fluctuations and uncertainities, but given the extremely inter-related nature of international capitalism, dominated by international corporations, the very stability of the whole seems dependent upon the preservation of the economic stability and prosperity of its separate major national units), this need now appears to frequently come into conflict with the often more immediate particular needs of the separate nations and economic blocs in their efforts to attain or maintain an 'adequate' share of the international market, investment opportunities and resource supplies to match their increasing individual productive capacities, production, investment capital and raw material requirements. In short, the difficulty in curbing economically upsetting inter-imperialist competition and monetary crises appears rooted in a general conflict in the capitalist world between longer range systemic interests and more immediate particular (national or regional) economic interests and necessities. The clear tendency for the growth of capitalism's productive capacities to outstrip the growth of effective demand on the world market is the central driving force behind this apparent dilemma.

The obstacles facing a 'permanent' solution to the monetary crises will be further discussed in a later section of this chapter.

While it is still far from clear which pressure will finally predominate, it is undeniable however, that with the emergence of productive capacity, production and money capital surpluses of serious dimensions, the unifying effect of the fear of the 'enemy' so crucial to Marcuse's analysis appears to have been significantly undermined. At a time of widespread and unilateral economic and diplomatic about faces on the part of the leading capitalist nations (70), at a time when the 'enemy' appears strobger than ever before, the validity of Marcuse's evaluation of its unifying effect on international capitalism should perhaps be re-assessed.

It has not been the intent of the preceding discussions to demonstrate the non-existence of inter-imperialist economic co-operation. On the contrary, neither this aspect of international capitalism nor the relative superiority of North American capitalism should be lost sight of. It should also be borne in mind that not all conflict is dysfunctional. Further it seems clear that the consequences for world capitalism of the economic collapse of one or another of its major 'partners'/'competitors' would be catastrophic for the entire system. Thus, the major blocs of world capitalism appear caught in a dilemma. The more immediate prerequisites for national and 'bloc' economic development and prosperity appear to increasingly necessitate effective and fierce competition for available world markets and investment opportunities. On the other hand, due to the complex and intrinsic trade and investment ties, the long-term economic disruption of one or more of the component nations as a result of sustained unsuccessful competition would appear to threaten the disruption of the entire system, and foster or feed forces working for socialist revolution. This contradiction between national and international, immediate and long-term interests, is reflected in the dual posture of cooperation and rivalry between the major capitalist powers. So long as productive capacity continues to expand faster than effective demand, an economically non-disruptive solution is difficult to envision. Therefore, as the scramble for markets, investment opportunities and control of sources of industrial raw materials grows in intensity, it would be equally short-sighted to fail to take into account the emergence of significant economic pressures which threaten to undermine the 'intercontinental political economy' projected by Marcuse as the long term tendency in international capitalism.

During the entire postwar period, centripetal forces have been at work —those pulling the leading capitalist countries together under U.S. hegemony, and competitive strains working to break up the system. Hitherto, the centripetal forces have been the more powerful. From now on, and increasingly as time goes by, the centrifugal forces may, well assume the dominant position (71)

Arms spending, the unproblematic safety-valve: further considerations

The notion that government spending on armaments provides North American capitalism with a unlimited and economically unproblematic 'safety-valve' for the traditional capitalist problems of uneven sectoral development, capital surpluses and surpluses of productive capacity, is yet another central premise in Marcuse's overall economic analysis and projections. Speaking of the once 'promising' inherent capitalist contradictions, Marcuse states (and he projects this as the most probable long range trend), 'They are frozen in the Western defense economy'. (72)

Thus, fear of the 'enemy' appears to not only provide the motive and rationale for transcending inter-imperialist competition and rivalry but at the same time it supplies the specific justification for the perpetuation of massive state expeditures on armaments. Preparation for defense against the 'enemy' thereby provides international capitalism with an unlimited and economically unproblematic 'safe-valve' for the expansionist pressures which had been deprived substantial outlet due to the 'voluntary' and permanent trans- cendence of inter-imperialist competition.

Clearly the medicative impact of American postwar arms spending has been profound and should not be underestimated. Indeed, extensive spending on 'defense' is the only really new feature of postwar U.S. capitalism with regard to state efforts at remedial economic intervention.

Apart from military spending, every other area of government expenditures is approximately the same percentage of the Gross National Product as in 1929 (73). After an initial postwar decline to 3.9% of the U.S.G.N.P., in 1947, it had climbed by 1953, under the impact of the Korean war, to a phenomenal 13.4% and has subsequently stabilized between 9–10% of the G.N.P.—a figure which represented approximately 78 billion dollars in 1968 (74). In the U.S. such expenditures account for approximately 90% of the demand for aircraft and parts, 60% of the demand for non-ferrous metal, more than 50% of the demand for chemicals and electronic products, and over 34% of the demand for communication equipment and scientific instruments, etc. Of the eighteen major industries in the U.S., government arms spending represented 10% or more of their total market. (75)

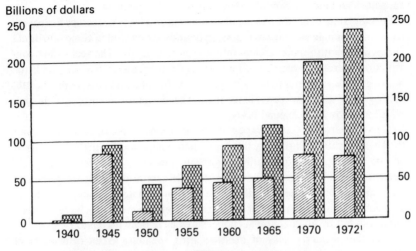

National defense and total budget outlays: 1940 to 1972

Billions of dollars

Fig. 2. ▨ Defense outlays ⊠ Total federal outlays

[1] Estimated.

Source: Statistical Abstracts of U.S., 1972, p. 249.

Even with the enormous postwar reconstruction and expansion, and especially since 1957 when this boom petered out (76), it has been the massive state 'defence' expenditures which have in large part kept the North American economy out of a postwar depression of 1930's proportions (77). With the more than 9% of the labor force dependent on military budget supported jobs (78) added to the current 4–6% unemployment rate (79), the nation would be suffering from an approximately 15% unemployment rate parallel to the depression years of the 30's.

Inasmsuch as expenditures on armaments represent expenditures for a 'self-perpetuating' market, it appears to be the ideal solution for the problems of over-production and surplus money capital accumulation (80). The rapidity at which modern weapons become technologically obsolete seems to guarantee a selfrenewing market, while the frantic, search for more technologically sophisticated weapons systems, sponsored and financed by the state, appears to ensure expanding areas for money capital investment. (81)

Quite apart from more ideologically motivated objections to alternative forms of state 'stimulant' spending, the apparently self-perpetuating market and investment field of the arms sector seems to be the central reason for the support such state expenditures receives from the business community. Not only do most alternate areas of state 'stimulating' expenditures (public housing, medical research and care, education etc.), conflict in large measure with the immediate interests of private capital, more importantly, they simply do not provide markets and investment opportunities on a scale and of adequate

87

renewability to meet the growing demands of the surplus of productive capacities and money capital of North American capitalism.

Further, state expenditures in public housing on a scale necessary to provide national economic stimulus in recession periods would tend to come into direct competition with private capital interests in this sector. The real estate/construction interests have a vested interest in maintaining a relative scarcity in the housing market in order to buoy-up prices. As for education and public health, neither of these sectors provide the market renewability and arbitrary flexibility afforded by arms expenditures.

Thus the virtues of state expenditures on arms has the multiple virtues of market renewability, arbitrary flexibility, non-competition with the interests of private capital, functional utility in the maintenance of foreign economic interests, and direct stimulation of the sensitive capital goods sector. These are the main factors influencing the disproportional state reliance on such an economic stimulant. This is not suggest that alternate measures, have not been employed but by comparison such measures have been minimal.

A further attractiveness of massive arms spending as an instrument of economic invervention (thorugh stimulation) is certainly its superiority at dampening the impact of cyclical crises. The nature and dynamics of the capitalist economic cycle are such that the capital goods sector is most sensitive to and generally the starting (and ending) point of economic downswings (82). Therefore, inasmuch as arms expenditures are primarily concentrated in this sector, they are significantly more immediate in their effect at 'rc-stimulating' the economy by placing a floor under the downward swing of the economic cycle. (83)

Inasmuch as government arms expenditure is primarily directed at the traditionally sensitive capital goods sector, state spending here has a more immediate effect at stimulating the economy. The virtues of the massivness, renewability, technological spin-off benefits, non-competition with private investment, and the domestic and foreign functional political utility of the product, all compliment the above mentioned fundamental advantage, to make arms expenditures the dominant form of state economic stimulation in North America.

These appear to be the general dimensions and economic rationales of American postwar arms spending, and, from the point of view of maintaining economic stability in North America, they have until now achieved significant successes. Nevertheless there exist certain current and potential obstacles and disadvantages to such an economic stimulant. It is a discussion of these factors which is singularly absent from Marcuse's analysis and overall image of the unlimited long-term and economically unproblematic nature of arms expenditures.

In an era of disproportionally slow growth of the world capitalist market, (a development which both leads to and intensifies competition between the leading imperialist centers) investment in the 'defense' sector appears to become an increasingly essential safety-valve (84) to match the growing productive and investment capacities of the capitalist world. Through foreign sales, the armament industry has long been a spearhead for international capitalist competition. The long postwar American superiority in this field has contributed immeasurably to the competitive edge it has enjoyed over its emergent rivals in Japan and Western Europe. Once outfitted with American weapons systems, the purchasing countries have largely become reliant upon the U.S. arms industry for further service, parts, resupply, etc., thus resulting in the effective consolidation of a long-term export market for the industry. Indeed, an indication of the priority given such sales may be seen in the U.S. pressure on Japan in the wake of the unfavorable balance of payments and intensifying monetary crises of 1970 to double its purchases of American arms (85). In the Third World too, North American economic and military aid frequently entails the same long-range market-ensuring consequences (86) as has its postwar assistance to Western Europe and Japan.

With the strengthening and expansion of the Western European and Japanese economies, North American capitalism is no longer alone with serious problems of surplus money capital and productive capacity. The relative shrinkage of the world market under the press of market outpacing increases in productive capacity and investment capital tend to place increasing pressures of Western European and Japanese economies to follow North America's postwar example and consider the possibility of utilizing state arms expenditures as an economic stimulant to take up the growing slack caused by money capital and productivity surpluses. Further, neither Germany nor Japan, for political reasons, have entered the arms market in a substantial way since the end of WWII. However, even in these areas, the pressure of growing surpluses as well as the loosening of allied imposed political restrictions, may well lead to the renewed utilization of this safety-valve by even these 'vanquished' nations.

Thus, the tendencial re-emergence of serious inter-imperialist economic competition will most certainly witness increased efforts by both Western Europe and Japan to undercut the North American monopoly even in this rather privileged market. Indeed, Nixon's recent threats to reconsider America's policy of policing Western Europe unless substantial economic conscessions are not forthcoming, may well mark the beginning of the erosion of the Nato alliance as now constituted and consequently the challenging of the monopoly position enjoyed by the U.S. arms industry in the European market. It seems unlikely that with American withdrawal from its 'peacekeeping' role in Western Europe, and in view of growing money capital and productive capacity surpluses in this area, European capitalism would long allow the continuance of the American monopoly in such a lucritive market and promising investment field.

The ability of arms spending to function as an unproblematic and limitless safety-valve in North America appears to be further jeapordized as inter-imperialist competition grows in dimensions. It may then be expected that (no longer-reliant on American produced arms), any move by one capitalist nation or bloc to expand arms spending and research for the purpose of domestic economic stabilization would be met for both competitive (because of the export market) and strategic reasons, by retalitory increases in arms research and production by other the major capitalist centers. Thus, the virtue of arbitrary flexibility, so long an attractive characteristic of arms expeditures in its utilization as a domestic economic stimulator to counteract periodic cyclical downswings, would seem to be substantially undermined as the struggle for strategic and economic advantage among the three main capitalist centers tended to perpetuate unabated growth of the this sector. –87)

Another problem and perhaps the most serious arising from sustained arms spending of the scale pursued in postwar North America is the tendency towards permenent inflation which it entails (88), a phenomenon which promotes a steady rise in the cost of living which is often not offset by rising incomes. Especially for the aged, the non-unionized and the unemployed, inflation brings intensified social suffering in its wake. The consequent decrease in purchasing power or 'effective demand', in turn may lead to increased unemployment as factories gear down to a lower rate of production. The social consequences of this phenomenon of inflation and other problems and contradictions in contemporary North American capitalism will be discussed further in chapter four. If there is a single outstanding characteristic of North American postwar capitalism, it is this sometimes slow, sometimes fast, but everpresent inflationary tendency (89). Particularly the inflationary surges of the early 50's and the '56–'58 period (90), as well as those of '65,, '67, and '68, are each in their particular way reflections of sharp increases in military outlays (91). But even apart from these spurts, inflation induced by massive state defence expenditures has been the hallmark of postwar North American capitalism (92). These expenditures have resulted in a steady rise in the amount of money in circulation without effecting a parallel increase in the amount of commodities on the market (93). While increased purchasing power may bring about the immediate re-employment of workers and the re-utlization of idle productive capacity, in the long run, when the wages of these workers and the profits of the concerned companies reappear on the market as demand for capital and consumer goods, without the production of these goods having been correspondingly increased, tendencial inflation is still the result (94). Furthermore it appears that in the postwar years a novel phenomenon of 'stag-flation' has tended to become characteristic of North American capitalist development. Thus, inflation does not lead to a higher level of economic activity via rising profit expectations, but rather, as suggested above, it tends to cut down aggregate demand. As monopolies succeed in shifting the burden of rising costs onto the consumers, the result appears to be a neutralization of the potential of increased consumer demand and a consequent tendency towards economic stagnation (see fig. 3).

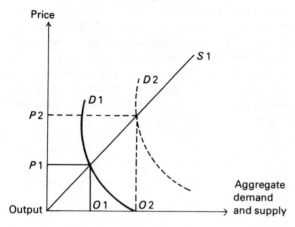

Assumed reaction to price inflation

Price

$S1$

$D2$

$D1$

$P2$

$P1$

Output $O1$ $O2$

Aggregate
demand
and supply

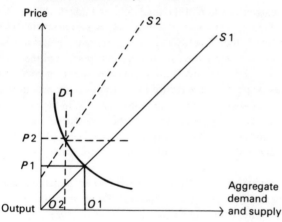

Actual reaction to price inflation

Price

$S2$

$S1$

$D1$

$P2$

$P1$

Output $O2$ $O1$

Aggregate
demand
and supply

Fig. 3. Source: Diagram formulations of Bo Gustafsson Ekonomisk-historiska institutionen, Uppsala.

Further, it may well be that nothing short of a prolonged period of stagnation with its ensuing chronic underutilization of industrial capacity and unemployment of dimensions of the 30's, will bring this inflationary spiral to a halt. (95)

Along these same lines, it would seem that if a situation were to develop where restricted supplies of basic raw materials, productive capacity, and/or manpower did not permit the free and parallel expansion of both the military and private sectors of the economy, then any further increase in military production would entail the transference to the military sector of raw materials, productive capacity and/or manpower necessary in the private sector. The ensuing process of protracted reproduction would lead to a shortage of

91

private consumer and capital goods (96), further antagonizing the inflationary spiral. The postwar years have not seen the emergence of this problem in North America in any serious dimension (97). However, gven the apparent intensification of inter-imperialist competition for many relatively scarce and/or inexpensive basic raw materials, and the growing insecurity of numerous crucial Third World sources, it is not inconceivable that the future may witness such problems of contracted reproduction due to restricted supplies of essential raw materials. It should be further noted that if and when such contracted reproduction does set in, it does not necessarily effect all economic sectors; rather it hits those in closest competition with each other for raw materials (98). For the present and immediate future however, it seems the most pressing problem arising from the inflationary tendency is the (potentially politically disturbing) undercutting of bargaining table wage gains made by the North American working class. (99)

On a different tact it is significant that the ability of further arms expenditures to alleviate unemployment and stimulate safe investment opportunities shows a tendencial decline. Technologically sophisticated weapons systems such as missiles, absorb a growing proportion of the total defense budget while at the same time requiring a steadily decreasing proportion of the nations manpower to construct and man them (100). Clearly such developments should not be overestimated, but it is nevertheless the case that as a proportion of the total defense budget, weapons, and weapons factories of high capital intensity (if such an expression may be permitted in regard to the former), are accounting for larger and larger shares of the billions layed out each year in the cause of North American defense (101). In terms of both the construction and the manning of the new weapons systems, developing technological sophistication implies a significant increase in the cost of creating employment through defense spending.

Thus, the labor consuming ability of the modern defense economy seems to show a marked tendency to decline as the technological sophistication of both the production and the nature of the new weapons increases. (102)

> Coupled with specialization, and partly as a consequence of it, go a rising capital and technological intensity in the arms industries. On both counts they become less able to underpin full employment even at the same level of relative expenditure. At a declining one, . . . their potency as an offset becomes increasingly questionable. (103)

The problem, of course, is not confined to the military producing sector of the economy. While up to 52% of all research conducted in the U.S. is done under the auspices and financing of defense research (104), most of this is conducted either in public universities or contracted out to private firms. The consequent transference to and use by the private industrial sector at large of the technological break throughs achieved by this 'free' research is further facilitated by the mobility of top personnel between the military, government, industrial and university sectors (105). Such government sponsored research has lead to enormous technological advances in nearly every field of production. (106)

This increase in the avaiability of new technology and scientific knowledge leads not only to the development of new products, but also to the 'technological' possibility for more rapid rates of increase in the organic composition of capital. Under increasing pressure from re-emerging inter-imperialist competition and a related narrowing of the technological gap between the rival centers, this 'technological possibility' may well in future be utilized to an increasing degree (107). Thus the relative (and often real) decline in demand for labor in the field of military production and operation is accompanied by a subsequent and similar decline in demand in industry at large, as labor intensive industries are steadily eroded and new capital intensive ones created. (108)

It therefore seems that in a certain respect, the enormous defence expenditures may be actually contributing to increasing unemployment, as numerous of the new products and technologies developed find direct applicability to the civilian sector and frequently lead to and hasten the increasing organic composition of capital and the ensuent relative decline in demand for labor. (19)

One final point should be made in relation to these developments. Spurred by the emergent inter-imperialist challenge and facilitated by technological break throughs (multiplied as a result of defense research), capital investments are more frequently replaced before they have become fully amortized. In those sectors defined by the state as 'strategic', the government guarantees the loss. However, in the non-military sector, this premature, but competitively necessary, industrial re-equipment tends to cause an unutilizable increase in total productive capacity and a potential threat to the stability of the average rate of profit* as the average life-span of capital goods continues to decline. Wherever possible the incomplete amortization is paid for either directly (through the elimination of labor content [increased unemployment], slower wage rises, or even outright wage cuts), or indirectly (through increased taxes and inflation). In either event, it appears to be the working class (both domestic and, wherever possible, foreign) which pays these added capital goods depreciation costs.

Further in connection with the attendant complications of sustained arms spending, it should be pointed out that North American military spending abroad in the form of military aid, base procurement payments, etc., has been a central factor contributing to the crisis in liquidity now confronting the American economy. (110)

Arms spending in North America has clearly been a major instrument for bottoming-out postwar economic downswings as seen by the statistics presented earlier on the actual and comparative extent of defense ezpenditures in

* Depending on whether or not this 'cost-burden' is shifted onto workers and consumers.

postwar North America. However, it should not be forgotten that even this massive stimulant has been inadequate to keep the economy prospering and maintain unemployment at 'politically resonable' levels (111). Even considering these expenditures, the limited prosperity and economic stability achieved seems hardly to have been possible without the considerable assistance of state deficit spending and a spiralling private debt (112). Not only the national government but state and local governments as well have become increasingly reliant upon debt in order to meet their governmental obligations and so contribute to economic prosperity and stability. (113)

Taken together, the short and long term limitations and adverse economic consequences of sustained arms spending on the scale pursued by the U.S. government during the postwar years (and increasingly necessary under rising pressure from emergent inter-imperialist competition) appear to suggest possible limitations on the long term efficacy of such an economic stimulant. What is more, Marcuse's singular exclusion of any consideration of the above-mentioned problems seems to detract from the validity of the monumental political-cum-theoretical dilemma he has erected on the basis of his projections of the long term stabilizing effect of extensive and sustained armament expenditures in North America. Surely one must appreciate the fact that such expenditures have in the past and indeed continue to effect a certain and often extensive economic stability and prosperity in North America. Nevertheless, limitations and problems do exist, and it is the exclusion of any consideration of these obstacles and 'disfunctional' consequences which depreciates the universal validity of Marcuse's analysis and the validity of his consequent justification for 'rethinking' critical theory to meet the demands of a qualitatively altered economic reality in North America.

> So far, the weight of the arms economy has been on the side of stability, charging and recharging the more immediate causes of high employment and well being. Within that stability, however, it has nurtured a set of problems as intractable as any. (114)

The containment of the Third World and the economic insignificance of national liberation movements on North American economic stability and prosperity: Further consideration

> ... the preconditions for the liberation and development of the Third World must emerge in the advanced capitalist countries. (115).

Therefore:

> The chain of exploitation must be broken at its strongest link. (116)

Yet another essential argument in the politico-economic dilemma Marcuse has portrayed is his estimation of the impossibility (117) of further successful nation liberation struggles in the Third World prior to the internal weakening and disruption of North American economy and society (118).

Third World national liberation struggles are apparently seen to be incapable of seriously disrupting 'smooth functioning' North American capitalism (119). Such a perspective appears to both underestimate the actual possibilities for successful national liberation in these areas as well as the increasingly vital role the Third World plays in U.S. capitalism. The term 'Third World' used here refers to those industrially underdeveloped nations whose external (and often internal) economic relations are dominated by one or more of the major imperialist centers (for Marcuse this means U.S.A.). National liberation struggles here refers not only to armed struggles but also to movements of a more exclusively political nature.

Marcuse's perspective on the chances for successful struggles in these areas as well as his assessment of their broader economic disruptive impact on the American imperialist system appears to unwarrantedly depreciate the political and military potentialities and disruptive economic consequences of these struggles.

The discussions which follow are not attempts to minimize the obvious and 'impressive' powers of containment available to and exercised by North America (120). They do, however, represent a brief attempt to consider certain factors and developments which are singularly lacking consideration in Marcuse's argumentation.

It is perhaps worth restating yet one more time that the underdevelopment of the Third World areas is not the result of an historical accident causing a delayed economic 'take-off'. Rather it seems to have been the direct and necessary consequence of the imperialist economic and political relationships prevailing in the past as well as present (121). While the major capitalist nations are characterized by extensive industrial development and the Third World areas generally reflect a gross lack of such development, it is important to appreciate that they do not exist in isolation from each other. Indeed, 'they are the top and bottom sides of one and the same world' (122).

The unevenness of development between the advanced capitalist world and the Third World was begun and is continually given renewed impetus by the unequal exchange which characterizes the economic relationships between these two areas of the capitalist world (123). This unevenness appears to continue to grow as the Third World steadily increases its share of the world population while, at the same time, receiving an ever diminishing share of the world's 'output' (124).

In the sixties, the dimensions of this discrepancy were seen in per capita income ratio between the advanced industrial countries and the Third World areas of 9/1 (in favor of the former of course) (125). Perhaps equally as telling were the ratios of 12/1 and 5/1 for per capita energy consumption and industrial steel consumption respectively (126).

In a situation where already the 'topside' of imperialism—the advanced industrial countries—account for only 20 % of the world population but 60 % of world output, while the 'bottom side'—the Third World—accounts for 50 % of world population and only 10 % of world production (127), further deterioration in both the relative and the real human conditions will in all probability become even less tolerable (and tolerated) than they are at present.

It is against this background that the potential success of Third World national liberation struggles and the importance of this part of the world for sustaining metropolitan 'affluency' should be assessed. Inasmuch as imperialism is a two-headed coin of development and underdevelopment, each intrinsically interwoven in a dialectical relationship, it then seems reasonable to conclude that any concerted and successful effort by the 'losing partner' to end this relationship would entail the undermining of the affluency of the 'developed partner'. While the instruments for political and economic repression and containment in the underdeveloped areas are 'impressive',

> . . . it does not necessarily follow that without and before the collapse of international capitalism nothing can be done about its liquidation. (128)

Important to understanding of the vital nature of the Third World in the world capitalist economy is an appreciation of the fact that this area has long been a major source of super-profits for capitalism with investments in these areas realizing average profit rates from 50 to 400 % greater than parallel investments in the advanced industrialized areas (129). The exploitation of relatively inexpensive sources of raw materials, as well as cheap land and labor, has traditionally complemented the lower profit rates realized by international capitalism's larger investments in the advanced industrial regions (130). But it is clearly the underdeveloped world's continually strengthening position as a supplier a numerous essential raw materials which gives it its most substantial potential disruptive power over the advanced industrial nations. Since the early postwar years, the U.S. has increasingly experienced a larger and more diverse shortage of basic industrial and 'strategic' raw materials. Indeed, this domestic shortage of basic industrial and strategic raw materials is perhaps the most novel aspect of contemporary North American imperialism (131).

The tables 7 and 8 give an *indication* of growing U.S. dependency on imported raw materials.

The tendency towards increased import dependency seems unlikely to cease or decline as the gap between Third World and Advanced capitalist domestic raw material production continues to narrow (132). It has been estimated that by the late 70's the U.S. will be a net importer of raw materials, and by the mid 80's it will be necessary to import 54 % of its annual oil consumption (133). Indeed, it is sometimes argued that breakthroughs in recycling techniques and in the production of synthetic substitutes will more than counter this growing import dependency. However impressive such achievements may be, they are

96

Table 7. *Selected minerals: net imports as a percent of domestic mine or well production*

	1937–39 Average (percentages)	1966 (percentages)
Iron Ore	3	43
Cooper	− 13	48
Lead	0	131
Zinc	7	140
Bauxite	113	638
Petroleum	− 4	31

Source: H. Magdoff, The Age of Imperialism, New York, Monthly Review, 1969, p. 50.

seldom able compensate with a supply which is both large enough to meet the demands of the massive North American industrial apparatus and/or produce at a cost comparable to the foreign supplies (134). If there is one consistant characteristic of capitalist enterprise, whether monopolistic or not, that is that it seeks to maximize profit rates, in this case by exploiting the cheapest possible sources of necessary raw materials.

Thus, apparent profound synthesizing achievements in the laboratory are usually nevertheless a far cry from being of an order able to supply North American industry with the quantities of raw materials necessary and at a cost low enough to enable U.S. industry to maintain, gain a competitive edge on the world market (135).

Therefore, the increasing reliance of U.S. industry on Third World raw material sources places these latter areas in a position of significant economic

Table 8. *Classification of strategic industrial materials by degree of dependence om imports*

Number of Materials	Ratio if Imports to New Supply (Percent)
38	80–100
6	60– 79
8	40– 59
3	20– 39
7	Less than 20
62	

Source: H. Magdoff, the Age of Imperialism, New York, Monthly Review, 1969, p. 48.

leverage. Should strategic areas of the underdeveloped world realign themselves politically and economically, raise their prices substantially, or utilize significant proportions of their raw materials domestically as a result of industrialization, it could have substantial economic reprecussions for North American capitalism. The result would probably be a serious undermining of both the super-profits earned in these areas as well as the productive potential of industry in the advanced industrial areas. Such a development would most certainly jeapordize North America's ability to 'buy-off' the industrial working class to the extent they have (136).

Without doubt, given the increasingly uncertain investment climate in numerous Third World areas, the U.S. would prefer to purchase its raw materials in the more stable areas of Western Europe (and Canada). Unfortunately, the geography of mineral deposits does not always coincide with the geography of political stability. Increasingly, necessary sources are found in the required quantities only in the Third World (137).

> ... it should never be forgotten that however heavily imperialist exploitation weighs upon the Third World this exploitation needs the Third World and cannot do without it ... the Third World is the sole or primary source of many products or raw materials without which many of the markets of imperialism would collapse and many of its most essential factories would come to a standstill. (138)

This increasing raw material dependence would seem to be further aggravated by the apparent re-emerging competition between imperialist rivals. The Western European 'aligned' Third World areas which were opened to direct and indirect American exploitation by North American investment in Western Europe (139) will in all probability become less accessible as the strength of European capitalism increases and manifests a more effective determination to protect not only their own domestic investment opportunities and markets but their priveliged raw material sources as well. Further, considering the rapid industrial growth rates of Western Europe and Japan it may be that the coming decades will witness an increasingly fierce struggle for access to, and control over the raw materials, cheap labor and land, and the markets of those Third World areas, which have for long been the more or less private domain of North American capitalism (140). Indeed, as mentioned earlier, Japan has already, made significant moves to establish an 'independent' source of raw materials (141). Thus, any evaluation of the importance of trade between the U.S. and the Third World must be assessed in light of the growing scarcity of adequate domestic supplies and the seeming resurgence of inter-imperialist competition. Often, and perhaps this has been the source of Marcuse's apparent miscalculation, the increasing overall proportion of world trade accounted for by inter-imperialist exchange as opposed to trade between the advanced industrial countries and the underdeveloped parts of the world (142), has lead to the conclusion that trade with the Third World is significantly diminishing in importance. Indeed, during the postwar years Third World share of world trade fell from 31.3% in 1950 to 20.8% in 1963 and to 18.5% in 1967 (143). The point to be bourne in mind however is that Third World trade has been largely (90%) (144) an exchange of primary products for the manufactured goods of the advanced capitalist countries; whereas inter-imperialist trade has been primarily an exchange of manufactured goods. There is a qualitative difference in importance between the two types of trade. Third World trade, while less, is perhaps equally or more important to the smooth functioning of the world capitalist economy inasmuch as it is primarily trade in basic industrial raw materials and bulk foodstuffs (145).

Thus, as P. Jallée points out,

> ... the Third World has an ace up its sleeve; its hand is on the tap controlling the essential flow, and thus it enjoys a position of strength in one respect which must not be underestimated in a dynamic and changing world. (146)

Apart from its increasingly essential position as a supplier of basic raw materials to the capitalist world, there are still other, perhaps at present less important, but nevertheless potential sources of economic disruptive power enjoyed by the Third World. In an era of shrinking economic maneuverability, it becomes more important to not only actively exploit the underdeveloped areas, but to also hold open the 'investment door' even if full advantage is not immediately taken of the available opportunities. Indeed, the Third World along with the old imperialist nations has offered North American capitalism a convenient and often flexible safety-valve for problems of surplus money capital accumulation and surplus production (147). Through this exporting of crises, economic downswings are further cushioned and boom periods better sustained.

Particularly in the area of capital goods (the most critical sector in the economy), North American exports to the Third World have played this role of safety-valve, complementing the medicative effects of arms spending (148).

In the case of steel, the Third World accounts for 30% to 40% of U.S. exports (149) and as C. B. Baker, administrative vice-president of the United States Steel Corporation, stated recently:

> ... it is largely due to the operation of our foreign aid program that the steel industry has managed to escape the full effects of the forces at work in the international market place. (150)

The role of the Third World as an area for substantial money capital export has been relatively limited by the generally small size of its domestic markets as well as by the fact that these markets are in large part already under

Table 9. *Production of Manufacturing Industries of Non-Socialist World (As Percentage of Total Value Added in 1958)*

Regions	All industry	Light industry	Heavy industry
Africa and the Middle East	1.5	1.7	1.2
Latin America	3.7	5.3	2.7
Asia, excluding Japan and socialist countries	2.1	3.5	1.1
Total	**7.3**	**10.5**	**5.0**
United States and Canada	49.9	47.5	51.5
Europe, excluding socialist countries	37.6	36.6	38.2
Japan	3.5	3.5	3.7
Oceania	1.7	1.9	1.6
Total	**92.7**	**89.5**	**95.0**

Source: P. Jallée, *The Pillage of the Third World*, New York Monthly Review, 1968, p. 20.

monopoly control by the usually more than adequate productive capacity of the American domestic productive apparatus (151). It is conceivable that under the press of aggravated inter-imperialist competition, the need to more fully exploit these available sources of cheap labor and land and to take advantage of the often closer proximity of raw materials, may become more urgent. In the past, wherever such North American sponsored industrial development of the Third World has taken place it has been predominantly aimed at export sales and therefore, apart from wages which necessarily remain low, is seldom or only coincidentally, of a nature appropriate to the domestic needs of the host country.

The preceding discussion has given some indication of the international division of labor characterizing the contemporary imperialism: The Third World supplying basic raw materials and the advanced industrial nations the manufactured goods. The table 9. gives an indication of the extent of this type of imbalanced development.

The underdevelopment of the Third World which appears to be an integral feature of imperialism is, for North America's part sustained and expanded through a complex of Aid programmes (152), trade restrictions, selective investments, economic blackmail, and direct and indirect political and military intervention in and manipulation of the affairs of the underdeveloped countries in its orbit. The increasing surplus money capital accumulation in North America, growing surplus productive capacity, diminishing adequate domestic supplies of basic industrial and strategic raw materials, and the apparent intensification of inter-imperialist competition, all act and react to make the maintenance of underdevelopment in the Third World of unprecedented economic urgency (153). Advancing industrialization in these areas threatens not only the export markets of U.S. monopolies (154) but as mentioned earlier, it jeapordizes the adequate supplies of inexpensive raw materials for its giant productive apparatus (155). While the obstacles to such industrialization are great, they are not perhaps as insurmountable this side of the internal weakening of North America as Marcuse supposes. Indeed, it may turn out to be a major cause rather than a consequence of that very weakening.

> The frightful differences in stand of living, the brutal subjection of one nation to another, prepare the way for the colonial revolution which in turn pushes forward the industrialization of the underdeveloped countries and intensifies the international contradictions of capital. (156)

Parallel to the tendencial growth in importance of the Third World to North American capitalism, is an increasing hesitancy on the part of American private capital to invest in the face of steadily worsening investment climate throughout the underdeveloped areas. Unless initial investment can be amortized within about five years, fewer and fewer corporations and businesses are prepared to take the five years, fewer and fewer corporations and businesses are prepared to take the risk (157). Even with substantial U.S. government investment guarantees, (an increasingly more costly program), the unfavorable investment climate has already curbed substantial private investment in these areas (158). The emergence of social, political and thus economic uncertainty in the Third World does not negate the economic and strategic necessity of its material and human resources for North American capitalism. The cost to the U.S. taxpayer of policing and keeping the underdeveloped world free for further intensified marketing and investment, may well continue to grow in step with the growth of Third World's discontentment with their lot. The devaluation of the dollar while at least temporarily enhancing the competitive position of North American capital, also raises the cost of maintaining a favorable investment climate in these areas (159). Thus the spread of political and economic uncertainty in the Third World through national liberation struggles as well as the aquisition of power by 'serious' national capitalist oriented governments would appear to threaten to undermine a key factor in the postwar prosperity enjoyed by North America.

To the extent that Marcuse appears to appreciate the potential disruptive power of Third World national liberation struggles on North American capitalist economy, it is based on a hope that the exemplary (but as yet only preparatory) struggle of the 'wretched of the earth', will in some way prick the consciences of the American citizenry and thus lead them to demand a stop to their country's role in suppressing and containing these struggles.

While the consideration of such developments should not be excluded (though given Marcuse's prior analysis of the *instinctual* 'cooling-out' of the underlying population in America, it is hard to believe he takes this proposal too seriously himself), it seems that the more direct adverse economic consequences of such liberation struggles may well play a more significant role in altering political consciousness in North America. It should be cautioned that the direction this stimulated consciousness will take is not always clear, and much of depends upon effective political action and propaganda (160).

Further, while the counter-revolutionary and general andi-development forces of North America should not be underestimated, nor should, as Marcuse appears to have done, the possibilities for meaningful successes this side of the internal weakening of the super-power.

For the peoples of the Third World with a steadily worsening living standard; a per capita food consumption rate that in Latin America fell 7% between 1958–1959 and 1963–1964; (161) a per capita income calculated inequality ratio between this part of the world and the advanced industrial areas which has dropped from 1/6 in 1900 to 1/12 in 1965 (162); the example of Cuba, and even more strikingly of China seems to be the great lession of our century.

> ... the peoples of the underdeveloped countries have learned, especially from the experience of China from 1949, that there is a way out of the trap in which they now find themselves. That way out lies through revolutionary national liberation struggles of the kind the people in Indo-China are now conducting against the United States. (163)

In the underdeveloped areas of the world, political awareness is advancing inexhorably (164) in the face of growing deprivation and repression and against the background of both the relative and absolute affluence of the advanced industrial countries. While, as P. Jallee has correctly predicted that the struggle for liberation in these areas will be as hard as it is long (165), it is improbable (especially after the domestically decisive Indo-China experience) (166) that North America's 6% of the world's population can indefinitely force 50% of the world's population to accept gross and worsening deprivation and humilation as a permanent 'way of life'. Indeed, it seems fair to say that

> ... the tide of world revolution against exploitation ... is flowing strong, much too strong to be turned back or halted. (167)

The rapid spread of national liberation struggles and the growing anti-imperialist consciousness throughout the Third World is in a certain sense indicative of how long the 'wretched of the earth' will be placated with imperialism's postwar granting of political independence coupled with apparent continuing and reinforced economic subservience. The postwar granting of political independence to large areas of the underdeveloped allowed North America to retighten the imperialist grip (168) for a decade or so. However, it is difficult to imagine what further 'peaceful' concessions can be

102

made in an era of seemingly renewed inter-imperialist competition and consequent shrinking economic elbow room, to placate a disillusioned and increasingly politically conscious people. The alternative of course would seem to be a forceful repression of emerging national liberation sympathies and movements. The example of Indo-China, however, while continuing to unfold, appears to indicate the problematic ability of the U.S. to repress and contain five to ten more Vietnams. It has also demonstrated the tremendously disruptive economic and political consequences which would probably follow such enterprises.

It should perhaps be noted too that inasmuch as U.S. foreign 'defence' spending appears to be a major cause of its chronic balance of payments deficit over the past decade (169), and consequently a central factor in the international monetary crises, the need for increased foreign military expenditures to curb the rising tide of national liberation struggles would in all probability further aggravate this problem.

Thus, the apparent growing importance of the Third World in world capitalist economy seems to imply a position of growing economic leverage and disruptive potential. The worsening conditions of its inhabitants increase the possibility that this leverage and disruptive potential may soon be utilized and reflected in a worsening economic situation within North America. The tendency toward economic stagnation in America, already noticeable, would seem to render North American capitalism still more sensitive to both the further restrictions of its ability to utilize the wealth of the countries of the Third World (170), and the adverse economic effects of widespread and sustained 'policing'.

Clearly it would be foolish to underestimate the ability of North America to continue to contain, repress and exploit vast areas of the Third World. Through the use of its enormous economic, political and military resources, it still holds the upper hand. Further, just as the export of military hardware tends to tie the purchasing or recipient country to the supplying nation for replacements, repairs, parts, etc., so, on a broader scale, the export of North American technology to the Third World tends to create a similar dependency, even when Third World areas effect significant capitalist industrialization. This technological neo-imperialism is still one more factor in the complex web of economic, political, military and even cultural relationships which effect the containment of the Third World within the world capitalist system. But limitations nevertheless do exist, and the failure to consider them may well lead to the underestimation of the real possibilities for successful national liberation struggles as well as the possible politicoeconomic disruptive effects such successes may have upon American capitalism.

> ... the relations between the Third World and imperialism are dialectical and not all the weapons are on one side. (171)
> ... one can say that there is as yet no reason to abandon belief in a

general crisis of capitalism—be it catastrophic or slow to develop. It is most likely to appear when the great revolution in the Third World passes from latency to reality. (172)

Thus, it would seem that Marcuse's discussions have failed to consider both certain apparent limitations on North America's ability to contain radical social change in the Third World as well as the potential disruptive impact such struggles may have on North American economic stability. Apart from numerous persistent anti-imperialist national liberation struggles, the capitalist Third World manifests a determination to more effectively compete with the capitalist metropoles in certain economic areas. The 'oil crisis', nationalizations, extensions of territorial boundaries at sea, etc., while not immediately taking the particular Third World areas involved outside the general framework of the world capitalist system, have nevertheless placed an added strain on the supposed long-term expanding affluency within North America. Even though B. Warren may be correct when he argues that Third World areas are tending to capitalist industrialization, such industrialization may well lead to conflicts, which, while not anti capitalist, have nevertheless often substantial unstabilizing effects on the dominant and affluent position of North America much in the same manner (though on a lesser scale) as does the inter-capitalist competition and economic-political conflict between North America and the 'older' capitalist nations.

Effective national economic planning and the management of cyclical crises: Further considerations

Traditional trouble spots are being cleaned out or isolated, disruptive elements taken in hand. The main trends are familiar: concentration of the economy on the needs of the big corporations, with the government as a stimulating, supporting and sometimes even controlling force. (173)
... we are faced with a novelty in history, namely with the prospect or with the need for a radical change, revolution in and against ... a well functioning society. (174)

A further key element in Marcuse's overall assessment of the long range tendencies of North American capitalism is his explicitly and implicitly expressed view that cyclical crises which had traditionally plagued capitalist development have to a very great extent come under effective management. Through the combined efforts of the large corporations and government, periodic cyclical crises have largely become a thing of the past. To the extent that they remain, such disturbances are rapidly being met with still more effective management. On the basis of subsided competition between former imperialist rivals under the domination of North American capitalism, sustained by the massive defence expenditures, the production of junk, and the

104

effective long range control of the Third World, such crisis management appears to be only the beginning of a long-term trend.

In this section, an attempt will be made to indicate some apparent shortcomings of such planning and management significantly absent from Marcuse's discussions. While the persistence of recessions does not necessarily imply immanent systemic collapse, it does indicate that the fundamental contradictions of capitalism are still unsolved.

During the postwar period, 'well-managed' and smooth dunctioning North American capitalism has experienced no less than seven recessions (in '48, '53–'54, '57–'58, '61, '67, '70 and '73), fundamentally as a result of the persistence of this eratic pattern of capitalist development and production (175).

Nevertheless, throughout the entire period a significant number of influential North American sociologists and economist were busy celebrating the 'end of ideology' and the beginning of a new era of effective economic management, a mood and atmosphere which did not fail to impress Marcuse. It appears that central to the notion that the 'blind anarchy' of capitalism has come under effective management, was the proposition that the dominant multinational corporations no longer placed profit maximization as their primary objective (176). Such writers as Berle and Means had early suggested that,

> It is conceivable—indeed it seems inevitable if the corporate system is to survive—that 'control' over the great corporations should develop into a purely neutral technocracy, balancing a variety of claims by various groups in the community and assigning to each a portion of the income stream on the basis of public policy rather than private cupidity. (177)

And later, along the same lines, Carl Kaysen argued,

> No longer the agent of proprietorship seeking to maximize return on investment, management sees itself as responsible to stockholders, employees, customers, the general public, ... there is no display of greed or graspiness; there is no attempt to push off onto workers or the community at large part of the social costs of the enterprise. The modern corporation is a soulful corporation. (178)

The traditional 'fast-grab' for as much as possible was said to have given way to the more socially responsible objective of profit optimization. In essence, however, the two objectives are the same, the latter appearing to be a somewhat weak attempt at using linguistic therapy to shore up the ideological front of contemporary capitalism. To point out that the modern corporation is more conscious of consolidating the long term possibilities of profit making is not to refute that the quest for profit remains the central objective of the modern corporation (199). This is all the more true when one realizes that this

105

consolidation is made precisely in order to guarantee normal or maximum profits. It should be noted however in passing that such longer-term profit outlooks would seem to have certain implications for the avoidance of periodic crisis.

Apparently gaining currency under the impact and ideological requirements of the cold war, the arguments of the proponents of the 'soulful' and socially responsible corporation have lent support and legitimacy to the notion of planned and effectively managed economy in North America. This argument has not failed to have a certain impact on Marcuse's analysis. The relative stability and affluence of the 50's appeared to further verify these conclusions and projections. However, E. S. Mason, professor of economics at Harvard and former dean of the graduate school of business administration there, has shown that such notions as the modern corporations declining interest in profit maximization, if taken seriously would undercut the whole structure of contemporary economic theory and is in general, 'hardly to be taken seriously'.

One side of the debate among liberal economists argues that if profit maximization is no longer the directing factor, then how are prices determined, what relation does price have to relative scarcity.

> Assume an economy composed of a few hundred large corporations, each enjoying substantial market power and all directed by managements with a 'conscience'. Each management wants to do the best it can for society consistent, of course, with the best it can for labor, customers, suppliers and owners. How do prices get determined in such an economy? (180)

Another extensive study of the objectives and goals of a sample of large and successful American corporations has shown that if anything, the modern corporation has become more profit oriented than its predecessor (181). It should be pointed out here that the persistence of the profit goal in the large corporations by no means excludes economic planning in the corporation. On the contrary, it demands it. While such planning at the corporation level has become increasingly sophisticated (182), it by no means implies planning of the overall economic system. Although several large corporations may occasionally act in concert, it should be borne in mind that even the largest of corporations contributed individually only about 1 % to the U.S. G.N.P. (183). This is large, but it nevertheless seems a far cry from a planned national economy of the nature suggested by Marcuse. However, even now, the market remains the central arena of the relationships not only between the large corporations but also between each of them separately and labor, suppliers, consumers, and smaller business (184).

State economic planning is primarly a matter of attempting to co-ordinate the previously formulated investment plans of large firms and corporations while at the same time proposing certain government priorites (185). Apart from the fact that it generally has no means for enforcing such 'planning', these attempts at state economic intervention appear to be further restricted by the basic uncertainty of the investment and market calculations and projections collected from the various economic aggregates (186). Much of this projected market and investment information is collected by polling big business (187), and thus suffers from the further defect that not all corporations are willing to cooperate. In the words of one state planner,

> To a great extent we still rely today largely on hunches and the anticipation of other people's behaviour. (188)

These tenuous estimates and 'enlightened guesses' (189), which appear to lie at the basis of the state's attempts at national economic management and planning would seem to suffer from the further uncertainties accruing from the apparent increased inter-imperialist competition and labor unrest.

While state intervention measures (primarily through arms spending) may decrease the severity of the dowward phase and temporarily sustain the upswing, these achievements have frequently lead to an overestimation of contemporary North American capitalism's ability to eliminate renessions (and depressions) (190) and the intensification of their more distant but also more adverse economic effects.

With the apparent re-emergence of inter-imperialist competition and monetary crises, international trade uncertainties coupled with difficulties of controlling wage costs serve to aggravate the already existing problems involved in planning for sectoral equilibrium targets (191).

The concerted efforts at economic planning in World War Two Germany and Japan offer striking examples of the limitations of capitalist planning in general (192). But perhaps more immediately instructive has been the postwar attempts and failures of economic planning in Japan and particularly of France. Without doubt these have been among the most comprehensive and prolonged efforts to effectively regulate advanced industrial capitalist economies. An example for other attempts at national planning (193), the prolonged French effort under the direction of a 'Planning Board', has proven a consistent failure (194). The scope and depth of the May '68 events in France should in themselves give some indication of the success of this economic management in the eyes of the working class. It might be noted also that in the case of Sweden, where state planning is more advanced than in the U.S. there persists a lack of correspondence 'planned', i.e. projected developments of G.N.P. and its components, and the actual development.

Nevertheless, attempts in postwar North America have not entirely been without success at dampening the downward swings of economic cycles. While a variety of measures are available to the state, each with its own particular advantages and disadvantages (195), the chosen option, as noted earlier has primarily been massive military expenditures which has resulted also in a swollen state debt, an unabated inflationary trend and the encouragement of increased consumer and corporate debt. The previous discussion of this form of state economic intervention has indicated both its obvious advantages as well as the more pronounced of its not so obvious short and long term disadvantages (196).

Even such a massive 'shot in the arm' however, complementing the postwar reconstruction and expansion and the expansion related to the Third industrial revolution, was not adequate to maintain the boom of the fifties (197), a 'boom' incidentally, which has not witnessed a reasonable rate of full employment since 1953 (198). What has been achieved is that the North American, indeed the world capitalist economy, has avoided a depression of the dimensions of that of the '30's. This in itself is a major achievement; whether these 'successes' can be maintained is another issue. In any event, the recessions and unemployment of the postwar years is a far cry from the planned and smoothly managed developing economy portrayed by Marcuse.

As it did in 1970 by 6% (199), the state has attempted to complement the defence expenditure effort to dampen recessions by the creation of new purchasing power. While such measures may help solve the immediate problems, there are limitations to the amount of extra purchasing power the state may introduce into the economy (200), and to the extent that such 'money manufacturing' measures are chosen as the instrument of state economic intervention, it is the severity of the recession which determines the amount of new purchasing power to be created (201). The problem involved here, of course, that such 'money creation' results almost immediately in an additional spurt to the already 'creeping' inflation. Thus, the dilemma confronting the state appears to be the unavoidable choice between crisis or inflation (202).

Inflation can of course be tolerated within limits and until now at least that course has proven to be the more preferable. Limits there are however, and at that point the state must either find (and they become increasingly difficult to find as the inflation spiral continues), alternate anti-crisis measures or accept a severe economic crisis.

One of the fundamental contradictions which arises here is that between the inflationary use of the dollar as an anti-crisis instrument in the American economy on the one hand, and the dollar's use as a reserve money in the international monetary system on the other (203). Thus, in its role as an economic moderator in the state's efforts to dampen cyclical economic downswings and sustain upswings, it is important that there are as many dollars as possible in circulation, which implies a flexible supply. These requirements, however, lay the basis for the general instability of the dollar's value due to the ensuing inflationary tendency. In its role as a money of account on the world market, however, it is important that the dollar's value be as stable as possible. Herein is manifest a fundamental contradition between those capitalists engaged in trade with the US (importers or those outside the U.S.) wanting a flexible (and inflationary) supply of dollars, and other capitalists such as central and private banks, holding large dollar reserves and credits, whose primary interest is in a stable dollar value (204). This conflict of interest makes more difficult the achievment of a commonly acceptable long-term solution to the monetary crises which have emerged during the past half decade.

The spiralling corporate (205) and consumer debt in the postwar years has added to the illusion of perpetual boom and spreading prosperity. While in 1951 only 14% of consumer income went to debt servicing, by 1963 it had risen to 21% (206). The trend did not end there as the 1960's witnessed a growth of consummer debt at a rate 50% faster than income growth (207). To the short sighted this rapid increase in corporate and consumer debt appeared to go a long way in buoying up an economy with a steadily growing surplus produc- tive capacity. So it did. However, while it may be difficult to deliniate the precise limits of the percentage of income going to servicing debts, it is clear that there must be a maximum percentage. Inasmuch as such a limit exists it implies a final restraint on an economy which relies on increasing debt to keep it stable (208).

As for corporate and business debt, the servicing of this growing indebted- ness necessitates both and expanding gross profit and/or rate of profit. The dilemma slowly creeping up on North American business is how to be realize such profit increases precisely at a time of the shrinking adequacy of markets and investment opportunities under the impact of stiffening inter-imperialist competition, increasing productive capacity, a worsening investment climate in the Third World and continually pressing wage demands. Indeed the problem is how to increase profits in a semi-stagnant economy which boasts the lowest, and still worsening postwar industrial expansion rate in the ad- vanced capitalist world (209). Undoubtedly, a primary remendial measure will be a concerted effort to reduce labor costs not only by further increases in the organic composition of capital, but by more direct and indirect forms of wage cuts of a working class that at least since 1965 has had the lowest rate of wage increase in the advanced capitalist world (210). However, such measures would seem to indirectly further aggravate the worsening economic situation inasmuch as workers, whose credit spending also helps sustain the economy on a steady keel, require rising wages to service and extend this debt (211).

While helping to curb recessions, the expansion of government, corporate and consumer debt has tended to steer the economy towards a far more serious dilemma. It seems that that problems 'solved' in one area, only result in the emergence of economic difficulties in another or in the prolongation and intensification of the original problem. The 'managers' appear to have forgot- ten the necessary (under capitalism), therapeutic effects of depressions. What used to bring the debt spiral to halt was the depression slump with its attendant price drop and the subsequent 'squeezing out' of the financial superstructure (212). In the present epoch, however, while the disproportional growth of debt and income is not a new phenomena to capitalism(213), the crucial difference lies in the fact that with the mitigation of the cyclical slump, no drop in prices occurs, nor a consequent 'squeezing out' of the financial structure. Consequently, state, corporate and consumer debt continues to swell resulting in a situation where even mild economic setbacks shake the entire highly sensitized financial super-structure (214).

The apparent dilemma facing the economic planners is that the cost of avoiding a crisis now is a steady worsening of the debt/liquidity squeeze which becomes even more explosive (215).

In the short run, however, these efforts have been successful in converting what were (in their initial phases) depressions of the dimensions of that of 1929–1930 to relatively mild and manageable 'recessions' (216). This was particularly true of the 1957–1958 recession.

It should be noted further, that in addition to any other adverse long range consequences of cyclical crisis management measures, the gains made in mitigating their severity appeared to be countered by their increased frequency and in the disappearance of real 'boom' phases (217).

Generally due to the postwar shortening of the business cycle, recessions increased from a prewar average of one every ten years or so to a postwar rate of roughly one every 3–4 years. The recession (or depression) phase of the cycle is characteristically a time for the renewal and expansion of fixed capital or productive machinery. In the postwar years several factors lead to a shortening of the business cycle. First, as a result of the development of more rapid construction methods and techniques, new and old factories were more quickly built and rebuilt and thus put into operation than previously (218). Second, spurred by the hastened rate of scientific and technological breakthroughs achieved through massive military and private research, the Third Industrial (or technological) revolution has resulted in a more frequent obsolescence of productive machinery (219). Third, in the U.S. the government policy of aimed at strategic industries (and this was a very large scope) allowed them to deduct from their profits depreciation sums which were often in excess of 2 or 3 times the actual wear. Thus these industries were permitted to write-off the fixed capital of their plants in five years or less at the expense of the taxpayer and so further increased the frequency of the cycle (220). Somewhat as a complement to this later point it is worth nothing that 2/3 of the new capital investments in the U.S. during the last decade went for the replacement and modernization of existing plants (221).

The apparent re-emergence of inter-imperialist competition has only served to further aggravate this tendency toward a shortening cycle. Thus, even with the underemployment of current productive capacities and substantial actual production surpluses, the hastened increase in the organic composition of capital under the press of revived inter-imperialist competition and facilitated by massive defence research reinforces the new tendency toward a drastically shortened cycle. The rise in productive capacity which nearly always accompanies the reduction of labor costs through increases in the organic composition of capital appears only to aggravate the already pressing problem of surplus production and under-utilized productive capacities (222). Not only has the frequency of crisis in postwar America increased, but it seems that the upswing phase of the business cycle has been seriously reduced and occasionally eliminated completely (223). Even though more frequent and extensive state economic intervention (stimulant spending) has clearly effected a dampening of the downward phase of the business cycle, Varga has observed that,

> we may expect subsequent crises to deepen in comparison with the first postwar periods the postwar crises in the U.S.A. exhibited a definite tendency to deepen. (224)

The main objective of the discussion which has been pursued here has been to indicate certain limitations to Marcuse's view of well managed and disappearing periodic crisis in North American capitalism. While state efforts at economic intervention aimed at smoothing out postwar economic development have achieved noteworthy successes, the problem of periodic cyclical crisis appears far from solved. Indeed it may well be that the relative success in this area, as a long range tendency towards ever more frequent and deepening cyclical crisis sets in. Repeated state efforts to counteract the jerking pattern of capitalist development and production have met either failure or only limited and short term success (225). If a major depression has been averted in North American/world capitalism (no small achievement), through extensive state economic intervention (swelling state and private debt, sustained arms spending, inflationary monetary policies, etc.), it does not appear too unreasonable to conclude that, "a capitalism which knows 'only' recessions is certainly not a crisis free capitalism" (226) and therefore hardly of the qualitatively new order portrayed by Marcuse.

Summary: general crisis of North American capitalism

Inasmuch as capitalist prosperity depends upon the conjunction of expanding markets, investment opportunities and a high or stable rate of profit (227), the continuance of the relative prosperity of the postwar years grew more uncertain (particularly since 1966) and events began to increasingly undermine the possibility for such conjunctions (228). The rising surpluses of money capital, production and productive capacity may be due to the non-realization of commodities in increasingly competitive and overcapitalized domestic and world market, rising labor costs, and necessary replacement of not fully amortized fixed capital. The problems may be further witnessed in the growth of structural unemployment and the under-utilization of economic productive capacity (229). Thus, with a productive apparatus geared to supplying 'the world it calls free', substantial signs of unrealized commodities and productive capacity have already begun to appear (230). Further, the rise in structural unemployment in North America, itself a consequence of surplus production and productive capacity, tends to aggravate the problem as the unemployed worker's role as consumer is drastically undercut (231). Welfare and social assistance checks in North America hardly compensate the loss of purchasing power suffered by prolonged unemployment.

With the shrinking economic elbow room effected by intensified inter-imperialist competition, and Third World unrest and hostility towards North American imperialism, the safety-valve of world trade for periodic capitalist overproduction is being seriously undermined (232). Inextricably related to problems of overproduction and surplus productive capacity are the growing surpluses of money-capital. The factors which lead to an increasing squeeze on marketing possibilities result also to a relative and sometimes real decline in investment opportunities both at home and abroad. While North American money capital export remains large, this capital export itself tends to exacerbate the surplus money capital problem inasmuch as foreign investments are not simply opportunities for the export of domestically generated surplus money capital. These foreign investments themselves pay dividends, the transfer of which to the money capital exporting country in the long run results in a further aggravation of the initial problem of money capital surpluses (233).

As for domestic investment of this growing money surplus, the already monopoly controlled market and the still growing surplus productive capacity in these areas restrict investment possibilities of a scale necessary to counteract the tendencial and disproportional rise in capacity, commodity and money capital surpluses. Furthermore in a domestic market which is coming under increased competitive pressure from the revitalized imperialist rivals, it is unlikely that large American corporations will see any advantage in building new plants to compete in a market which their present productive capacity more than matches. Monopolists are not known for going into competition with themselves.

Coupled with this, the unabated and disproportional rise in government, corporate and consumer debt and military expenditures has given rise to an inflationary spiral which continued right through the 1970 recession (234). This problem is well recognized even by those economists whose apparent interest is primarily the propping-up of the system. P. Samuelson stated in 1971,

> Creeping inflation is the malaria of the modern mixed economy. Like malaria it is uncomfortable to live with and just will not go away. But unlike malaria, there seems to be no known cure for creeping inflation that is better than the disease (235).

112

'No known cure better than the disease' indeed, letting the crisis 'run its course' at this stage would in all probability mean running the risk (by government calculations) of from 15–20 million employed (236). The probable political consequences of unemployment of these dimensions is more than North American capitalism cares to risk. Thus, it appears that it is caught in a dilemma between on the one hand solving the immediate problems of surplus capital, productive capacity (and production) and high structural unemployment, and, on the other hand, letting itself in for a general worsening of the overall economic situation as a significant consequence of measures employed to ensure short-term stability (237).

This creeping inflation coupled with a chronic balance of payment deficit over the last half decade (largely the result of capital export and foreign military expenditures (238) has resulted in a gradual undermining of the American dollar (239), in its role as a money of account on the world market.

Thus state efforts to mitigate cyclical crisis by the expansion of overall credit spending and inflationary monetary policies appears to lead to an emergent contradiction between the dollar's use as an instrument in the struggle against cyclical crisis, and its role as a reserve money in the international monetary system (240). Resulting in a proneness to monetary crises. It was not long before that 'proneness' was realized, as the monetary crises of the late sixties and early seventies upset the 1944 Bretton Woods agreement (241) and shook the world capitalist system to its very roots (242). The apparent uncorruptable stability of the postwar years was suddenly threatened with an economic turmoil not witnessed since the depression of 1929 (243). In 1963, Per Jacobsen, the then director of the International Monetary Fund, addressing a group of economists cautioned,

> ... a new situation has arisen which shows certain similarities with what happened in the early 1930's ... I do not intend to convey the idea that we must repeat the sad experiences of those years, but I do think we will have to take definite measures to see that they are not repeated. (244)

The intervening ten years not only have not seen any successful 'measures' to curb this situation, but on the contrary, they have witnessed a gradual worsening of the problems then present and the addition of several new ones. The long range prospect seems far from promising for capitalist expansion and prosperity.

The arguments presented in this chapter have been in the first instance an attempt to assess the validity of Marcuse's self-declared justification for seeking a new route to socialism and rethinking critical theory. At base it appears to be Marcuse's views on current realities and probable long range tendencies in North American capitalism which motivate and justify this shift in perspective and for that reason an assessment of the main features of his economic analysis seemed of primary importance.

Further, the discussions in this chapter make no pretense at being exhaustive treatments of the phenomena considered. Rather, they have been attempts to balance-out, with the consideration of certain heretofore unconsidered (by Marcuse) developments and tendencies, the propositions he would have us accept as we follow the development of his discussions regarding the necessary nature and method of liberation from the advanced industrial society in North America. The overall objective of macro-economic planning appears much further from realization than Marcuse supposes. The prerequisities of such planning, predictable prices and supplies of raw material, predictable markets, full information on individual corporation's long term plans, effective control of that planning, predictable labor costs and stability, etc., are difficult indeed to achieve. Particularly in a world where increases in productive capacities are steadily outstripping increases in effective demand, the awakening of the Third World (a vital source of basic industrial raw materials) to their adverse position vis-a-vis the metropolis and both capitalist and socialist attempts to 'reset' the scales of exchange, the competition, contradictions and uncertainties which flow from this unreversed development seem to promise a future of declining successes for the capitalist economic planners. Nevertheless, the opening of the Soviet Union and China to Western economic penetration may well prove to be one significant stabilizing factor. The vast markets in these areas if substantially opened to capitalist expansion may well supply the vital, predictable and secure room for the increased export of money capital, and capital and consumer goods by the leading capitalist powers. Both obstacles and opportunities exist. But to the extent that they do exist, they appear to be in large measure neither the obstacles to nor the opportunities for long term capitalist expansion, stability and affluence proposed by Marcuse.

While the arguments presented in this chapter are limited, they should however be sufficient to cast substantial doubt upon the universal validity of Marcuse's central positions and thus give an indication of the general validity of the argument he has subsequently constructed on their basis. This perhaps would not have been so obviously the case had Marcuse not insisted that the developments he perceived were merely the beginning of probably permanent trends in this direction. While he appears to have drawn his economic conclusions largely on the basis of developments and economic apparent tendencies in the early and mid-fifties, the criticism still applies. Both explicitly and implicitly (through his continued insistence on the necessity for a 'revised' critical theory to meet the 'unique' situation) Marcuse continues to affirm the validity of that analysis and the consequent long-range projections he has made on that basis.

Further, the above discussions have not been intended to replace Marcuse's picture of 'gloom' with one of capitalist 'doom'. Rather, the intent of the preceeding discussions is to point out certain apparent limitations, weakenesses, and gaps in the argument Marcuse has made supporting the notion of the unforseeably long term stability, management, and expanding affluence of North American capitalism. Advanced capitalism in general and North American capitalism in particular are undoubtedly a long way from complete collapes and no doubt the future will hold further surprises of its already well demonstrated tenacity and 'flexibility'. However, it also seems clear that the long period of relative postwar stability and prosperity which so impressed (or depressed) Marcuse, shows significant signs of strain. Still further, the structure, goals and dynamics of contemporary North American capitalism seem hardly to have changed in the postwar years to anywhere near the 'qualitative' degree Marcuse insists upon. In short it does not appear to have 'outgrown' the conceptual structure of critical theory. If the objective is to be a realistic evaluation of the conditions and tendencies of North American capitalism, then those who not always without cause are quick to criticize the often flippant 'doomsday' predictions aimed at that economic system, would do well to show equal critical scrutiny of their own often ill-formed evaluations of its elasticity, stability and general 'staying-power' of that system. The point is that the task of assessing the future direction of North American capitalist development and the crises and contractions it may be heading for is an extremely difficult one to accomplish and one which the foregoing discussions make no claim to realizing. What should be clear however, is that the often conjunctural and undialectical economic analysis offered by Marcuse should be approached with caution. It can and has lead in Marcuse's case, to apparently premature and untimely social and political conclusions and subsequent unnecessary theoretical revisions. The complexity of contemporary world capitalism militates against such *ahistorical* and uncritical analyses.

Chapter Four:

The Critique of the Fundamental Social and Political Propositions and Implications

Introduction

The discussions in this chapter will focus upon main features of Marcuse's social and political analysis of tendencies and realities in North American society. Building upon his economic analysis they complete the political dilemma which Marcuse sees confronting critical theory and revolutionary praxis and consequently represent further arguments for his insistence on and proposals for a new route to and conception of socialism.

Unemployment and poverty: Further considerations

> ... a rising standard of living is the almost unavoidable by-product of the politically manipulated industrial society. (1)

Thus,

> ... it is the sheer *quantity* of goods, services, work and recreation in the overdeveloped countries which effectuates this containment. (2)

Consequently,

> The achievements of progress defy ideological indictment. (3)

It should be made clear at the outset that this discussion is not an effort to deny the existence of substantial affluence and employment opportunities in North America. It does however, represent an attempt to balance out Marcuse's analysis by pointing out certain facts and tendencies singularly absent from his study and projections. Marcuse does not simply suggest that the North American working class has its basic requirements met and has reasonable opportunities to acquire 'normal' working class employment. Far from it, he apparently suggests that the affluence of the North American working class is of the rapidly expandings, 'two-car', 'split-level home', and abundant 'purchasing-power' variety, while employment opportunities are not only numerous but also of a rewarding, stimulating nature offering substantially increased leisure time. Thus, it is more the dimensions and quality of working class affluence and employment portrayed by Marcuse which seems exaggerated—particularly inasmuch as he interpretes the developments which he depicts as only the beginning of unforeseeably long-range tendencies in these directions.

The postwar years in North America have seen a vast revolution of expectations (4), a development which the sociological and economic 'celebrationist' literature of the fifties and early sixties contributed to in no small way. Despite the rhetoric however, the hard fact remains that vast numbers of Americans still suffer from chronic unemployment and/or live in varying degrees of poverty and deprivation. The officially pronounced ideal as well as the existence of substantial affluence serves only to make the plight of these 'outsiders' that much more difficult to accept (5).

Under the impact of a worsening international economic situation, structural unemployment continues to rise slowly but steadily, while the increasing frequency and intensity of cyclical economic fluctuations and the everpresent seasonal unemployment bursts, periodically aggravate an already bad situation (6), usually leaving it worse than it found it. If there is any validity in the economic tendencies discussed in the previous chapter, then the dimensions of unemployment and poverty which will be shown here, may well be viewed as only a prelude of worse things to come in the not too distant future.

Despite all government efforts to curb it, structural unemployment has steadily worsened since 1953 (7). While bad in the mid-sixties (8), the worsening world financial situation and multiplying trade uncertainties pushed it by 1971 to serious proportions (9). Combined with and related to these developments, the growing organic compositions of capital (in 1970, 65% of the West's total capital investment went toward increased technological productive efficiency (10), and thus frequently at the same time to labor displacement), and diminishing market and investment expansion opportunities appears to evermore permanently exclude the growing pool of reserve labor from the civilian job market (11). According to official statistics, which take no account of the massive slacks taken up by direct military employment (12), unemployment in the U.S. in the early seventies was set at 6.2% of the total labor force (13). It should be noted here; as several economists have convincingly argued (14), that these figures take no account of those workers (particularly women and younger workers), who in the face of recessions and generally rising structural unemployment, drop out of the labor market and in so doing drop out of official unemployment statistics. Indeed, if these 'vanished' unemployed, that is workers who are in their prime working years but not seeking employment, are included in the calculation, then it seems clear that at the end of 1970 not 6.2% but 9.1% of the total U.S. work force was unemployed (15).

Hardest hit by the steadily rising structural unemployment have been the youth, suffering a 1971 overall unemployment rate of 17.2% (16), even after the massive 'holding' functions performed by both the military and post secondary educational institutions (17). Since the mid-fifties, working age teenagers who represent just 8 % of the U.S. population had, by the end of the 60's, come to account for 45 % of the increase in unemployment (18).

To the 9.1% unemployed in the early seventies one might fairly add a reasonable proportion of the 5–6 million students registered in post secondary educational institutions (19) whose continued presence there was due largely to their desire to stay of an unfavorable job market for as long as possible.

Further it should be noted that the frequently applauded though often exaggerated (20) shift in the labor force from the industrial to the service sector implies most often not only a drop in income and status (21) but also the obliged acceptance of a part-time job to compensate for the loss of a full time one in the industrial sector (22). In 1962, (and there have been no indications that this trend has been subsequently altered, on the contrary), of the $2\frac{1}{2}$ million (23) persons employed in sales work in the U.S. 1/3 (24) close to a million were employed on a part-time basis, and of the nearly 3 million service workers (25) more than $\frac{1}{2}$ (26) or $1\frac{1}{2}$ million worked on a part-time basis. According to official statistics however they were simply registered as 'employed'.

Thus, considering those who stay in school to avoid inevitable under-or unemployment, the more direct labor market drop-outs (those who have given up looking but don't spend their time in universities or the like), the part-time workers, to say nothing of the more complicated problem of the military drain off, a figure of 10% unemployment in the early seventies would appear indeed modest. P. Sweezy has estimated that had such an anti-crises and unemployment softing measures as government arms spending not been pursued, unemployment in 1970 would probably have stood at about 22.3 million (27). Again, it is worth restating that these current 'serious' dimensions of unemployment may well be in for further growth as a result of a general long term worsening of the North American economy. All of which comes precisely at a time of an accelerated growth of the labor force in general. It has been estimated that due to the birth rate explosion of the early postwar years and projecting from present population growth patterns, the U.S. labor force between '70–75 will grow at 200 % the rate it had between 1950–1960 (28).

It would seem reasonable to conclude that if the relative 'boom' period of the fifties and early sixties was unable to absorb the growing labor force, boasting a steady tendential rise in structural unemployment since 1953, then the semi-stagnant condition of the North American economy in the seventies will in all probability only cause to aggravate the situation further. Thus the prospects for a continuation of 'the sheer quantity of ... work' envisioned by Marcuse in the mid- and late fifties, seems at least a little tenous.

But what of the steadily expandning affluence of the working class—those who manage to get and hold jobs? Clearly, significant sections of the North American population enjoy just that quantity and quality of 'affluence' Marcuse attributes to them. The question is, has it expanded at a rate, in the quantity and to the proportions of the population which Marcuse suggests?

No. A far better characterization of the pattern of income distribution in postwar North America is stability rather than the notion of an income revolution (29), though this in itself does not deny the possibility of an overall rise in prosperity and affluence. In a recent and thorough study of class in the U.S., R. Hamilton, using government statistics, has arrived at the following picture of the size and rate of increase of North American working class affluency throughout the postwar years (at least until things began to get worse economically in the mid-sixties).

> The spendable average weekly earnings (for the family of four in 1957–1959 dollars) figures are available for the years from 1947–1967. In most of these years there is an increase in the average, in some, however, in recession years 1957, 1958 and 1960 and in the years 1951, 1966 and 1967, there were slight fall-offs registered. If we take the entire period and calculate the average yearly increase we find that it amounts to just over one dollar per week per year. That means that the average family of four earning say $70 per week in a given year would be earning approximately $71 per week in the subsequent year (30).

This is hardly the picture of rapidly expanding affluence portrayed by Marcuse. Further, as a consequence of the worsening economic situation discussed in the previous chapter, the period from 1966 (the above mentioned calculation covered a period ending in 1967), to 1971 (and recent indications make it reasonable to assume that this trend has continued to present), saw almost no increase in the average 'real' income of the North American worker (31). In the words of Milton Freidman, one not especially known for understimating the achievement of North American capitalism and society,

> Since then [1966]* however, there has been almost no gain [in U.S. workers' real wages]—a major cause of labour's militance at the bargaining table. (32)

Considering the previously mentioned growing debt servicing drain on consumer incomes (33), affluence hardly seems to be galloping forward, appeasing the masses at the rate and to the degree that some (Marcuse) would have us believe. As late as 1968, more than 10 million workers in the U.S. received less than $1.60 per hour and the prospects for further substantial rates and sizes of wage increase, decline as North American capitalism under pressure from emerging intense international competition, rising raw material prices and increasing uncertainty of sources, seeks to make good its losses and regain or consolidate its international competitive edge by containing or even pressing back the 'real' wages of the North American working class (34).

* my insertion.

Further, reference should be made to discussions in the previous chapter on the probable consequences which renewed inter-imperialist competition will have on the future wage patterns of the American working class (35). Already they have the slowest rate of increase (and that in gross income) of all in the advanced capitalist countries (36).

To the extent that the working class do achieve 'affluency' it has been observed that it is at a far greater effort (37). Unlike the affluence of their middle class brothers, working class affluence usually implies not only that both husband and wife *must* work, but it also implies that the type of work they must engage in is far less satisfying and, far less secure. The probability of seasonal or cyclical layoffs and the consequent disruption of the family economy and jeopardization of its tenuous hold on the 'affluence' life is an everpresent and ever more appreciated threat.

Further, inasmuch as there has been no substantial reduction in the forty-hour week which was in general universally introduced in North America in the very early postwar years (38), it seems far more probable that the clear increase in to-and-from work travelling time since this early period as a result of a population shift to the suburbs has lead to a net decrease in leisure time rather than the supposed substantial increase made so much of by Marcuse (39).

In addition to this 'not so rampant and conspicuous' affluence, the postwar years have witnessed a marked increase in the rate of exploitation of the North American working class (at least until 1963 and if earlier discussions are correct then the trend would probably not have been altered-), as American capitalism appropriated from $20\% - 30\%$ larger a share of the surplus product than it had in 1948 (40).

If the steadily employed secton of the working class is not as affluent as Marcuse supposes, then at least their lot (apart from a sizable number of working poor) (41) is better than the unemployed (both temporarily and chronically) and other poverty groups in North America. The dimensions are sobering. In the mid-sixties $\frac{1}{2}$ of the aged persons in the U.S. lived below the officially designated poverty line (41). Further, the report of th Conference of Economic Progress, Poverty and Deprivation in the United States which summed up the situation, demonstrated that in 1960 (when Marcuse's 'split-level' home affluency was well established), 38 million people were living in poverty and 39 million lived in what is officially termed 'deprivation' (43). That means that 77 million people (2/5 of the total population of the United States) were a long, long way from the 'good-life' portrayed by Marcuse.

Further, by the latter half of the 60's, it has been estimated that $\frac{1}{2}$ of the U.S. population lived below what was officially defined as 'adequate for minimum comfort' (44).

Indeed, there has been improvement since the early postwar years, but in light of the probable long-range economic trends in North America, Magdoff and Sweezy appear more than generous in their calculation of it taking at the present rate of improvement, another 90 years to abolish poverty in North America (45).

H. P. Miller's comments are illuminating in this matter:

> In summarizing the results of a three year study of poverty ... Oscar Ornati concluded that between 1947–1960 there was some reduction in the proportion of families living at or below the subsistance levels, but there was no change in the proportion living in poverty just above bare subsistance. (46)

Well if the poor were not quite as poor as before, they were nevertheless a far cry from the 'split-level home and two-car garage' affluency of Marcuse's indicators of prosperity or affluency (47) in America.

In areas lacking adequate public transportation (and anyone familiar with North America will know this is the rule than the exception), automobile ownership becomes not only an essential factor in enabling travel to and from work, but in addition, an added burden on an often already strained working class budget (48). Thus, it hardly seems appropriate to draw overly broad conclusions regarding increased working-class affluence on the basis of the postwar increase in private car ownership.

As for home ownership as an indicator of prosperity and affluence, it should be noted that the sharp increase in home ownership during the postwar years has been accounted for by homes of extremely modest value (an average in 1964 of $13.327) (49) and that particularly in the 60's, much of the increase may be attributed to the purchase of 'trailers', which are classified by the Survey of Consumer Finances (the general source for analyses focusing on home ownership rates), as normal home ownership (50).

Marcuse appears to have significantly over-estimated both the overall dimensions (individual quantity and proportion of the population enjoying it), as well as the rate of expansion of affluence in North America. This seems particularly true of his assumptions of the extent of working-class affluence. Further, and this may be due to his particular conception of contemporary North American capitalism, he appears to have failed to consider the fact that poverty is not only a general consequence of the functioning of a capitalist society (51) but it is often a very functional aspect of it as well (52) (providing of course it is kept within politically acceptable dimensions). Its presence provides a surplus labor pool for capital to draw upon during periods of rapid economic expansion or periodic 'booms'.

The fact nevertheless remains that substantial unemployment and poverty persist in comtemporary North America. Since 1953 structural unemployment has been a growing problem and in view of the apparent tendencies in North American capitalism, 'the problem of achieving full employment must become increasingly difficult' (53). As for the continued existence of poverty of serious dimensions (1/3 of the U.S. population) (54), Morril and Wahlenberg point out that while:

> Many voices today predict a quick disappearance of poverty, . . . experience, and the findings of this study, should help us to appreciate its cruel persistance. (55)

Aggravated by an apparently long range and overall and worsening North American economy, the current serious dimensions of unemployment and poverty appear further than ever from being 'taken in hand'. If the citizenry of NorthAmerica is far from starving to death, as a whole, they appear to be equally as distant from the type and scope of affluence Marcuse insists upon attributing to them and it is far from clear that either the immediate or the long-range future under capitalism will see them move substantially closer to that goal. Further, the stability, dimensions and rapidity of increase of working class affluency appear to be significantly overstated by Marcuse. Indeed, it is far from clear that,

> "The achievements of progress defy ideological indictment." (56)

The new working class and working class structure: further considerations

> The long-range tendency which in large areas of material production, tends to replace heavy physical labor by technolical and mental energy, increases the social need for scientifically trained and intelligent workers. (57)

Further,

> This tendency is strengthened by the changing composition of the working class. The declining proportions of blue collar workers, the increasing number and importance of white collar employees, technicians, engineers and specialists divide this class. (58)

Therefore,

> The chances for promotion decline as management prefers engineers and college graduates. (59)

Thus,

> The intelligentsia attains an increasingly decisive role in this process (productive process). (60)

122

Owing to their key positions this group really seems to represent the nucleus of an objective revolutionary force. (61)

This section will focus on Marcuse's notion of the changing proportional composition of the North American working class and the consequent steadily rising demand for and premium placed on the highly educated, trained and skilled. Further, the discussion will turn on certain unconsidered developments and tendencies regarding the 'objective' revolutionary potential of this NEW working class due to their position in the newly revolutionized means of production. Marcuse suggests that the working class becomes increasingly 'split', as this 'new group', because of qualitatively different work experiences (i.e. responsiblity, satisfaction, etc.) develops a consciousness 'apart' from the traditional working class. Again, for Marcuse's part all of these conclusions and propositions are suggested as the beginning of long-range trends. The discussion thus attempts to consider some aspects of the new working class phenomenor, and working class structure and consciousness, significantly absent from Marcuse's analysis. Marcuse's conclusions appear to be based upon the assumption that the third industrial or technological revolution which began in the early 50's will entail a long term unabated rise in the demand for highly educated manpower.

The 50's and early 60's witnessed a far reaching revolution in the fundamental character of the overall productive apparatus in North America, indeed in all advanced industrial countries. As early as the 1940's the first indications of this third industrial revolution began to emerge (62). Whereas the first industrial revolution was based on the steam engine, and the second on the electric and internal combustion motor, the third was based upon computers and electronic machinery in general.

The ensuing qualitative break in numerous areas of industry resulted in a rapidly spiraling demand for highly educated and scientifically trained manpower to carry out the basic research, development construction and installation necessary facilitate this transformation. Entire new areas of knowledge and skill suddenly aquired central importance in the further development of North America's productive apparatus. The universities and immigration policies were quick to anwer the call as the early fifties saw the beginning of an increase in the 'production' of highly educated manpower and a less enduring but equally steep rise in the immigration of the highly educated to North America.

Increased industrial demand was not the whole cause of this increase however (63).

It was complimented by the cold war arms race (exacerbated by the 'Sputnik' shock) in making both the American public and policy makers accutely aware of a substantial technological gap, which for reasons of industrial competitiveness as well as defense, needed to be closed as rapidly as possible (64). Apparently proven by this situation and giving theoretical coherence to

123

the necessary solutions, a novel theory of economic development know as the Human Capital Thesis rapidly gained adherents among influential public policy makers. In a nutshell, R. Lockhart outlines this theory as follows:

> ... the Human Capital hypothesis saw knowledge as a super-critical new input factor in advanced industrial economies. It was argued that once high levels of physical capital formation and advanced industrial infrastructures are achieved, further growth is almost entirely dependent upon an accelerating rate of technological innovation. This in turn was a function of formally institutionalized knowledge production. (65)

The intrinsically related rapid rates of technological change and innovation taking place in industry and defense under the combined impetus of the general technological revolution (hastened by rising inter-imperialist competition), and massive and sustained government arms expenditures, developed in a dialectical relation to the increasingly influential Human Capital thesis as the latter not only spurred the former developments but appeared to be validated by their very scope and progress (66). There were few indeed who questioned that it was the egg (increased knowledge production) which came before the chicken (industrial progress).

What was apparently not appreciated by those (and here Marcuse must be included), who heralded the coming of a long range trend towards a change composition of the 'working class' and a consequent unforeseeably long range upward spiralling premium on the highly educated university trained scientific workers, was that what they were witnessing in the fifties and early sixties was indeed an industrial *revolution*. Consequently, once the first feverish burst of research, development, construction and installation was completed, the demand for the highly educated would begin to level off and even decline. In the case of this third industrial revolution, this initial research, development and installation phase began to draw to a close as early as the mid-sixties (67). As in the case of past industrial revolutions, the accelerated growth rate of the first transformation phase soon comes to an end once the basic technological problems are solved, production of the 'new' machinery has been routinized and general installation has been achieved. From that point on, while further scientific research advancement and installation of improved machinery certainly continues, the rate of innovation, development and installation declines and consequently *so does the exaggerated demand for highly educated scientifically trained personnel.*

Further, the logical extension of the application of the new technology to more and more areas of labor leads eventually to a further fall-off in the demand for just those scientists, technicians and engineers who first designed and built the new technology (68). It appears that the long range impact of the new technology on the work force of modern factory and office is not quite what Marcuse had anticipated. In an extensive study of the impact of automation on

124

the work force of 13 factories, J. Bright concludes that the significant long range effect of automation on the work force is the substantial reduction of the skill requirements of the overall work force (69).

Both at the level of direct (70) and indirect (71) labor as well as in maintenance work (72), Bright's study showed that apart from exceptional instances (73) the overall tendency in newly automated plants is towards a downgrading of the skill requirements of the work force (74). Further, he noted that as a result of this unexpected tendency the composition of the factory work force generally remained stable or showed only a slight shift in favour of what is traditionally termed unskilled or semi-skilled labor.

A further consequence of the introduction of automation was a related diminishment of the need for prolonged training periods for new workers (75). Rather than resulting in a premium being placed on high levels of education and skill, the new machinery placed emphasis on the general qualities of alertness and physical and mental ability (76). And, of special significance to Marcuse's conclusions, it was observed that the introduction of the new and highly sophisticated electonic machinery did not lead to a particular or relative decline in opportunities for the unskilled work force (77) (those of course that the new plant had numerical room for). Indeed, in most cases the newly automated factories studied utilized their old unskilled and semi-skilled work force in the new factory (78) and the training formerly required of operators and maintenance personal has become far less complicated and time consuming (79). Instances of increased training time were the exception rather than the rule (80). Thus it appears that in general as a result of the introduction of automation to a factory including devices for measurement, design and machine control, the skill and training requirements of the former traditional work force are, apart from exceptional instances, significantly reduced (81).

The table 10 and fig. 4 give an indication of the fluctuations in skill, education, etc. requirements of the work force in an automatic factory.

In Bright's words:

> The significant conclusion arising out of this study is that it is not true that ... automation ... inevitably means a lack of opportunity for the unskilled worker and/or tremendous retraining problems. On the contrary, automation often reduces the contribution of the individual at the machine. Automated machinery reqires less operator skill, after certain levels of mechanization are passed. It appears as though the average worker can more quickly and easily master new and different jobs where highly automatic machinery provides the skill, effort and control required. Furthermore, some 'key' skilled jobs currently requiring long experience and training, are reduced to easily learned machine tending jobs. (82)

One is reminded here of Marx's observation that the long range tendency in

Table 10. *Changing contribution required of operators with advances in levels of mechanization*

Worker contribution[a] or sacrifice traditionally receiving compensation	1–4 Hand control	5–8 Mechanical control	9–11 Variable control, signal response	12–17 Variable control, action response
Physical effort	Increasing-decreasing	Decreasing	Decreasing-nil	Nil
Mental effort	Increasing	Increasing-decreasing	Increasing or decreasing	Decreasing-nil
Manipulative skill (dexterity)	Increasing	Decreasing	Decreasing-nil	Nil
General skill	Increasing	Increasing	Increasing-decreasing	Decreasing-nil
Education	Increasing	Increasing	Increasing or decreasing	Increasing or decreasing
Experience	Increasing	Increasing-decreasing	Increasing-decreasing	Decreasing-nil
Exposure to hazards	Increasing	Decreasing	Decreasing	Nil
Acceptance of Undesirable job conditions	Increasing	Decreasing	Decreasing-nil	Decreasing-nil
Responsibility[b]	Increasing	Increasing	Increasing-decreasing	Increasing decreasing or r
Decision making	Increasing	Increasing-decreasing	Decreasing	Decreasing-nil
Influence on productivity	Increasing	Increasing-decreasing or nil	Decreasing-nil	Nil
Seniority	Not affected	Not affected	Not affected	Not affected

[a] Refers to operators and not to setup men, maintenance men, engineers, or supervisors.
[b] Safety of equipment, of the product, of other people.
[c] Refers to opportunity for the worker to increase output through extra effort, skill, or judgment
Source: James Bright, "Does Automation Raise Skill Requirements?" *Harvard Business Review* July–August (1958), p. 92.

industry is to relegate labor to the role of bystander and watcher (83). The outcrop of these developments seems to be that with the advent of the new technology, skill and training are becoming increasingly less critical factors in industry (84) (and office). The qualification should be made here that this apparent tendency applies only to those workers who remain employed after the impact of automation. Thus, it is not the higher skill and education requirements of automation that deprive the traditional working class of jobs in industry, rather it is more precisely the decline in the overall numbers required to man the new productive apparatus. It is in short, far more a question of quantity than quality.

126

**How total contribution required
of operators may vary with levels of
mechanization**

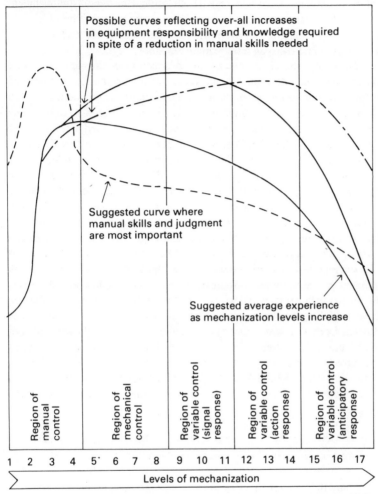

Possible curves reflecting over-all increases
in equipment responsibility and knowledge required
in spite of a reduction in manual skills needed

Suggested curve where
manual skills and judgment
are most important

Suggested average experience
as mechanization levels increase

Region of manual control

Region of mechanical control

Region of variable control (signal response)

Region of variable control (action response)

Region of variable control (anticipatory response)

1 2 3 4 5˙ 6 7 8 9 10 11 12 13 14 15 16 17

Levels of mechanization

Fig. 4. Source: James Bright, "Does Automation Raise Skill Requirements?" Harvard
Business Review, July August (1958). p. 92.

As Varga has observed:

> In the factories of today there are very few skilled workers in the old
> sense of the term. Technological progress ... has led to the skill of the
> worker being no longer of decisive importance in production. (85)

This tendencial decrease in skill and training requirements should come as no surprise if one pauses to reconsider that one of the basic factors motivating automation is the effort to diminish overall labor costs or costs of constant capital. Such reductions may be effected both through the overall diminishment in the size of the labor force (increasing the organic composition of capital) as well as by minimizing the proportional requirements for highly skilled, highly educated and consequently high priced labor.

The plants engaged in the design and production of the new automatic machinery are well aware of this and consequently of their own enhanced marketing possibilities for automatic machinery which not only reduces overall labor costs and improves production efficiency, but which also reduces the need for (and the expense of) a highly educated and skilled work force to operate it. There is therefore a steady effort being made in this branch to trivialize the skill requirements of the new electronic machinery (86).

Thus from the beginning of the third industrial revolution to the present, the nature and sophistication of automatic machinery has progressed. Whereas the automated plant of the early fifties may have required an increase in the skill, education and training level of operators and maintenance personnel, the logical extension of the new technology to more and more areas of labor has witnessed a long range decline in such skill requirements (87). Therefore, it would seem that the pioneering studies on the impact of automation on the skill requirements of the factory workforce (C. Walker for example whose study was conducted in the late forties and whose conclusions have had explicit effect on Marcuse's thinking on these matters) (88), focused on and drew long range conclusions from what was in fact a conjunctural tendency of the first phase of the third industrial revolution, a tendency which was soon to be arrested and even reversed as higher stages of automation began to be achieved by the late fifties to mid sixties (89). Indeed, Bright, reflecting on the increased mental strain characteristics of the different levels of automation, states that in the early stages,

> Increased mental strain had resulted—not because the equipment was more automatic, but because it was not automatic enough! (90)

A tendency that applies likewise to 'responsibility' requirements (91).

Until now the focus of our discussions of the impact of automation on the work force has been largely concerned with the traditional working class (as opposed to the so-called new working class). As has been indicated however, just as automation hastened forward under its own dynamic (92) and the underlying pressure of the competitive and profitability squeeze to decimate the ranks of the traditional working class (as opposed to the so-called new working class). Neither was it long before the engulfing wave of automation began to hit the ranks of the scientists, engineers, and technicians (93). By the mid-sixties, it was clear that even their indispensibility was in question. The long range trend of a steadily rising demand for university-trained per-

128

sonnel projected by Marcuse and central to his assessment of the objective strength of this potential new working class must be reconsidered in view of the findings of the studies of R. Lockhart (94), P. A. Schon (95), B. B. Seligman (96), and J. Bright (97). They have shown that, on the contrary, the long range trend appears to be a trivializing of functions of these jobs and a consequent drastic reduction in the demand for such professionals in both office and factory. The general consensus is that once the initial installment and 'trouble-shooting' of the new automatic factory is complete, the demands for technicians, engineers, etc. either returns to its pre-automation proportions or is actually reduced (98). Not that these skills in themselves are no longer generally necessary, but it seems that in the not so long run, computers can not only do their work more quickly and effectively, but once a certain scale of operations is reached, less expensively as well. It is worth quoting at length B. B. Seligman's observation on these developments for it gives a glimpse of precisely what kinds of advances are being made in this area.

> Not only is the skilled craftsman automated out of his job, but the engineers who dream up the new machines are not immune either. The most sophisticated examples of automation are turning upon their masters and taking over traditional engineering work ... Original design problems involving variations of standard product lines can be solved by a computer in thirty minutes, compared with six days for a man with a slide rule. In one technique the design method itself rather than past solutions, is stored up in the computer, it uses its stored knowledge to generate design plans and also to produce all the paper work required to start the manufacturing process. (99)

Increasingly employers are turning to training 'housewives, ex-meatcutters, office sweepers, etc.' to operate the most advanced automatic factories and offices (100), as they recognize that highly educated manpower is to a substantial degree becoming an unnecessary expense in their overall labor costs.

In a test conducted by IBM (101) it was clearly demonstrated that high educational and professional background is a largely irrelevant factor in learning to operate the equipment and machinery of the most technologically sophisticated plants and offices. Indeed, chronic *underemployment* is a constant cause of complaint among the highly educated work force that remains (102). The example of 'scientific' workers in the communications industry is a particularly illustrative example. Here, in one of the most technologically advanced areas of production, one would expect to find the conditions suggested by Marcuse, however, even here (or perhaps, particularly here) extensive automation has resulted in work being organized along more mechanical lines. Responsibility, skill and education requirements have been drastically

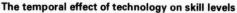

The temporal effect of technology on skill levels

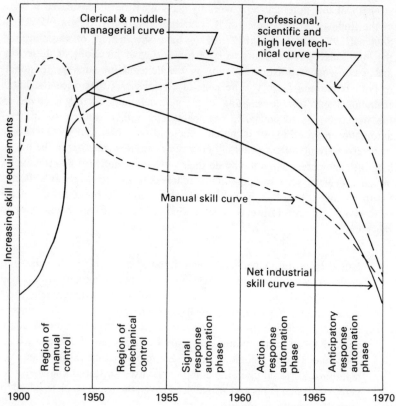

Fig. 5.

Source: R. A. Lockhart, *The Effects of Recent Techno-Economic Changes on the Mobility Patterns and Opportunities of the American Middle-Class, with particular Emphasis on Emergent Contradictions between Occupational and Educational Factors,* unpublished M. A. Thesis, Simon Fraser University, Burnaby, B. C., Canada, August, 1970, p. 187.

reduced, and the remaining 'scientific' workers 'complain bitterly' about their under-employment and demeaningly simple and mechanical tasks (103).

Figure 5 gives an indication of the initial rise then subsequent fall-off in professional skill requirements.

In addition to the decline in demand for highly educated manpower due to the 'petering-out' of the first feverish research, design, and development stage of the third industrial revolution, and further as a consequence of the logical dynamic of continuing sophistication of newer automatic machinery which 'trivializes' previously indespensible human tasks, the evidence shows that the initial high demand for engineers, technicians, etc. was in large part the result of the 'novelty' of the new equipment rather than of real and continuing industrial need (104).

Thus, the combined result of these factors, along with the general worsening of the overall economic situation seems to indicate a probable long range decline in the necessity of and so demand for highly educated and scientifically trained manpower in the 'new' means of production. Indeed, considering the basic motivation of capitalist production it is not at all surprising at this stage to find, as R. Lockhart has (105), that employers are apparently looking with increasing disfavour on the over-educated and over-trained. Not only are the wage demands of the less educated significantly lower, but not having internalized the higher income and occupational mobility expectations characteristic of the more highly educated, they are far less likely to be as frustrated by the workplace realities than their more 'privileged' counter-parts. By the midsixties, therefore, with university output still climbing, the first indications of a general fall-off in the demand for the highly educated began to appear (106). The impact of the automatic office brought with it a parallel decline in demand for traditional white collar workers (107) which was only further aggravated by the overall economic slowdown which began to make itself felt also by the mid-sixties. Thus the disproportional growth rate of the white collar work force experienced during the 50's had by the early 60's tapered off to return to a very slow rate of change.

One of the most significant results of the third industrial revolution has been the consequent steady undermining of the power of the so-called 'middle manager'. Inasmuch as professional 'new working class' employment had come to be a first rung in the ladder towards management positions (108), the objective revolutionary potential attributed to this group of workers appeared all the more enhanced. However, the advent of the full implications of the computer in the automatic office and factory seem to clearly indicate that this particular avenue to management 'power' is increasingly limited.

> The tightening of the executive lines stems from the new philosophy of centralization engendered by the computer. This process has been going on for a number of years in many American corporations. The result is a lesser need for middle class manager skills. (109)

While in the initial stages of automation it was necessary for top management to recruit 'allies' among the professional scientists, technicians, engineers, etc. (110), the long range and largely unanticipated tendency of the technological development characteristic of the third industrial revolution was toward a 'routinization' and 'trivilization' of more and more of the tasks performed by this group. This trend is greatly facilitating the return of much of the decision making power which top management was earlier obliged to surrender under corporate expansion of the postwar period. The centralizing characteristics of the computer which effects a major shift of decision making power from middle to top management (111) paves the way for such a reversal (112) and make possible major cutbacks in middle management personal (113).

Indeed, quite apart from this computer facilitated recentralization of decision making, it seems wrong to too easily equate necessary expertise with real decision making power. The fact that one is necessary to the functioning of a system, or the fact that one advises a decision-maker, should not too readily lead to the conclusion that final authority rests with that advisor, or in that necessary role. Indeed, as functional sociology has taken great pains to demonstrate, "most parts of any system are necessary" (114).

Nevertheless, to the extent that expertise and middle management did enjoy independent decision making power, the long range tendencies of the new technology soon began to rapidly undermine that power. Considering that stock ownership is "not so dispersed that it is meaningless" (115), and further that there is considerable evidence (116) to demonstrate that the largest shareholders in corporations are usually also active in top management (117), it seems reasonable to conclude that the re-centralization of decision making power made possible by the computer, implies a significant return of direct decision making power to the owners of the means of production. Indeed, it has been estimated that this shift in the center of gravity from middle managers to the front office facilitated by the computer has in the final analysis placed control at major corporations in the hands of fewer than 1.5 % of the population (118).

This increasing exclusion of the white collar work force from the 'management team' (119) and the consequent decline in the ranks of 'management' at first appears at odds with tendencial rise in the U.S. bureau of statistics figures on professionals, managers, and the overall white collar work force. However, as already pointed out, not only had the rate of increase tapered off sharply by the early 60's, but also much of the overall rise in the ranks of white collar workers is accounted for by an increase in non-professional and partime sales and service employment which in terms of both status and income represents a lesser quality of employment than industrial blue collar employment. Further, R. Lockhart has argued convincingly that not only is the apparent increase in professional, management and technical jobs almost exclusively restricted to the service sector, but also, "very few are professional or managerial in the normally accepted sense" (120).

The overall long range trend for the new 'inteligentsia' working class seems to be a gradual decline in numbers, indispensibility, and decision making power. Consequently, Marcuse's conclusions regarding the long range increase in their numbers, growing indispensibility and the expanding potential decision making power—their increasingly strengthening objective revolutionary potential—appears to be rather questionable.

What then of the altered structure of the North American working class and the increasing proportion, indispensibility and power of the white-collar workers and new working class. It seems clear that not only are there now

Table 11. *Nonfarm occupational trends: 1950, 1960, and 1969* (*employed males*)

	Year					
	1950		1960		1969	
	N	%	N	%	N	%
White collar (in 1000's)						
Professional, technical, and kindred	2 696	7.5	4 766	12.0	6 751	14.7
Managers, officials, and proprietors	5 439	15.1	5 968	15.0	6 726	14.6
Cerical and kindred	3 035	8.4	3 145	7.9	3 422	7.4
Sales	2 379	6.6	2 544	6.4	2 675	5.8
Total	13 459	37.7	16 423	41.3	19 574	42.5
Blue Collar, service						
Craftsmen, foreman, and kindred	7 482	20.8	8 332	21.0	9 854	21.4
Operatives and kindred	8 810	24.5	8 617	21.7	9 883	21.4
Laborers	3 435	9.6	3 471	8.8	3 526	7.6
Private household workers	125	0.3	30	0.1	39	0.1
Service workers	2 560	7.1	2 814	7.1	3 257	7.0
Total	22 412	62.3	23 264	58.7	26 520	57.5

Source: R. Hamilton, *Class and Politics in the United States*, New York, John Wiley and Sons Inc., 1972.

more blue collar workers in North America than ever before, but in the long run (between the early postwar years and the end of the 60's),

> ... as a percentage of the work force, the number of blue collar workers has remained amazingly constant (121). (See also table 11.)

Indeed, in the manufacturing industries in general, the decline of the representation of the 'old' working class has been far from drastic, nor has the rise of the technical worker. Projecting in 1960 it was estimated that between 1960 and 1970 the growth of technical, scientific, and professional workers would be only 4.3% and the drop of semi-skilled and skilled workers only 1.3% (122). Here it should be bourne in mind that this projection was made before the reversal in the demand for highly skilled and educated workers began to be felt in earnest in the mid-sixties. The real change in working class structure appears to have been more in the replacement of both skilled and unskilled workers by the semi-skilled (123).

133

What it more, it seems as was hinted at earlier, that white collar work is increasingly coming to resemble blue collar factory work. Seligman's statement deserves to be quoted here in full.

> A 1961 O.E.C.D. report on office automation suggested that traditional relations between management and clercs were coming to resemble those existing in the factory ... the speed, the need for close attention,and the reduction of work to repetition duplicate the boredom of the assembly line. In time, *the white collar becomes tinged with blue** and the status that once sustained the office worker in his endless shifting of papers and ledgers evaporates. (124)

A far more probable development in overall working class structure, when professional and general white collar workers begin to experience more consistantly and frequently (as have their blue collar brothers for long) the alienation, depressed wages, occupational insecurity and general frustration of under- as well as unemployment, there may well develop a growing objective and subjective homogeneity of the proletariat rather than the incerasing division envisioned by Marcuse (125).

The basis and existence of working class consciousness: further considerations

> In the advanced capitalist countries, where the radicalization of the working classes is counteracted by a socially engineered arrest of consciousness, and by the development and satisfaction of needs which pereptuate the servitude of the exploited, a vested interest in the system is thus fostered in the instinctual structure of the exploited. (126)

Under the impact of such novel developments,

> Hatred and frustration are deprived of their specific target, and the technological veil conceals the reproduction of inequality and enslavement. (127)

Thus, it appears to Marcuse that even the re-emergence of,

> ... impoverishment does not necessarily provide the soil for revolution. (128)

The following dicussion will focus on certain fundamental aspects of working class consciousness in North America. Specifically it will be a consideration of those factors which appear to be most critical in the emergence of class consciousness. Further, some reference will be made to areas in North

* Emphasis added.

134

America where radical working class consciousness has and does manifest itself even now, in the age of supposed expanding affluence. In brief, it is an attempt to consider the limitations of Marcuse's proposition that not only is radical working class consciousness generally absent from the North American labor scene, but also and more importantly, that the impact of sustained affluence and effective mental manipulation have effected an instinctual alteration of the underlying population which militates against, indeed negates the impact of those social, political and economic factors which were traditionally responsible for motivating the emergence of working class consciousness.

Like most other aspects of his social and economic analysis, Marcuse's conclusion regarding working class consciousness in North America appears to rely on those studies of class consciousness associated with the "end of ideology ideology" of the fifties. If there is one central fault to these studies (and Marcuse's) it is that they lack an historical perspective (129) and thus their conclusions are of a unnecessarily high conjunctural nature (130). Such studies, appear to focus largely on sectors of the working class which have experienced relatively long periods (throughout the fifties) of stability and relative affluence (131) incorrectly view the working class as a single group (132) thus drawing unwarranted generalizations from what are not only historically peculiar periods but also from often unrepresentative sectors of the entire class. It would seem more appropriate if studies of working class consciousness selected areas where conditions were likely to favor the emergence of militant class consciousness (133), only then could one assess the validity of Marcuse's assertions regarding the instinctual/biological undermining of working-class consciousness. Further, and Marcuse appears particularly guilty of this, class consciousness is too frequently considered to be a quality either present or absent. Rather, it would seem to due more justice to the phenomenon to view it 'ordinally'-varying in strength and militancy depending upon time, group and conditions (134).

Viewed in this manner and in consideration of the probable long range economic tendencies, the facile generalizations about a long range undermining and decline in working class consciousness and the conditions which give rise to it appear somewhat questionable (135).

It has been earlier pointed out that the postwar period in North America has witnessed, if not the universalization of affluence, then at least a far reaching revolution of expectations (136). Nor has this rise in expectations been confined to the steadily employed workers. The U.S. government promise of jobs and social assistance in its anti-poverty programs of the late 50's and early 60's served only to raise expectations of economic security which could not be met as government spending priorities gradually shifted to foreign aid (137). Thus the rising expectations of both the employed and unemployed of the North American working class promised by the relative prosperity of the fifties, the unmet promises of adequate state assistance and jobs and, the general image of universal and rightfully deserved affluence perpretated by the media, led to a consequent further sensitizing of the working class to any eventual economic back-slides or government renegging on previous promises of jobs and assistance (138). Rather than the fear of the 'enemy' or the depth of instinctual repression being responsible for the relative 'cooling-out' of the North American working class, it would appear that,

> ... the working classes of the advanced capitalist countries have made no revolution because their past has always been a little worse than their present, and their future has promised to be a little better yet. (139)

As for the basis of working class consciousness, both Leggett's study of the Detroit working class in the mid-sixties (140), and a similar but as yet unpublished study of working class consciousness in Vancouver, Canada conducted by him in the late 60's indicate that the factors most critical to the emergence of such consciousness are: 1) economic insecurity (141) caused either by seasonal cyclical, or long term structural unemployment; 2) occupational insecurity—(142) resulting both from direct unemployment as well as being the result of technological alterations at the work place; 3) uprootedness (143) resulting from rural to urban or urban to urban migration (frequently resulting in unmet expectations by the uprooted); and, 4) Working class marginality (144).

Clearly the inter-related nature of these factors implies that workers are often subject to a combination of them at the same time. The unavoidable conclusion of Leggett's studies indicate that along with unpleasant and hazardous working conditions and general alienation, the above are still the ciritical factors in motivating the fluctuations of class consciousness in North America.

Further, Leggett observed that while radical differences in the working class often presented obstacles to the formation of a common working class front, this goal was far from impossible. Indeed, in the Detroit study he observed that, as white working-class militancy increases, so does their willingness to co-operate and join the struggle of minorities for equal rights. At these times 'class consciousness proves more important than inter-ethnic hostility'' (145). Along these same lines it was also observed that the marginality of the racial minorities did not lead simply to race consciousness but also to militant working class consciousness.

As for the often assumed racism of the poor whites, and more generally the notion of working class authoritarianism, R. F. Hamilton's study (146) revealed that there is very little evidence to support such notions. Indeed, available data tends to dispute this notion (147).

This conclusion is in harmony with T. B. Bottomore's view that the continuing struggle of the Chicanos, Blacks and other ethnic minorities in North America will lead to a gradual diminishment of ethnic divisions and an ever more homogeneous class consciousness (148).

These then appear to be the basic factors which continue to influence the rise of working class consciousness. It is on this basis that the politically activating role of unions and other working class organizations and political parties attain decisive importance (149). Especially in areas where unions have in the past carried out successful struggles, their importance in sustaining and perpetuating class consciousness is high (150). While it is often correctly protested that Union leadership in North America has been effectively co-opted by the establishment, what is seldom appreciated in estimations of the political significance of labor unions is the relatively insecure position of the leadership. Unlike the major stockholders of corporations, union leaders owe their power in the last analysis to an either apathetic or actively supportive constituency. Not infrequently in North America, tense labor strife has led to the re-radicalization of that constituency and the quick casting off of leadership who remain out of step with the new levels of consciousness and demands (151).

The current trend towards union radicalization in parts of Canada as well as areas in the United States is witness to the historically temporary nature of 'establishment' unions and union leadership.

These critical factors in the emergence of radical working class consciousness should be considered against the apparent long range worsening situation of North American capitalism and the consequent aggravation of already significant structural unemployment, occupational insecurity, uprootedness and social marginality. Doing so gives a substantially different picture of things to come in the working class than is portrayed by Marcuse. Further 'progress' in automation will undoubtedly give rise to new dimension of occupational and economic insecurity.

Further, when one considers that one half of the present U.S. working class had middle-class or farm backgrounds until reaching working age (152), it seems clear that the 'uprooted' (153), the 'occupationally insecure' and the 'socially marginal', precisely those groups identified by Leggett as the most prone to radical class consciousness (154), are represented in large proportions in the present composition of the North American working class.

It might also be noted that a study conducted by Ulf Himmelstrand and Jan Lindhagen (155) in Sweden has revealed that in that national context, the upwardly mobile members of the working class and the affluent workers have either retained or even strengthened their sympathies for the Social Democratic party. Furthermore, R. F. Hamilton arrived at similar conclusions in a study of North American working class (156). This is contrary to Marcuse's correlation between working class affluence and upward mobility on the one hand and political conservatism on the other. It might be worth noting here, that by comparison with North American social democratic parties, the Swedish counterpart is significantly further to the left.

The uncertain economic future will in all probability multiply precisely those factors which have traditionally been critical in stimulating class consciousness. Thus, the uncertain economic future would appear to promise significant intensification and increases of the critical factors and a consequent widespread re-emergence of working class consciousness in North America. Under such conditions, the growing class and union militancy in Quebec, and other parts of Canada as well as manifestations of growing radicalization in Detroit, Akron (155), Flint and New York (158) can only contribute to the rest of the working class, examples of alternate political perspective and alternate forms of struggle. Further the rise of white collar unionism in Quebec (159) and in New York (160) indicates that the tendency is not wholly confined to the blue collar work force.

Just as the events in France in May ''68 shook many students of society who had become overly occupied with stability, so may the coming decades witness the same 'disturbing' events in large areas of North America. Indeed, som leading socialist scholars in North America who for long have minimized the potential revolutionary role of the North American working class are beginning to make definite adjustments to that assessment (161).

Viewed at a time of apparently worsening economic conditions and increasing class consciousness in significant areas of North America (with the probability of more to come), Marcuse's confidence in the ability of fear of the 'enemy', expanding affluence and ample opportunities for employment, and instinctual modification to curb the rise of working class consciousness in North America, seems a trifle dubious.

> At once objective and subjective, the class conflict is perpetual, though sometimes only latent and hidden and sometimes overt and explosive. It never stops, though it sometimes appears to have done so. (162)

**The subjective and objective revolutionary potential of
the North American student movement: further considerations**

> The role of students today as the intelligentsia out of which, as you know, the executives and leaders of even existing society are recruited, is historically more important than it perhaps was in the past. (163)

Thus,

> The student rebellion hits this society at a vulnerable point (164). What we have here is ... the simple refusal to take part in the blessings of the 'affluent society'. (165)

They have,

> ... with their bodies and minds experienced the horrors and oppresive comforts of the given reality. (166)

138

But for them, this is not a question of choice; the protest and refusal are parts of their metabolism. (167)

For,

... prior to all political strategy and organization, liberation becomes a vital 'biological' need. (168)

Marcuse's analysis of the basis, depth and political significance of the North American sutdent and general youth (or counter-culture) movement of the mid-and late 60's and early 70's rests heavily upon his new ontological point of departure—Freud's later theory of instincts. While the chapter immediately following attempts to consider the epistemological merits of that 'theory', the present discussion focuses on what appears to be a more appropriate structural analysis of the *basis* of student unrest and general youth disenchantment in North America. The arguments which follow should be considered against the background of preceeding discussions of this and the chapter immediately previous. Of the deluge of opinions and analyses of the 'student phenomenon' and the counter-culture, few have been as incisive as the implications of a study conducted by R. Lockhart (169).

Under the spur of the of the third industrial revolution and the accompanying predominance of the human capital theses, North America had succeeded in doubling its college population between 1950 and 1964 (170), and over the decade of the 60's had doubled university enrollment of undergraduates and tripled enrollment of graduates (171). By the mid-60's close to 50% of the university aged population (18–26) were either enrolled in or had spent some time in university or some similar post-secondary educational institution (172).

However, knowledge and training were not the only thing gained in the universities and like institutions. The opening of universities to such a large percentage of North American youth, entailed also the inculcation of higher expectations in this swelling number of young people. Complementing the previously discussed general rise in expectations in the postwar years, the elite-tinged universities acted as effective institutions for socializing the youth to the expectation of even higher consumption patterns (173) than they had experienced in their generally middle class childhood and adolescent milieu. Increasingly they came to expect as their 'right', not only higher consumption, after leaving university, but also more stimulating, responsible and satisfying employment. Institutions, in this case the university, in advanced industriaal societies are effective transmitters of values. They provide a 'social road network' connecting various origins to various social/occupational destinations (174). Thus high social and occupational expectations appear to be as much a part of a university degree as the specialized knowledge gained (175).

Had these expectations continued to be fulfilled as they had been throughout the 50's and early 60's, the 'mean-ends' connection would have been veri-

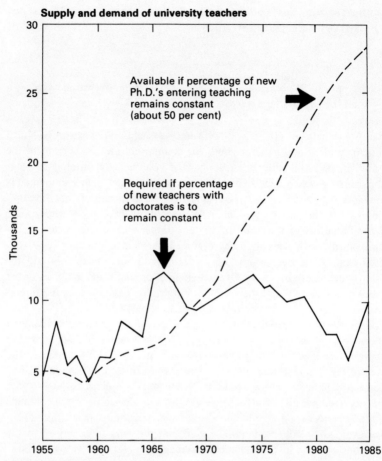

Supply and demand of university teachers

Available if percentage of new Ph.D.'s entering teaching remains constant (about 50 per cent)

Required if percentage of new teachers with doctorates is to remain constant

Fig. 6. Source: R. A. Lockhart: "The Effects on the mobility Patterns and Opportunities of the American Middle class with particular Emphasis on the Emergent Contradictions between Occupational and Educational Factors", p. 223.

fied and effective socialization achieved (176). However, under the combined impact of the worsening economic situation and the 'petering-out' of the first research, design and installation phase of the Third industrial revolution, the consequent fall-off in demand for the highly educated began to be seriously felt in the mid-60's, and the still increasing numbers of students pouring out of North-America's education mills found themselves facing an ever worsening job market (177).

With the educational institutions still in high gear as a result of previously increasing industrial and government demand as well as from the impact which the attendant Human Capital thesis had had upon educational policies, the sharp mid-60's fall-off in demand (despite the obsorbtion function of the

Table 12. *Ph.D.'s: Supply and Demand*[a]

Field	Registered Ph.D.'s	Vacanies
Business Administration	30	27
Sociology and Anthropology	109	87
French	80	34
Psychology	197	49
Political Science	228	31
Physics	243	12
English	372	69
History	394	43
Chemistry	347	29
Religion	263	14

[a] Ph.D.'s in search of available academic posts at 315 liberal arts colleges as of March 1, 1970.

Source: R. A. Lockhart, The Effect of Recent Techno-Economic Changes on the Mobility Patterns and Opportunities of the American Middle Class With Particular Emphasis on the Emergent Contradictions Between Occupational and Educational Factors, p. 223.

Vietnamese conflict), failed to curb the steady output of university graduates. Even by the late 60's, graduate and post-graduate output continued to increase at an annual rate of upwards of 10–15 % while during the same period, demand continued to decline by at least a parallel amount (178).

Thus, by the mid-60's, Marcuse's 'essential' new members of the working class began to experience some of the highest levels of structural unemployment (and under-employment) (179)—a situation which was to be further aggravated as employers, ever conscious of the need for profit and labor tranquility, began to recognize the 'inappropriateness' of hiring the highly educated (180). Indeed all available evidences suggests that empoyens are decreasingly inclined to hire the 'over-qualified (181).

In face of enormous hiring cutbacks in government and big business (10 %–40 %) (182) the 'big' employers and professional organizations began to caution new aspirants, encouraging them to look elsewhere. This appeared to be only the beginning as the long range prospects looked even less promising (see table 12 and fig. 6) given an indication of the dimension of the drop off in demand and over production.

What is more, it seems increasingly the case that, of those finding employment, a growing proportion are so *'underemployed'* that they feel their university degree is useless (183). As H. LeFebvre has observed, "The youth may be said to define themselves by their relationship to the world" (184), and it is precisely that relationship which is becoming increasingly problematic. The intensive socialization of North American youth which has

Table 13. *Libertarianism by major subject area and sex*

	Proportion highly libertarian			
	Men		Women	
Major Subject Area	Percentage	Number of cases	Per centage	Number of cases
Applied social sciences (social welfare, criminology, etc.)	–	(9)	45	(20)
Social sciences (political science, sociology, etc.)	63	(30)	34	(32)
Humanities (literature, philosophy, history, classics, etc.)	62	(45)	34	(112)
Life sciences (medical and biological sciences, pure and applied)	41	(37)	35	(60)
Physical sciences (and mathematics)	39	(31)	–	(17)
Engineering and other applied physical sciences[a]	30	(245)	–	(2)
Education[a]	29	(24)	23	(73
Business administration	24	(33)	–	(10)

Source: S. M. Lipset and S. S. Wolin (ed) p. 512.

prepared them for a life of expanding consumption, comfort, stability and satisfaction runs headlong into social reality increasingly characterized by economic and occupational insecurity, social marginality and general frustration of goals and ambitions (185). Socialization, no matter how thorough or intensive, cannot long sustain society's prescribed and defined ideals and legitimate objectives unless they are at least minimally verified by social reality. The heightened expectation of the student group along with and related to their generally middle-class background seemed to serve only to further aggravate the sense of frustration and let-down experienced when the anticipated rewards were not forthcoming and the expected goals proved evermore unattainable (186). Thus, the social marginality experienced by students (187) is the direct result of an actual marginal existence resulting from the closing of anticipated avenues of 'success' to them.

In view of the previous discussions of the critical factors determining the emergence of radical working class consciousness, it should be not at all surprising to find that precisely the period from the mid-60's one witnesses the rise of widespread unrest and radical political consciousness among this group (see table 13 and 14). The worsening economic situation, the impact of the continuing development of the new technology and increasing overproduction of university graduates all resulted in a broadening of the un-

Table 14. *Libertarianism and Year in University*

	Undergraduates				Graduate Students %
	First year %	Second year %	Third year %	Fourth year %	
Highly libertarian	21	29	34	40	54
Moderately libertarian	47	44	50	30	
Slightly libertarian	32	27	16	14	16
Total	100	100	100	100	100
Number of cases	(131)	(226)	(216)	(266)	(50)

Source: S. M. Lipset and S. S. Wolin (ed) p. 503.

and under-employment of this group, placing them in a marginal position in North American society—a situation which their previous socialization hardly prepared them for. Further, it might be expected that students in the social sciences and humanities, because of the nature of their major subject area, would be more aware of any contradiction between the theory and practice of their society whereas students in the natural science disciplines, might, on the basis of a less critical perspective of dominant values, tend to see their occupational and social failure in more personalistic terms and thus be less political or socially rebellious in their discontent.

> ... those youths who conformed to, and apparently succeeded within, the institutionally prescribed means, but failed to receive the socially defined end results, are caught in a personal crisis which must inevitably make them aware of a massive systematic contradiction. This awareness comes at a critical time in the individual's life. Every society has its formal or informal rites of passage ... To be denied such entry after preparation, ... is to have one's legitimacy within the social order denied. (188)

In brief, it is the confrontation of North American middle-class students, holding high social and economic expectations, with the stark reality of increasingly scarce avenues to and opportunities for success' as a result of the technological and economic developments and tendencies discussed in the previous chapter, which seems to lie at the basis of the widespread student and youth unrest and dissatisfaction of the mid and late 69's and early 70's.

Certainly the Vietnam conflict played a decisive role in sparking and sustaining this unrest, but here too is detectable a further compounding of the original factors of unrest. In addition to the reneging of their promises to youth, U.S.

society appeared to have little else to offer to the disillusioned than employment in a war machine involved in the nation's most unpopular and socially divisive conflict.

Thus, rather than affluence and opportunity, frustration and social exclusion appears to be a far more probable basic explanation of the widespread youth and university unrest of the last eight years. While it may be argued that the 'rebels' had not yet 'personally' experienced this social closure, it is clear that one need not personally experience the closed door to know that it is closed. The experience of those who went before was more than adequate to convince many students that the quantity and quality of employment awaiting them did not match their previous expectations nor the institutionally promised rewarxs.

Further, once begun, the culture of rejection (of established society) took on a dynamic of its own. The ensuing social, economic, political and cultural critique became a force on its own right. As the dialectic between the emerging counter-culture and the conditions which fostered it developed, it was clearly not always necessary for each student to be personally rejected. Indeed, even if opportunities were available in the 'promised form', the cultural dynamic often led nevertheless to a refusal to take part in the 'blessings of the affluent society'. The outcome may have been similar, but the initial motivation seems to differ substantially from Marcuse's interpretation.

While the preceding discussion of the new working class and class structure called into question the objective revolutionary potential of Marcuse's proposed revolutionary vanguard or nucleus, the present arguments have indicated in part the non-validity of Marcuse's explanation of the basis of their revolt as lying in the manifestation of Eros, and consequently the limitations of his views on the unique subjective revolutionary potential of this group. This latter point will by implication, be further assessed in the discussion of the next chapter, which focuses on the credibility of libido.

The above arguments should not be interpreted as an overall dismissal of the revolutionary potential of the youth of North America—far from it. Rather, it is an attempt to view more clearly some general estimations of the subjective and objective revolutionary potential of the student movements. It should be added with haste that the suggestions made here obviously pretend to be no more than a minimal basic analysis of the issue and aim primarily at evaluating Marcuse's views of these phenomena.

The discussions pursued in this chapter represent an attempt to assess those aspects of Marcuse's overall social and political analysis which, taken together with his views on the long range trends of North American capitalism, lead him perceive a nearly insurmountable political and, consequently, theoretical dilemma.

It has not been the purpose here to deny the existence of substantial affluence, working-class acquiscence, or the importance of the 'new working class' in the productive process in North America. Rather, the arguments presented here attempt to illuminate certain aspects and tendencies of these several phenomena singularly unconsidered by Marcuse, and hence endeavour to demonstrate the lack of universal validity of his analysis.

Thus, they indicate further limitations on Marcuse's justification for rethinking, and in many respects abandoning, critical theory (Marxism). Inasmuch as that rethinking was necessitated by qualitative changes in the nature of certain central aspects of contemporary capitalist economy and society, the demonstration that the contemporary situation is not quite as qualitatively different and unique as Marcuse supposed would seem to imply that rather than 'traditional' critical theory being ill-equipped to correctly analyze the current situation, it is rather Marcuse's 'new improve brand' which is perhaps conceptually inadequate for the task.

Chapter Five:

The New Ontology

> Phantasy plays a most decisive function in the total mental structure: it links the unconscious with the highest products of the consciousness (art), the dream with reality; it preserves ... the tabooed images of freedom. (1)

The argument in this brief chapter focuses upon Marcuse's new ontological perspective—Freud's later instinct theory. As this notion is the central point of departure for his 'reinforcement' of the political dilemma as well the cornerstone in his revised theoretical, analytical and political perspectives and proposals as was demonstrated in chapter two, its validity deserves special attention. Indeed, once the ontological shift had been effected, the entire structure of the new theoretical perspective, as well as his cultural and political analysis, and the subsequent proposals for liberation, come to rest on the notion of psychic energy-libido.

Thus, the objective here is not to attempt to fault the internal logic of psychoanalysis or Marcuse's use of it. Rather, the focus is exclusively upon the now indispensible notion of libido, and an assessment of its epistemological status. Such an assessment should by implication indicate the validity of all those notions, concepts and conclusions built upon it.

The notion of instincts is far from new and at least as old as the 'active principles' of Greek philosophy (2). Indeed, a salient characteristic of the pre-scientific mind is that it fills the world with mysterious forces and irreducible agencies which crank the machinery of man and his environment, setting in motion and sustaining the dynamic phenomena of experience (3). Indeed, although refined and depersonalized by generations at philosophers and logicians, these mysterious causal agencies are still replenishing language with their symbols (4).

The positing of libido was a logical consequence of the lack of biological and physiological knowledge on the functions of the brain (5), the consequently prevalent 'motivation paradox' (6) and, most importantly, of the very structure of Freud's psychoanalytic schema. On this latter point, R. R. Sears has observed that,

> If a consistent theory is laid down along the lines of psychoanalysis, it must include a concept like libido. (7)

A conclusion which simply concurs with Freud's own view on the necessity of 'positing' libido. He states:

> ... without *assuming* the existence of a displaceable energy of this kind we can make no headway. (8)

Certainly Freud was aware of the arbitrary and assumptive nature of this notion of libido (9), nevertheless he also perceived that the situation of psychology at the time, appeared to justify the arbitrary positing of such assumptions as seemed necessary (10). Even given the demands of expediency, Freud was nevertheless painfully aware of the weak epistomological status of the very instinct assumptions he used as the basis for his subsequent theoretical conceptions. No wonder R. R. Sears concluded after an extensive study of the validity of the concept of libido, that the "source of this drive is not clear" (11), for indeed, Freud himself was obliged to confess of this 'scarcely known' force (12).

> The theory of instincts is, as it were, our mythology . . . The instincts are mythical beings, superb in their indefiniteness. (13)

It is often suggested that 'Freud's opting for the use of libido was at first prompted and later verified as the result of clinical research, but as Freud said himself, libido was posited not on the basis of the findings of 'scientific research' but rather to satisfy the demands of psychoanalytic theoretical experiency. At a later period Freud stated,

> The conceptions I have summarized here I first put forward only tentatively, but in the course of time they have won such a hold over me that I can no longer think in any other way. (14)

However this bit of self analysis would seem to demonstrate nothing other than the fact that conceptual habits, like all others, tend to become habitual. It seems that the one lasting strength of the notion of libido is that it is the type of theoretical construction which can be neither proven nor disproven (15). Indeed, it appears to be quite simply the first article of faith in the acceptance of the theoretical structures built upon it. So it is also in the case of Marcuse. It is, in the traditional scientific sense, an untestable hypothesis.

Further, the notion of libido and its attendant and related concepts with their constant resort to hydraulic analogy (16) are clearly reminiscent of the pre-Einsteinian concepts of physical energy which were predominant and conceptualy influential in the 1890's- the time of the 'birth' of psychoanalysis (17). Indeed, the social sciences appear to have had more than their share of mechanoporphism (18) (the ascription of mechanical characteristics to humans and the interpretation of human behavior in concepts and processes indiginous to machines).

Fundamentaly however, the great weakness of the idea of libido (and like derived and formulated notions), stems from their uncertain epistemological status (19) which is in turn a direct consequence of the manner in which such notions are initially arrived at and subsequently sustained (20).

In the case of both the 'spirits' and 'demons' of old and in the case of psychoanalysis's libido, the procedure is essentially the same. Initially one observes some form of regular activity (in this case human activity), and from this observation(s) infers an instinct or disposition (21). This inferred instinct is then theoretically abstracted from the observed activity and 'posited' in the organism as an independent force, and consequently as the dynamic cause of the originally observed behaviour. Thus, the description serves also as the explanation, as the procedure simply treats an attendant name for some particular activity as the explanation of it (22). Such 'explanations' are tautological. They attempt to explain one mystery by positing an even greater one. They are in fact second order constructs set up to explain first order constructs which are set up to explain some observed behaviour (23).

While it is sometimes objected that such a criticism is invalid on the grounds that these instincts (in this case libido) are not meant to refer to 'discrete entities' or 'things', being rather merely descriptive concepts (24), such a counter-critique, as weak as it is initially, simply does not apply to Marcuse's use of the notion of libido and the subsequent notions of Eros and Thanatos. For, aside from all hedging, the fundamental content and character of his socio-political analysis and proposals for liberation, the explicit theoretical and methodological implications of this new concept of essense make it crystal clear that for Marcuse this is no mere 'interesting way of looking at things'. It is incorporated, at first cautiously, then later unreservedly as an actual 'discrete entity'—a Thing.

It should be further added as E. Ellis has illustrated, that the same behaviour may be more satisfactorily analyzed in a variety of alternate and less 'mythical' ways (25).

Consequently it appears that neither Freud nor his critics viewed the notion of libido as being the best basis upon which to build a psychological theory; at best it was a necessary expedient, a tentative assumption to be later clarified or discarded as physiological and biological knowledge progressed (26). It was as he once confessed, his 'mythology'.

The point of the discussion here however is not whether Freud held a critical eye to this arbitrary and highly speculative assumption, but rather how Marcuse has utilized the notion. The discussions pursued in chapter two have illustrated the far reaching implications libido has had upon his further work. As stated before, while the first steps into the realm of the 'mythical', superbly indefinite' libido and its attendant concepts were cautious and tentative, the work of the sixties reveals a growing confidence in the 'reality' of this source of psychic energy. Indeed, Marcuse's work of the last decade appears to reveal an increasing preoccupation with the impact and consequences of the manifestation of this energy in social and individual life (27).

148

While the very nature of the concept renders it unprovable by any scientific criteria, it seems that for the 'initiated', that particular weakness is in fact its greatest strength. However, the pronouncements of its formulator, the manner in which it was formulated, the apparent influence of pre-Einsteinian theories of physical energy and hydraulic principles on its formulation, and, indeed, the tautological nature of such explanations (to which group it clearly belongs) all point to the highly dubious epistemological status of the notion of libido. At the level of theoretical speculation it certainly does no harm. But as we have seen earlier, Marcuse's utilization of it takes us far beyond the philosopher's armchair and into the world of concrete social, cultural, and political analysis and praxis. It seems a frightfully weak basis upon which to build such serious and concrete endeavor as he proposes. All the more so when we recall that on the basis of the foregoing counter-analysis of trends and realities in contemporary capitalist economy and society, the necessary new critical theory for which it serves as a base is perhaps not so necessary after all.

Conclusion

As stated at the outset of this study, Marcuse's influence, particularly on the North American left, has been substantial. The protracted, sometimes difficult socio-economic analysis, as well as the far reaching theoretical and political consequences of his revision of critical theory (Marxism) have been the central factors motivating this analysis.

The study has had two central objectives. First, it has been an attempt to both elaborate and interpret the main features of Marcuse's economic and socio-political analysis while discussing the nature and implications of the revision of Marxism he has effected on the basis of this analysis and with the instrumentality of Libido. In the second place, it has been an attempt to 'balance-out' as it were, the main features of Marcuse's social and economic analysis and his evaluation (or lack of it) of the epistemological status of libido, by considering certain relevant factors and tendencies singularly absent from Marcuse's work. This latter task has been pursued in an attempt to reasses the necessity and justification for revising critical theory to meet the demands of a supposedly qualitatively new socio-economic and political constellation in North America. Further it has aimed at an assessment of Marcuse's 'revised' critical theory by critically considering the epistemological status of its ontological point of departure—Libido.

Thus the study aims first at an elaboration and interpretation of Marcuse's social and economic analysis and the theoretical consequences and implications which arise from that analysis. It then turns to an assessment of the universal validity of the analysis, his consequent justification for revising critical theory and the credibility of the theoretical structure he raises in its stead.

The discussions in chapter one revealed the central features of Marcuse's social and economic analysis of realities and tendencies in North America. In brief, Marcuse appears to have concluded that under the impact of the fear of the 'enemy'—international communism—formerly competing imperialist nations agreed to put aside any economic competition or rivalry which might weaken the world capitalist system as a whole. There emerged therefore an inter-continental political economy susceptible to planned regulation. Markets, investment opportunities and sources of essential raw materials were increasingly and effectively allocated on the basis of a common assessment of national economic need conjunction with the expediencies of containment.

The traditional tendencies towards surpluses of money capital, produced commodities and productive capacity (and consequently manpower surpluses) were seen to be increasingly manageable through the economic stimulant of sustained massive state expenditures on 'defence' (and to a lesser but significant degree through the production of 'junk' consumer commodities and the sophistication of planned obsolescence). This defence safety-valve was seen to be effectively sustained by a populace ever-fearful of and anxious to contain the 'enemy'. The periodic cyclical crises were also seen to be decreasing in severity and frequency—effectively eliminated under the impact of extensive state/corporation economic management and planning. On this stable economic base, Marcuse argues that the ability and determination of the powers that be in North America to contain national liberation movements in the Third World was irresistible and resolute. He further seems to imply that even the existence of highly improbable success of these liberation struggles would have no serious disruptive effects upon North American capitalism.

Largely grounded in the unproblematic safety-valve of the defence economy, further strengthened by technological advances and assured supplies of adequate and inexpensive Third World raw materials (and labor), the stability and prosperity of North American capitalism seems guaranteed for the foreseeable future, guaranteeing in turn and increasing degree of affluence to a steadily growing proportion of the population. The political tranquilizing effect of this sustained affluence and occupational security is completed by a constant fear of the 'enemy' and the effective media-induced indoctrination of the underlying population, stifling any manifestations of radical working class consciousness in North America for the forseeable future. Further the traditional working class appears to be well along in the process of being ousted from the strategic positions in the productive apparatus, as the new technology places a neverending spiral on the demand for highly educated and scientifically trained workers—a new working class. While this new working class occupies a critical objective position in the productive process, its members too are 'cooled-out' by the same factors which lead to the political aquiscence of the traditional working class.

Inasmuch as Marcuse views the basic economic developments and the indoctrinating abilities of the media as merely the beginning of long-range development in this direction, the resultant political dilemma appears nearly insurmountable. It is at this point that Marcuse begins to have doubts about the continuing vitality of critical theory (Marxism). If his analysis is correct, then there appears to have emerged an historically unique social, economic and political situation—a situation which traditional critical theory is conceptually inadequate to deal with. Inasmuch as the need for revolution remains, it thus becomes essential to revitalize critical theory. Only a fundamental revision of its basis concepts can render critical theory once more conceptually adequate to the task of radical social analysis and of directing liberating political praxis.

It is in the face of this political-cum-theoretical dilemma that Marcuse

151

turns to Freud, to Libido to be precise. By moving from a Marxian concept of human essence to a Freudian one as represented by the latter theory of instincts, Marcuse lays the ontological basis for a far reaching revision of Marxism. A revision intended to render critical theory adequate to the task of critically analyzing the qualitatively unique smooth functioning prosperous North American society. While the incorporation of Libido leads to a certain reinforcement of the already perceived political dilemma—from dilemma to vicious circle—by introducing the notion of instinctual repression which takes the political acquiesence of the North American working class to a new dimension, it neverthelses provides the basis for a potential break with the vicious circle.

The introduction of the notion of basic and inherent instincts and a constant pool of 'interchangeable' energy, seems to provide the needed dynamic in an otherwise politically stifling environment. It lays the metaphysical basis for a voluntarism and re-enforced idealism, completely absent from marxism. It suggests a glimmer of hope in that while radical political consciousness has been suppressed by the achievements of society, the unconscious (and particularly Eros), although subject to increasing repression, may—just may —in some disparate groups and individuals, escape that repression and become manifest in 'authentic' liberating thought and political activity. Thus Eros provides the necessary dynamic, the *internal* motor force to break with an otherwise unbreakable circle of political repression. Inasmuch as Eros is a manifestation of the true and authentic essence of man, by its measure the achievements of the 'achieving' society may now be accurately assessed. Hence, Marcuse calls for the return of moral criticism to a central place in the critical theory of society. Indeed, inasmuch as the society is so stable and achieving, it appears to be the only criticism which has any grounds. Again, this is no Judeo-Christian or even traditional socialist moral critique. It is rather the critique arising from the very essence of man against the false and perverted happiness and harmony which prevails. Further, given the instinctual, even biological, manipulation of the underlying population, Marcuse suggests that even if the improbable did happen and economic deprivation and uncertainty re-emerged, mental manipulation has now reached such a stage that even these conditions would fail to rekindle militant working class consciousness. And again, even if that doubly improbable event did occur, inasmuch as their very instinctual structures have been perverted (Eros having lost ascendency to Thanatos), a revolution carried through by such thoroughly sublimated men and women would be incapable of overcoming the Psychic Thermidor, the return of the repressed. Thus the new society constructed would not be built in harmony with the demands of the life instincts. Hence *authentic* liberation would not have been achieved.

The solution he suggests, indeed insists upon, is a revolution led and directed by men and women who had achieved the ascendency of Eros over Thanatos and are thus able to construct a society in harmony with and complementary to the Demands of the Life Instincts—the true essence of man. Here, the desire to resurrect Plato, the Form and the Philosopher King, as well as Hegel and the World Spirit (Mind) is painfully obvious.

In an apparently totally repressive society it is difficult to imagine where such men and women may be found. But, due to altered postwar child rearing practices, prolonged and affluent adolescence, and the extension of university education to greater proportions of the American population, Marcuse locates them in the middle-class youth of North America. It seems to be upon this group that not only the liberation of North America depends but indeed that of the entire world.

Not only has this group authentic subjective revolutionary potential as a result of relatively unrepressed life instincts, but also due to their inevitable future position in the new means of production, they seem destined to achieve objective revolutionary potential as well. Because of both the 'goods delivering' ability of the affluent society and the media-induced Psychic Thermidor (the internalization at the instinctual biological level of the demands of the 'masters'), it is essential that the revolution be achieved in many respects against the will of the vast majority of the underlying population. This is made potentially realizable as a result of Marcuse's assessment of the instinctual/biological bond which has been created between the underlying population and the productive apparatus which satisfies its perverted needs—needs which have been created to facilitate the sustained growth of the system. Inasmuch as the middle-class students in their future role as managers of the new means of production will gain control of that process, they will simultaneously gain complete (instinctual/biological) control over the masses which it 'serves'. Herein lies the glimmer of hope.

This is the political-cum-theoretical dilemma which confronts Marcuse, and his subsequent efforts to overcome it. But what of the basis for that dilemma? Was Marcuse really as justified as he supposes in 'rethinking' critical theory? In short, has North American society and economy changed so fundamentally in character that the categories and concepts of traditional critical theory are no longer adequate to the task of further analysis? And further, is Libido—the new ontological point of departure and essential cornerstone of all Marcuse's further theorizing, analysis and political proposals—of such sound epistemological status to warrant this confidence and theoretical centrality? It has been the central objective of the last three chapters to cast some light on the above questions.

The discussions pursued in these chapters were in essence attempts to *balance-out* Marcuse's analysis insofar as they appeared to lack sufficient validity. While they make no pretence at being exhaustive counter-analysis, the arguments and further considerations of the central phenomenon do appear to cast significant doubt on the completeness of Marcuse's analyses and the validity of certain of the long range projections he makes on their bases.

153

On the question of Marcuse's insistence of a permanent end to inter-imperialist economic competition it seems that not only is reference to the 'enemy' an inadequate explanation for the temporary lull of such competition in the early postwar period, but further, events, particularly of the last half decade, appear to indicate that serious interimperialist competition for markets, investment opportunities and sources of raw materials may be once again emerging. The 'anarchy of capitalist production' in which Marx saw the root of capitalist contradictions but which Marcuse saw transcended with the emergence of a well planned intercontinental political economy, seems to be once again threatening the cohesion and stability of international capitalism. While the 'enemy' continues to gain strength, it seems that the surpluses of money capital, production and productive capacity as well as the related growing scarcity of inexpensive basic industrial raw materials are straining the bonds of the united capitalist front against the threat from without. Increasingly it appears that the 'threat from within', inter-imperialist competition for relatively shrinking markets, investment opportunities and cheap adequate sources of raw materials, is proving to be the dominant fear. This is not to suggest that competing capitalist nations do not recognize and work towards common overall interests and objectives, nor that Nixon, Brandt, et al. have overcome the cold war mistrust and hostility. It does appear however that in a toughening and tightening world market, the unusual postwar cohesiveness of the several imperialist powers are forced by more immediate economic interests and necessities to be less critical of who they trade with and how many economic concessions they 'willingly' give each other.

All of which seems to imply that defence expenditures in North America, while enormous, have been in the long run not completely adequate in guaranteeing economic stability and prosperity. In brief it has been brought up short against the surplus money capital and productive capacities of North American capitalism. While such expenditures have achieved clear successes in keeping the economy out of severe depressions of the order of the 1930's, there appear nevertheless to be limitations to its capacity to absorb these growing surpluses. Further, arms spending on the sustained scale pursued in postwar U.S.A. has not been without serious long-term adverse economic effects, not the least of which has been a tendency towards permanent inflation. While successes have been achieved, it seems that in the past, and even more so in the future, arms spending will not prove to be as unproblematic and limitless a 'safety-valve' as it may earlier have been.

As to the smooth running economy free from cyclical crises due to effective state/corporation economic planning and management, Marcuse's assessment of capitalism's successes in this area appear to have failed to consider numerous persistent obstacles to such planning and management. Indeed, it may well be that given the apparent rise in inter-imperialist competition, the more apparent problematics involved in the sustained use of arms spending as an

154

economic stimulant, even such successes as were achieved in the past may be harder to come by in the future.

As to Marcuse's confidence in North America's will and ability to contain any further national liberation struggles (after Cuba), events in Indo-China alone have demonstrated that both political and economic limitations do exist. While the days of North American counter-revolutionary intervention are clearly far from over, and the powers for political containment it possesses are awesome, it would seem that the writing-off of chances for further national liberation successes in the Third World prior to the internal weakening (due to internal factors) of North America is a substantial underestimation of the dimensions and strength of such movements.

Further, whether they are completely successful or not, Marcuse seems also to have minimized the actual and potential disruptive economic-political effects which the sum total of these struggles may have on the prosperity of North American capitalism. Insofar as these struggles are being carried out in apparently increasingly essential raw material rich areas of the world, even their existence, whether finally successful or not, would seem to threaten to detract from America's ability to exploit these areas. If and when such struggles are successful, they often threaten essential and inexpensive sources of basic raw materials, sources which become increasingly vital in the emerging competitive struggle between America and her capitalist 'partners'. Added to this, the consideration of the adverse economic effects (to say nothing of the decisive domestic political consequences) of extensive military intervention on the Third World it seems to suggest that Marcuse's assessment of the relatively insignificant impact which national liberation struggles will have on the overall stability of North American capitalism, is somewhat unjustified.

In sum, it appears that Marcuse's present analysis and long term projections regarding the stability and prosperity of North American capitalism significantly excludes consideration of numerous and often serious economic contradictions facing the system both now and in the future. Indeed, overall Marcuse's economic analysis seems to be a trifle too conjunctural, reflecting the apparent and real conditions of the fifties. Nevertheless he clearly continues to hold to that analysis, using it as the basis for his socio-political analysis and consequently as the justification for revising critical theory.

His analysis of long range projections regarding employment, affluence, the new working-class and working class structure and consciousness and the basis and nature of the student movement in North America appear also to lack the degree of validity he attributes to them. Inasmuch as these propositions and projections rely heavily upon the correctness and comprehensiveness of the main features of his economic analysis, the limitations and errors which have been pointed out in that analysis would seem to substantially detract from the credibility (especially in the long-run) of his image of the affluence, and occupational security of the North American working class.

While Marcuse has argued that increasing affluence and sustained adequate employment possibilities are the present general features as well as the most probable long range prospects for the North American working class, the arguments in chapter four indicate certain limitations to such a proposition. Significantly absent from Marcuse's discussion is any consideration of the persistent and often increasing dimensions of structural unemployment and poverty in America. Apparently relying upon the developments of the 'boom' period of the fifties, he appears to have projected an unabated growth of working class affluence and employment prospects for the long-term future. Rooted in his conviction of the sustained, indeed increasing, prosperity and stability of North American capitalism, he passes lightly over the substantial dimensions of poverty and unemployment existent even in the 'golden age' of the fifties, and fails to take seriously the possibility of any substantial reversal of the tendency towards increasing affluence which he sees those developments manifesting.

But serious structural, cyclical and seasonal unemployment does exist. Indeed, since 1953 (except for the manpower absorption of the Vietnam conflict), structural unemployment has shown in marked persistence at serious proportions and a tendency towards a long-term increase. In view of the tendencial worsening of the economic situation it is not completely improbable that the future may witness a further aggravation of this problem. The same factors are likely to slow down (or perhaps even reverse) the already limited progress being made in the elimination of the persistent substantial dimensions of poverty in North America. Indeed, the Nixon administration has in the past four years introduced numerous cutbacks and curbs on the already not overly impressive 'war on poverty' programmes, and the construction of the 'great society' launched by the Democrats under Johnson and Kennedy. It is worth noting the hard line taken against federal welfare spending by Gerald Ford in his first general policy statement after being sworn in as U.S. president in early August, 1974. (C.B.S. News, August 12, 1974). Even if the late sixties' rate of poverty elimination persisted, a development increasingly less probable in view of the financial restraints imposed by accumulating economic problems, it has been suggested that it would take a further 90 years to completely eliminate this social plague. Marcuse's concurrence with the most optimistic of liberal economists and 'celebrationist' sociologists of the fifties appears to have resulted in his underestimation of the actual dimensions and persistence of poverty and unemployment in North America.

As to his projection of a long term spiralling demand for highly educated and scientifically trained work force due to the altered nature of the means of production, here too Marcuse, relying heavily upon the works of D. Bell and C. Walker in the late forties and early fifties, seems to have too hastily drawn long-range conclusions on the basis of what now appears in fact to have been a largely conjunctural phenomenon arising from the initial peak demands of the first phases of the Third industrial revolution and the relatively unsophisticated charactered of the initial levels of automation. This is certainly not to suggest the elimination of the need for scientifically trained and highly educated manpower. However the exceptional inflation of the demand for such workers during the fifties, now shows clear signs of falling off to more 'normal' rates of absorption. Marcuse seems not to have fully appreciated the long range consequences of the new automatic machinery on even the 'new working-class'. With the continuing tendency towards the trivialization of even the most complicated tasks, the completion of the major research, development and installation phase of this Third Industrial Revolution, and the over-production of highly educated manpower, the demand and opportunities for the instrumentalist intelligentsia began to show a marked decline as early as the mid-sixties. This development appears to have been further aggravated by the general economic slowdown of North American capitalism which began to set in about the same time. Further, given the high social and economic expectations characteristic of this group as a result of the institutional transmission (through the university) of values, employers wherever possible are showing increased reluctance to employ the highly educated. From the point of view of wages and worker satisfaction and contentment, employers appear to be grasping the wisdom of employing the less educated to carry out the operations of the highly sophisticated new means of production made increasingly possible through the trivialization of even the most complex tasks.

It is clear that the Third Industrial Revolution has eroded the ranks of the traditional working class required in the maintenance and operation of the new means of production. However, apart from the initial phase (the fifties) of this revolution in productive techniques, the *proportion* of the traditional working class in the total work force has remained remarkably constant. At the plant level, the ratio of traditional to 'new' working class, after the introduction and 'jelling' of the automated machinery, has either remained constant or shown a slight increase in the representation of the traditional working class (even though the overall number of employees has shown a marked decline).

Marcuse's insistence that working class consciousness in North America is by and large absent and, in light of his long-range economic projections, not likely to re-emerge in the foreseeable future appears also to inaccurately reflect the total reality of the North American Labor movement and to somewhat overestimate the ability of capitalism to perpetually pacify the working class. Indeed, having effected the ontological shift at the theoretical level, Marcuse has reinforced this particular aspect of the political dilemma by insisting that even a re-emergence of those factors (economic and occupational insecurity, deprivation, etc.) which have traditionally motivated the intensification of working class consciousness will, in all probability, not affect the emergence of a radical class consciousness. The perversion of the fundamental instinctual (even biological) structure of the underlying population has altered and under-cut the traditional basis of class consciousness.

Several recent studies of the existence and basis of militant working class consciousness in North America have shown however that not only is such

157

consciousness still existent but also the critical factors (economic and occupational insecurity, social marginality etc.) remain unaltered. While working class consciousness is far from widespread in North America, contrary to Marcuse's assessment, the effects of both the fear of the 'enemy' and the instinctual manipulating power of the media, have neither eliminated it nor altered the factors which have traditionally been critical in motivating its emergence. Indeed, considering the incompleteness and oft-times conjunctural nature of Marcuse's economic analysis and projections, it is not improbable that the future may witness an aggravation of just those critical factors and a consequent intensification of working-class consciousness in North America. Manifestations of such developments are in fact already present in numerous of those areas of North America hardest hit by recent recessions and structural displacement.

Finally Marcuse's estimation of the objective and subjective revolutionary potential of the North American student movement appears somewhat exaggerated. Inasmuch as the previously discussed decline in demand for the highly educated as the first phase of the Third Industrial Revolution has petered out, and with the continuing trivialization of complex human tasks which were previously thought to be incapable of mechanization and automation, the indispensibility of this potential new working class seems to be increasingly undermined. This development appears further aggravated by the apparent general worsening of the overall economic situation and the massive overproduction of highly skilled and educated manpower. In sum, the student movement seems far less able to hold the system for ransom because of its functional indispensibility than Marcuse supposes. Indeed, this closing of opportunities for intellectually and economically rewarding employment and upward social mobility, expectations fostered and reinforced by the institutional perpetuation of values (primarily effected through the university in this case), seems a far more adequate explanation of the basis of the North American counter-culture and student movement than Marcuse's reference to permissive child-rearing practices, the unsublimated manifestation of Eros and youths' subsequent rejection of the ever-abundant opportunities for increasing affluency and professional security. In fact, it is more probably largely those same critical factors centrally responsible for the emergence of militant working class consciousness that have motivated the rejection of the system. The student movement and general counter-culture thus appear more actually a response to societal rejection after a prolonged period of preparation for institutionally promised social and economic rewards, than a manifest rejection of affluency due to its antagonism to the demands of the life instincts. It should be hastily added here that this alternate explanation of the origins of the student movement and the counter-culture, is meant to suggest what seem to be the basic motivating factor. However, the problem is certainly more complex than this, embracing most obviously the impact of the civil rights movement and the Vietnam intervention.

In sum, Marcuse's economic and social analysis, the essential justification (by his own criteria) for the revision of critical theory, appears to have overlooked or minimized numerous and substantial limitations to the conclusions he draws and the long-range tendencies he projects. His discussions often reflect a failure to consider a variety of developments and tendencies which tends to reveal severe limitations to his analysis.

There is much of value in Marcuse's analysis of North American economy and society. However the political-cum-theoretical dilemma he has formulated appears significantly exaggerated. It seems clear therefore that inasmuch as developments in North American society and economy are not as qualitatively unique as Marcuse supposes, the necessity for revising critical theory due to its resultant conceptual inadequacy is hardly as pressing as he has insisted. In short, a central conclusion of this study is that by Marcuse's own criteria, the revision of critical theory he has demanded and effected seems inadequately justified on the basis of both short and probable long-term developments in North America. Indeed, considering the 'non-so-novel' nature of North American society and economy, it now appears that it is Marcuse's revitalized' critical theory which is the more conceptually inadequate for the task of further analysis and the direction of liberating political praxis. While subjective factors are of importance, his subsequent elevation of them to a position of central and necessarily prime concern appears somewhat out of harmony with the reality of North American society and the actual requirements of appropriate critical theory.

His particular reversal of the relationship between base and superstructure (particularly subjective factors) appears hardly justified in view of the apparent limitations of his basic social and economic (and psychoanalytical) analysis.

Furthermore, while absolute disproof is not possible given the very nature of the concept of libido, which is in effect the indispensible cornerstone of his revised critical theory, appears to be of such questionable epistemological status that the theoretical structure, social analysis, and political proposals which Marcuse develops and pursues on its basis are of a parallel value and credibility. Indeed, it seems far more likely that, as suggested at an earlier point in this study, the metaphysical nature of this 'material base under the material base', more accurately represents a weakly justified return to idealism in the face of a vicious circle which in reality is hardly as vicious as suggested. Thus the return to Fourier from Marx appears necessitated more by Marcuse's lack of analytical rigor and justified by his too uncritical acceptance of an ontological point of departure of dubious epistemological status. While the problems involved in assessing how, when and in which manner, further economic, social and political developments in North America will unfold are enormous, and all conclusions seem necessarily shaded with an unavoidable tentativeness due to the complexity of the problems, it should at least be clear that the comprehensiveness and correctness which Marcuse both explicitly and implicitly ascribes to his socio-economic and political analysis is far from justified. Therefore, and by that same measure, so is his insistence on the need to revise critical theory in the manner proposed.

It seems a striking paradox indeed that Marcuse, the champion of 'critical thinking', should have accepted so uncritically the conclusions and observations of the numerous studies he has relied upon to build his arguments on social change. Despite his attempts to challenge the sociological, political and economic 'celebrationism' of the fifties and early sixties, he appears to have significantly failed to appreciate the often a historical nature of their studies and conclusions. Not that he has applauded these developments, on the contrary, his challenge to the 'authenticity' of the attained prosperity, affluence, stability and progress has been incisive, often beyond parallel. His failure lies not in the fact that he was 'impressed' by the achievements and quality of bourgeois culture and society for he wasn't, but rather in the fact that he too uncritically accepted the establishment's own analysis of its dimensions, effectivity, and durability. Instead, he appears to have given up the argument on those grounds conceding that, by its own measure, the 'system' had in fact been and would in the foreseeable future continue to be 'successful'. He attempted instead, with the help of libido, to demonstrate that while these successes were real, they were nevertheless 'inauthentic'. No mere Judeo-Christian moral critique, for now with the authority of Eros as the only true measuring rod, he had found a material basis for such a moral critique. Increasingly, Marcuse's analyses have followed this tact. He appears to have abandoned any further re-assessment of those factors which first led him into the dilemma in the fifties.

There is nevertheless much of value in Marcuse's analyses, but it should be scrutinized as critically as he admonishes us to be in assessing the 'given facts'.

> The mark of dialectical thinking is the ability to distinguish the essential from the apparent processes of reality and to grasp their relation. (Reason and Revolution, p. 146.)

References

Chapter 1

1. H. Marcuse, One Dimensional Man, p. xiv.
2. Ibid, p. 21.
3. Ibid, p. 21.
4. Herbert Marcuse, Soviet Marxism, p. 21; see too p. 156.
5. Ibid. pp. 19–20; see too p. 60.
6. Herbert Marcuse, An Essay on Liberation, pp. 84–85.
7. Soviet Marxism, op. cit., p. 60; see too An Essay on Liberation, op. cit., pp. 84–85.
8. For an excellent discussion of the Soviet Unions generally 'defensive' politico-military posture vis-a-vis the West, see D. F. Flemming, The Cold War and Its Origins, 2 vols., New York, Doubleday, 1961.
9. Soviet Marxism, op. cit., p. 83, see too pp. 60 and 154.
10. Soviet Marxism, op. cit., p. 83.
11. An Essay on Liberation, op. cit., p. 84.
12. One Dimensional Man, op. cit., p. 34.
13. Soviet Marxism, op. cit., p.83.
14. One Dimensional Man, op. cit., p. 34.
15. Soviet Marxism, op. cit., p. 60.
16. Soviet Marxism, op. cit., p. 60; and One Dimensional Man, op. cit., p. 54.
17. One Dimensional Man, op. cit., p. 49; see too Herbert Marcuse, Negations, p. 248.
18. Negations, op. cit., p. 248.
19. Negations, op. cit., -. 248.
20. One Dimensional Man, op. cit., p. 49.
21. Negations, op. cit., p. 217.
22. For example, the work of Daniel Bell and John K. Galbraith.
23. Negations, op. cit., pp. xv–xvi, and 215; see too One Dimensional Man, op. cit., p. 49; and Negations, op. cit., pp. 13–14.
24. One Dimensional Man, op. cit., p. 11.
25. One Dimensional Man, op. cit., pp. 11–12.
26. One Dimensional Man, op. cit., p. xiii; see too pp. 17, 18, 241–242.
27. Negations, op. cit., pp. xv–xvi.
28. Negations, op. cit., p. 248.
29. One Dimensional Man, op. cit., p. 34; Negations, op. cit., p. xv–xvi; An Essay on Liberation, op. cit., 80.
30. Negations, op. cit., p. 248; An Essay on Liberation, op. cit., pp. 13–14; Soviet Marxism, op. cit., pp. 19–20.
31. One Dimensional Man, op. cit., p. 19.
32. One Dimensional Man, op. cit., p. 38.
33. An Essay on Liberation, op. cit., p. vii.
34. Herbert Marcuse, Five Lectures, p. 93.
35. An Essay on Liberation, op. cit., p. 80; Herbert Marcuse, "The Containment of Social Change in Industrial Society", pp. 477–8, 480.
36. An Essay on Liberation, op. cit., pp. 81–82.
37. Five Lectures, op. cit., p. 95.
38. An Essay on Liberation, op. cit., p. 81.

39. Five Lectures, op. cit., p. 93.
40. An Essay on Liberation, op. cit., p. 81.
41. Five Lectures, op. cit., p. 93.
42. An Essay on Liberation, op. cit., p. 81; see to "The Containment of Social Change in Industrial Society, op. cit., p. 478.
43. An Essay on Liberation, op. cit., p. 82.
44. One Dimensional Man, op. cit., p. 36.
45. One Dimensional Man, op. cit., p. 35.
46. Five Lectures, op. cit., p. 98.
47. One Dimensional Man, op. cit., p. 16, see too pp. 36–37.
48. Five Lectures, op. cit., p. 66, see too p. 98.
49. One Dimensional Man, op. cit., -. 17.
50. An Essay on Liberation, op. cit., p. 7.
51. An Essay on Liberation, op. cit., p.5.
52. One Dimensional Man, op. cit., p. 17.
53. Negations, op. cit., p. 188.
54. The Containment of Social Change in Industrial Society, op. cit., p. 482.
55. One Dimensional Man, op. cit., p. xv.
56. One Dimensional Man, op. cit., p. xv.
57. An Essay on Liberation, op. cit., p. vii; see too One Dimensional Man, op. cit., p. 257.
58. One Dimensiona Man, op. cit., p. 2.
59. An Essay On liberation, op. cit., p. 59.
60. An Essay on Liberation, op. cit., p. 55; see too One Dimensional Man, op. cit., p. 25.
61. One Dimensional Man, op. cit., p. 30.
62. An Essay on Liberation, op. cit., p. 55.
63. Five Lectures, op. cit., p. 85.
64. An Essay on Liberation, op. cit., p. 66.
65. An Essay On liberation, op. cit., p. 54.
66. An Essay on Liberation, op. cit., p. 55.
67. Five Lectures, op. cit., p. 85.
68. Five Lectures, op. cit., p. 15.
69. Five Lectures, op. cit., p. 85.
70. Five Lectures, op. cit., p. 85.
71. Negations, op. cit., p. 224.
72. One Dimensional Man, op. cit., p. 38.
73. See for example, Five Lectures, op. cit., p. 66.
74. Herbert Marcuse, Reason and Revolution, p. xiv.
75. An Essay on Liberation, op. cit., p. 55.
76. An Essay on Liberation, op. cit., p. 16; see too "The Containment of Social Change in Industrial Society", op. cit., p. 479.
77. Five Lectures, op. cit., pp. 99, 85.
78. One Dimensional Man, op. cit., pp. xiii–xiv.
79. One Dimensional Man, op. cit., p. xiii.
80. One Dimensional Man, op. cit., p. xiii.
81. One Dimensional Man, op. cit., p. xiii.
82. One Dimensional Man, op. cit., p. 25.
83. One Dimensional Man, op. cit., p. 26. These views reflect the impact of the conclusions of D. Bell and C. Walker on Marcuse's thinking.
84. One Dimensional Man, op. cit., p. 31.
85. One Dimensional Man, op. cit., p. 32, see too An Essay on Liberation, op. cit., pp. 11–12.

86. One Dimensional Man, op. cit., p. 21, see too p. 51.
87. One Dimensional Man, op. cit., p. 226.
88. One Dimensional Man, op. cit., p. 50.
89. One Dimensional Man, op. cit., p. 9.
90. An Essay on Liberation, op. cit., pp. 82–83.
91. An Essay on Liberation, op. cit., p. 53; see too "Herbert Marcuse, Re-examination of the Concept of Revolution", p. 482.
92. One Dimensional Man, op. cit., p. xiii.
93. One Dimensional Man, op. cit., p. xiii.
93. One Dimensional Man, op. cit., p. 257.
94. Negations, op. cit., p. 42.
96. Herbert Marcuse, Eros and Civilization.
97. One Dimensional Man, op. cit.
98. One Dimensional Man, op. cit., p. 252..
99. One Dimensional Man, op. cit., p. 17, see too pp. xv, 23 and 253; see too Eros and Civilization, op. cit., pp. 90–91.
100. One Dimensional Man, op. cit., p. 253.

Chapter 2

1. Paul Robinson, in The Freudian Left, has noted this shift, and E. Fromm points out well the fundamental difference in the two positions when, speaking of the varying notions of the "mainsprings of man's actions", he states: "according to Freud they are rooted in Man's Libidinal strivings: according to Marx, they are rooted in the whole social organization of man which directs his consciousness in certain directions and blocks him från being aware of certain facts and experiences." (Erich Fromm, Marx's Concept of Man, p. 21.
2. Negations, op. cit., p. 193 (1938), see too p. 86.
3. On this point see also Paul Robinson's discussion of Marcuse in The Freudian Left, esp. pp. 183–4.
4. Negations, op. cit., p. 74, see too p. 86.
5. Negations, op. cit., p. 77.
6. Negations, op. cit., p. 121.
7. Herbert Marcuse, "Art as Form of Reality", pp. 57–58.
7 A. Eros and Civilization, op. cit., pp. 130–131.
8. Eros and Civilization, op. cit., p. 90.
9. Negations, op. cit., p. 86 (1936): Note the emphasis placed on changing essense.
10. Negations, op. cit., p. 90 (1938).
11. An Essay on Liberation, op. cit., p. 21.
12. An Essay on Liberation, op. cit., pp. 88–89.
13. Art as Form of Reality, pp. 57–58 (1972), see also reference to the same sentence in Marx in Herbert Marcuse, Counter-Revolution and Revolt, p. 74. This appears to be the only manifestation of Marx's 'vision' that Marcuse is able to come up with; see too Soviet Marxism, op. cit., pp. 114, 115, 118.
14. One Dimensional Man, op. cit., p. 23.
15. An Essay on Liberation, op. cit., p. 2, further and more comprehensive discussions of this point will be given in the following chapter.
16. Eros and Civilixation, op. cit., pp. 96–97.
17. Soviet Marxism, op. cit., pp. 114–115.
18. Eros and Civilization, op. cit., p. 113.
19. His doctoral work and much of his work in the thirties and forties was devoted to or centered around the ideas and notions of numerous of these philosophies. His views both implicitly and explicitly reflects the influence of many of the 'provocative' ideas of these philosophers.

20. See for example, Negations, op. cit., p. 51 (prelude to Eros); Eros and Civilization, op. cit., p. 177; Reason and Revolution, op. cit., p. 162 (Note the parallel to the notion of the tension between the reality principle and the pleasure principle.); Eros and Civilization, op. cit., p. 177; Negations, op. cit., pp. 174–176 (prelude to instinctual repression and false sensitivity); Reason and Revolution, op. cit., p. 21, (prelude to 'new rationality') and p. 149, (prelude to contrast between Pleasure Principle and Reality Principle).
21. Eros and Civilization, op. cit., p. 114.
22. Negations, op. cit., p. 151.
23. Eros and Civilization, op. cit., p. 114; Negations, op. cit., pp. 174–176.
24. Reason and Revolution, op. cit., pp. 149, 162.
25. Negations, op. cit., p. 51.
26. An Essay on Liberation, op. cit., pp. 28, 37–38.
27. Eros and Civilization, op. cit., p. 180.
28. Reason and Revolution, op. cit., pp. 20–21.
29. Eros and Civilization, op. cit., p. 130, see too p. 177.
30. Reason and Revolution, op. cit., p. 145.
31. One Dimensional Man, op. cit., p. xiv.
32. Reason and Revolution, op. cit., p. 113.
33. One Dimensional Man, op. cit., p. 13.
34. An Essay on Liberation, op. cit., p. 86.
35. One Dimensional Man, op. cit., p. 225.
36. Reason and Revolution, op. cit., p. xiv.
37. An Essay on Liberation, op. cit., p. 14.
38. Five Lectures, p. 96.
39. Negations, op. cit., p. 182.
40. Negations, op. cit., p. 182.
41. One Dimensional Man, op. cit., pp. 255, 253.
42. An Essay on Liberation, op. cit., p. 28.
43. Eros and Civilization, op. cit., p. 5, see too p. 12.
44. Negations, op. cit., pp. 57–58.
45. Five Lectures, op. cit., pp. 25–26.
46. Five Lectures, op. cit., pp. 6–7.
47. Negations, op. cit., pp. 257–8.
48. Eros and Civilization, op. cit., p. 24.
49. Five Lectures, op. cit., p. 3.
50. Five Lectures, op. cit., p. 7.
51. Five Lectures, op. cit., p. 21.
52 Five Lectures, op. cit., p. 21.
53. Negations, op. cit., p. 248.
54. Negations, op. cit., p. 57; see too Eros and Civilization, op. cit., p. ix.
55. Five Lectures, op. cit., pp. 6–7.
56. Eros and Civilization, op. cit., p. 14.
57. Eros and Civilization, op. cit., pp. 127–8.
58. Soviet Marxism, op. cit., p. 230.
59. See for example: An Essay on Liberation, op. cit., p. 16.
60. See for example: An Essay on Liberation, op. cit., p. 16.
61. See for example: An Essay on Liberation, op. cit., p. 10.
62. Five Lectures, op. cit., pp. 3, 11.
63. One Dimensional Man, op. cit., p. 23, see too pp. 6, 246.
64. An Essay on Liberation, op. cit., pp. 9–10.
65. Five Lectures, op. cit., pp. 45–47.
66. Five Lectures, op. cit., pp. 59–60, see too pp. 16–17.

67. Five Lectures, op. cit., p. 59, see too pp. 36–37.
68. One Dimensional Man, op. cit., p. 34.
69. Five Lectures, op. cit., pp. 55–56.
70. Soviet Marxism, op. cit., pp. ix–x.
71. Five Lectures, op. cit., pp. 55–56, see too p. 58.
72. An Essay on Liberation, op. cit., pp. 18–19.
73. An Essay on Liberation, op. cit., p. 13.
74. An Essay on Liberation, op. cit., p. 11, see too p. 5, and also Five Lectures, op. cit., p. 84.
75. One Dimensional Man, op. cit., p. 9.
76. An Essay on Liberation, op. cit., p. 7.
77. An Essay on Liberation, op. cit., p. 25.
78. An Essay on Liberation, op. cit., p. 15.
79. An Essay on Liberation, op. cit., p. 16.
80. An Essay on Liberation, op. cit., p. 15.
81. Five Lectures, op. cit., pp. 55–56.
82. Eros and Civilization, op. cit., p. 82, see too 83, 84.
83. Five Lectures, op. cit., p. 80, see too p. 99.
84. Soviet Marxism, op. cit., pp. 4–5.
85. See for example: Five Lectures, op. cit., pp. 4–5; and An Essay on Liberation, op. cit., p. 68.
86. An Essay on Liberation, op. cit., p. 15; One Dimensional Man, op. cit., p. 9.
87. Eros and Civilization, op. cit., p. 82,
88. An Essay on Liberation, op. cit., pp. 9–10.
89. An Essay on Liberation, op. cit., p. 53.
90. Negations, op. cit., p. xx.
91. An Essay on Liberation, op. cit., p. 83.
92. Five Lectures, op. cit., pp. 62–63, see too pp. 3–4, 53.
93. An Essay on Liberation, op. cit., p. 52.
94. It should of course be noted that the term 'subjective' factors has taken on a meaning somewhat different (or broader) than it had under the rubric at the traditional Marxist perspective.
95. Five Lectures, op. cit., p. 60.
96. An Essay on Liberation, op. cit., pp. viii–ix.
97. One Dimensional Man, op. cit., p. xiv.
98. One Dimensional Man, op. cit., p. 11.
99. Five Lectures, op. cit., pp. 5–6.
100. An Essay on Liberation, op. cit., pp. 20–21.
101. Five Lectures, op. cit., pp. 62–63.
102. Eros and Civilization, op. cit., p. 77.
103. Five Lectures, op. cit., p. 3, see too p. 24.
104. Five Lectures, op. cit., p. 20.
105. Five Lectures, op. cit., pp. 41–42.
106. Five Lectures, op. cit., p. 42.
107. Five Lectures, op. cit., p. 78, see too p. 24.
108. Eros and Civlization, op. cit., p. 196.
109. Eros and Civilization, op. cit., p. 140, see too 183.
110. Five Lectures, op. cit., p. 41.
111. Five Lectures, op. cit., pp. 4–6, see too p. 37.
112. But is it really 'Utopian' in the Marxist sense if techno-economic developments do in fact fully warrant such projections? Perhaps it is rather against certain 'reluctant' Marxist that Marcuse is levelling his critique.
113. An Essay on Liberation, op. cit., pp. 3–5.

114. Five Lectures, op. cit., p. 65.
115. An Essay on Liberation, op. cit., p. 23.
116. Eros and Civilization, op. cit., pp. 174–5, see too p. 183.
117. An Essay on Liberation, op. cit., p. 51.
118. Five Lectures, op. cit., p. 66.
119. An Essay on Liberation, op. cit., p. 53.
120. An Essay on Liberation, op. cit., pp. 9–10.
121. Herbert Marcuse, "Repressive Tolerance", p. 112.
122. Five Lectures, op. cit., pp. 46–47; see too Negations, op. cit., p. 258.
123. Repressive Tolerance, op. cit., p. 111.
124. An Essay on Liberation, op. cit., pp. 30–31.
125. Five Lectures, op. cit., p. 74.
126. An Essay on Liberation, op. cit., pp. 88–9.
127. Five Lectures, op. cit., pp. 65, 74.
128. Marcuse, as we have already seen, is not without appreciation of the unfortunate contradiction existing between what he sees as 'necessart' and the actual state of affairs, see Five Lectures, op. cit., p. 80.
129. An Essay on Liberation, op. cit., p. 7.
130. One Dimensional Man, op. cit., p. 6, see too p. 55.
131. One Dimensional Man, op. cit., pp. 40–41.
132. Five Lectures, op. cit., pp. 55–56, see too p. 38.
133. Eros and Civilization, op. cit., p. 206.
134. Repressive Tolerance, op. cit., p. 121; This line of thinking is reminiscent of numerous philosophers from Plato and his 'Philosopher Kings' to Karl Mannheim and his 'detached intelligentsia'. Now of course the notion has the 'firm basis', the 'truth' of Eros as its source of indisputable legitimacy.
135. An Essay on Liberation, o. cit., pp. 30–31.
136. Five Lectures, op. cit., p. 98.
137. An Essay on Liberation, op. cit., p. 84.
138. One Dimensional Man, op. cit., p. 17.
139. Five Lectures op. cit., pp. 14–15.
140. One Dimensional Man, op. cit., pp. 245–6.
141. One Dimensional Man, op. cit., p. 49.
142. Eros and Civilization, op. cit., p. 96.
143. Eros and Civilization, op. cit., p. 180; see too Five Lectures, o. cit., pp. 40, 56.
144. One Dimensional Man, op. cit., p. 246.
145. An Essay on Liberation, o. cit., pp. 27–28.
146. One Dimensional Man, op. cit., p. 252.
147. An Essay on Liberation, o. cit., pp. 3–5.
148. Art as Form of Reality, op. cit., pp. 54–57.
149. Soviet Marxism, op. cit., p. 120; see too An Essay on Liberation, op. cit., pp. 28, 37–38; and Negations, op. cit., pp. 154–5; and Reason and Revolution, op. cit., p. 21.
150. For examples of these 'new needs', see Five Lectures, op. cit., pp. 81–82, 65; and Negations, o. cit., p. 258.
151. An Essay on Liberation, o. cit., pp. 23–24.
152. An Essay on Liberation, op. cit., p. 23.
153. An Essay on Liberation, op. cit., p. 24.
154. An Essay on Liberation, o. cit., p. 24.
155. An Essay on Liberation, op. cit., p. 30.
156. Five Lectures, op. cit., p. 65.
157. An Essay on Liberation, op. cit., p. 88.
158. An Essay on Liberation, op. cit., p. 63.

159. Five Lectures, op. cit., pp. 75, 83; see too 'Art as Form of Reality', op. cit., p. 52; and An Essay on Liberation, op. cit., p. 60.
160. Five Lectures, op. cit., p. 97.
161. An Essay on Liberation, op. cit., p. 6.
162. An Essay on Liberation, op. cit., p. 46.
163. Art as Form of Reality, op. cit., p. 52; see too, An Essay on Liberation, op. cit., pp. 7, 60.
164. Art as Form of Reality, op. cit., p. 52.
165. Five Lectures, op. cit., p. 112; and An Essay on Liberation, op. cit., p. 61.
166. An Essay on Liberation, op. cit., p. 51.
167. Eros and Civilization, op. cit., pp. 87–89; see too Five Lectures, op. cit., p. 14–15.
168. Five Lectures, op. cit., pp. 45–47.
169. Repressive Tolerance, op. cit., p. 113.
170. An Essay on Liberation, op. cit., p. 61; and Five Lectures, op. cit., p. 112.
171. An Essay on Liberation, op. cit., p. 46.
172. An Essay on Liberation, op. cit., p. 30.
173. Soviet Marxism, op. cit., p. x.
174. Five Lectures, op. cit., p. 85.
175. Negations, op. cit., p. 224.
176. One Dimensional Man, op. cit., p. 30.
177. Five Lectures, op. cit., p. 71.
178. Negations, op. cit., p. 224.
179. An Essay on Liberation, op. cit., p. 59.
180. One Dimensional Man, op. cit., pp. 250–1.

Chapter 3

1. Soviet Marxism, op. cit., pp. 19–20, see too p. 60.
2. One Dimensional Man, op. cit., p. xiv.
3. E. Mandel, Europe vs. America, p. 476.
4. M. Kidron, Western Capitalism Since the War, p. 1.
5. Joseph D. Phillips, "Economic Effects of the Cold War", p. 189.
6. R. Kalko, The Roots of American Foreign Policy, p. 40.
7. P. Sweezy, Modern Capitalism and Other Essays, p. 12.
8. E. Mandel, The Decline of the Dollar, p. 82.
9. G. Adler-Karlsson, Western Economic Warfare 1945–1967, p. 5.
10. Ibid., p. 5.
11. Ibid., p. 5.
12. Ibid., p. 5.
13. Ibid., p. 6.
14. Ibid., p. 7.
15. Ibid., p. 7.
16. Ibid., p. 7.
17. Ibid., p. 3.
18. Europe vs. America, op. cit., p. 11.
19. Ibid., p. 11.
20. Ibid., pp. 11–12.
21. See Charles Kindelberger, Europe's Postwar Growth.
22. Europe vs. America, op. cit., p. 13.
23. E. Mandel, Marxist Economic Theory, pp. 393–4.
24. Europe vs. America, op. cit., p. 13.
25. Ibid., pp. 13–14.
26. Modern Capitalism, op. cit., pp. 12–13.

27. Nixon on C.B.S. News, March 15, 1974.
28. J. Connally quoted in U.S. News and World Report, June 14, 1971, pp. 52–53.
29. Europe vs. America, op. cit., p. 13.
30. Bob Rawthorn, "Imperialism in the Seventies—Unity or Rivalry?", p. 33; see too H. Magdoff and P. Sweezy, The Dynamics of U.S. Capitalism pp. 198–199 for a discussion of the recent U.S. shift to just such a policy.
31. H. Magdoff, The Age of Imperialism, pp. 41–42.
32. Bob Rawthorn, op. cit., p. 41; see too E. Mandel, "Where is America Going?", p. 13; and also G. Novack in E. Mandel and G. Novack, "The Revolutionary Potential of the Working Class", p. 31.
33. "Where is America Going?", op. cit., p. 57, see too Marxist Economic Theory, op. cit., p. 146; and "On the Revolutionary Potential of the working Class:, op. cit., p. 31.
34. R. B. Sutcliffe and A. Glyn, British Capitalism, Workers, and the Profit Squeeze, p. 57.
35. C. Levinson, Capital, Inflation and the Multinationals, p. 113.
36. See also J. Halliday and G. McGormack, "Japan and America: Antagonistic Allies", p. 70, regarding this possibility, and G. W. Domhoff, "Who Made American Foreign Policy 1945–1963?", p. 201.
37. "Where is America Going?", op. cit., p. 12.
38. Europe vs. America, op. cit., p. 16; see too Y. Varga, Politico-Economic Problems of Capitalism, pp. 229–230.
39. Bob Rawthorn, op. cit., p. 35.
40. Ibid., p. 35.
41. Ibid., p. 35.
42. Politico-Economic Problems of Capitalism, op. cit., p. 229; see too Europe vs. America, op. cit., p. 9.
43. C. Levinson, op. cit., p. 171; see too Decline of the Dollar, op. cit., p. 83; and "Japan and America: Antagonistic Allies", op. cit., p. 70.
44. Bob Rawthorn, op. cit., p. 70.
45. Decline of the Dollar, op. cit., p. 83; see also Europe vs. America, op. cit., pp. 9, 16; and also Politico-Economic Problems of Capitalism, op. cit., p. 229.
46. Bob Rawthorn, op. cit., p. 45; see too "Japan and America: Antagonistic Allies", op. cit., p. 70.
47. Europe vs. America, op. cit., p. 28.
48. "Japan and America: Antagonistic Allies", op. cit., p. 66.
49. Decline of the Dollar, op. cit., p. 11.
50. H. Magdoff, "Is imperialism Really Necessary?", p. 9.
51. T. Szentes, The Political Economy of Undevelopment, pp. 168, 173; see too, "Is Imperialism Really Necessary", op. cit., p. 229.
52. P. Kolko, op. cit., p. 86.
53. The Age of Imperialism, op. cit., p. 166.
54. The Age of Imperialism, op. cit., pp. 166, 173; see too "Is Imperialism Really Necessary?", op. cit., p. 9.
55. Japan and America: Antagonistic Allies, op. cit., pp. 68–69.
56. Jon Halliday, "Washington vs. Tokyo: Wall Street vs. Maranouchi", p. 46.
57. "Japan and America: Antagonistic Allies, op. cit., pp. 64–65.
58. J. Halliday and G. McGormack, Japanese Imperialism Today, pp. 232, 237.
59. See C. Levinson, op. cit., for a discussion of this point.
60. Japanese Imperialism Today, op. cit., pp. 232¹/7.
61. Politico-Economic Problems of Capitalism, op. cit., p. 230; see too "Is Imperialism Really Necessary?", p. 9.
62. R. B. Sutcliffe and A. Glyn, op. cit., p. 90.

74. Automation and Management, op. cit., pp. 176–7; see too Most Notorious Victory, op. cit., p. 222; and The Effect of Recent . . . , op. cit., p. 182.
75. Automation and Management, op. cit., pp. 17, and 194–195.
76. Ibid., p. 179.
77. Ibid., pp. 176–177; see too 'Fortune' Jan–Feb 1965, Quoted in The Effects of Recent . . . , op. cit., p. 182.
78. Does Automation Raise Skill Requirements?", op. cit., p. 97.
79. Automation and Management, op. cit., p. 179.
80. "Does Automation Raise Skill Requirements?", op. cit., p. 86.
81. Most Notorious Victory, op. cit., p. 117.
82. Automation and Management, op. cit., pp. 176–177.
83. S. Aronoqitz, op. cit., p. 206.
84. Automation and Management, op. cit., p. 12.
85. 20th Century Capitalism, op. cit., p. 130.
86. Automation and Management, op. cit., p. 189.
87. Ibid., p. 177.
88. "Does Automation Raise Skill Requirements?", op. cit., p. 90; see also C. Walker, Toward the Automatic Factory, New Haven, Yale University Press, 1957; see too One Dimensional Man, op. cit., pp. 25–30.
89. "Does Automation Raise Skill Requirements?", op. cit., p. 90.
90. Ibid., p. 90.
91. Most Notorious Victory, op. cit., p. 223; see too, "Does Automation Raise Skill Requirements?", op. cit., p. 91.
92. The Effect of Recent . . . , op. cit., p. 163.
93. Most Notorious Victory, op. cit., pp. 212 and 216; see too, The Effect of Recent . . . , op. cit., p. 163.
94. The Effect of Recent . . . , op. cit.
95. R. A. Solon, Beyond the Stable State.
96. Most Notorious Victory, op. cit.,
97. "Does Automation Raise Skill Requirements?", op. cit.,
98. The Effect of Recent . . . , op. cit., p. 163; see too Automation and Management, op. cit., pp. 195–197.
99. Most Notorious Victory, op. cit., pp. 126–7.
100. Ibid., p. 216.
101. The Effect of Recent . . . , op. cit., pp. 132–133.
102. "Future Failure: the Unanticipated Consequences of Educational Planning, op. cit., p. 251.
103. G. Fischer, The Revival of American Socialism, p. 208.
104. Most Notorious Victory, op. cit., p. 223.
105. The Effect of Recent . . . , op. cit., p. 205.
106. Ibid., p. 184.
107. Most Notorious Victory, op. cit., pp. 211–212.
108. B. B. Seligman, Economics of Dissent, p. 185.
109. Ibid., p. 185.
110. Ibid., p. 186.
111. Ibid., p. 186.
112. The Effect of Recent . . . , op. cit., p. 197.
113. Economics of Dissent, op. cit., pp. 184–185.
114. G. W. Domhoff, Who Rules America?", p. 149.
1s5. Ibid., pp. 148–149.
116. Ibid., pp. 49–50.
117. Ibid., pp. 49–50.
118. Economics of Dissent, op. cit., p. 188; see too G. W. Domhoff, op. cit., p. 148.

119. The Effect of Recent . . ., op. cit., p. 197; see also, Most Notorious Victory, op. cit., p. 191.
120. The Effect of Recent . . ., op. cit., p. 190.
121. E. Geltman and S. Plastrik, "Labor's Decade . . . Maybe", p. 366.
122. S. Aronowitz, op. cit., p. 207.
123. Ibid., p. 206.
124. Most Notorious Victory, op. cit., p. 218.
125. An Essay on Liberation, op. cit., p. 55; see also "Workers and Permanent Revolution", op. cit., p. 176.
126. An Essay on Liberation, op. cit., p. 16.
127. One Dimensional Man, op. cit., p. 32.
128. An Essay on Liberation, op. cit., p. 15.
129. T. B. Bottomore, Classes in Modern Society, p. 77.
130. Ibid., p. 70.
131. J. C. Leggett, Class, Race and Labor, pp. 43, 70, 79.
132. Ibid., p. 3.
133. Ibid., p. 43, see too p. 79; see also Class and Politics in the United States, op. cit., p. 144.
134. J. C. Leggett, op. cit., p. 16.
135. T. B. Bottomore, op. cit., p. 30.
136. Poverty as a Public Issue, op. cit., p. 52; see also R. Sutcliffe and A. Glyn, op. cit., pp. 209–210.
137. J. C. Leggett, op. cit., p. 153.
138. Ibid., pp. 20 and 153; see also "Workers and Permanent Revolution", op. cit., p. 181.
139. M. Nicolaus, op. cit., p. 7; see too D. M. Gordon, op. cit., p. 74.
140. J. C. Leggett, op. cit.
141. Ibid., pp. 79, 94 and 139.
142. Ibid., p. 94.
143. Ibid., pp. 74–75.
144. Ibid., p. 143.
145. Ibid., p. 129.
146. R. F. Hamilton, Class and Race in the United States.
147. Ibid., pp. 104–105, see too p. 106.
148. T. B. Bottomore, op. cit., p. 46.
149. J. C. Leggett, op. cit., p. 15.
150. D. Drache, Quebec . . . Only the Begijning, p. xviii; see also J. C. Leggett, op. cit., p. 16.
151. I have personally been involved in and a witness to two such events as a member of the Western Canadian Section of the International Woodworkers of America.
152. Class and Politics in the United States, op. cit., p. 309.
153. J. O'Connor, "Merging Thought with Feeling", p. 25.
154. J. C. Leggett, op. cit., pp. 74–75, 116 and 94.
155. Ulf Himmelstrand and Jan Linhagen, "The Rejected Status Seeker in Mass Politics: Fact and Fiction»».
156. R. F. Hamilton, "A Note on Skill Level and Politics", Public Opinion Quarterly, 1968.
157. J. C. Leggett op. cit., p. 142.
158. "Workers and Permanent Revolution", op. cit., p. 76.
159. D. Drache, op. cit.,
160. S. Aronqitz, op. cit., pp. 190 and 213; see too "Workers and Permanent Revolution," op. cit., p. 176.
161. Modern Capitalism, op. cit., p. vii.

162. H. Lefebvre, The Explosion, p. 102; see too "Workers and Permanent Revolution", op. cit., p. 185.
163. Five Lectures, op. cit., p. 71.
164. An Essay on Liberation, op. cit., p. 59.
165. Five Lectures, op. cit., p. 75.
166. "Art as Form of Reality", op. cit., p. 52.
167. An Essay on Liberation, op. cit., p. 63.
168. Ibid., p. 51.
169. The Effects of Recent ..., op. cit.
170. T. Roszak, op. cit., p. 28.
171. "Future Failure: The Unanticipated Consequences of Educational Planning", op. cit., p. 24.
172. E. Kohák, "Being Young in Post-Industrial Society", p. 32; see too, The Effects of Recent ..., op. cit., p. 223.
173. G. L. Boggs, "Education: The Great Obsession", p. 23.
174. "Future Failure: the Unanticipated Consequences of Educational Planning", op. cit., p. 3.
175. Ibid., p. 24.
176. Ibid., p. 35.
177. S. Aronowitz, op. cit., p. 207; and The Effects of Recent ... op. cit., pp. 164–165.
178. "Future Failure: the Unanticipated Consequences of Educational Planning", op. cit., p. 30.
179. R. A. Lockhart, "Graduate Unemployment and the Myth of Human Capital", p. 253.
180. The Effect of Recent ..., op. cit., p. 205.
181. "Graduate Unemployment and the Myth of Human Capital", op. cit., p. 273.
182. The Effect of Recent ..., op. cit., p. 228.
183. Ibid., p. 251.
184. The Explosion, op. cit., p. 67.
185. See earlier discussions of economic stagnation, unemployment, and the impact of technology on the new working class.
186. E. Kohák, op. cit., p. 31. The author, however, has apparently not gr grasped the full implicatons and roots of the problem.
187. The Explosion, op. cit., p. 67.
188. "Future Failure: the Unanticipated Consequences of Educational Planning", op. cit., p. 32.

Chapter 5

1. Eros and Civilization, op. cit., pp. 127–128.
2. L. Henderson, "On Mental Energy", p. 1; H. K. Wells, Sigmund Freud, p. 69; see also S. Freud quoted on P. 70.
3. L. Henderson, op. cit., p. 1.
4. E. Fronm, Marx's Concept of Man, pp. 78–79.
5. See S. Freud, quoted in "Sigmund Freud" by H. R. Wells, pp. 71–72.
6. D. Shakow and D. Rapaport, The Influence of Freud on American Psychology, p. 114.
7. R. R. Sears, Survey of Objective Studies of Psychoanalytic Concepts, p. 1; see also H. K. Wells, 'Sigmund Freud', p. 71.
8. Quoted in H. K. Wells, The Failure of Psychoanalysis, p. 57.
9. Quoted in H. K. Wells, 'Sigmund Freud', p. 71.
10. Quoted in, Ibid., p. 71.
11. R. R. Sears, op. cit., p. 22.

12. R. Fletcher, Instinct in Man, p. 178.
13. Quoted in H. K. Wells, 'Sigmund Freud', p. 70.
14. Quoted in Ibid., p. 73.
15. A. E. Ellis, "An Introduction to the Principles of Scientific Psychoanalysis", p. 105.
16. L. Henderson, op. cit., p. 3.
17. A. E. Ellis, op. cit., p. 105; see also L. Henderson, op. cit., p. 1.
18. See L. Henderson, op. cit., pp. 6–7; see too A. E. Ellis, op. cit., p. 85.
19. L. Henderson, op. cit., p. 1.
20. A. E. Ellis, op. cit., p. 86.
21. L. Henderson, op. cit., p. 1.
22. H. K. Wells, Ivan Pavlov, p. 35.
23. A. Salter, The Case Against Psychoanalysis, p. 157.
24. See for example, Instinct. In Man, op. cit., p. 83.
25. A. E. Ellis, op. cit., pp. 105–106; see too L. Hendersson, op. cit., p. 1.
26. H. K. Wells, 'Sigmund Freud', pp. 70–71.
27. See particularly Five Lectures, op. cit.; "Art As Form of Reality", op. cit.; An Essay on Liberation, op. cit.; and Counter-Revolution and Revolt, op. cit.

Bibliography

Adler-Karlsson, Gunnar, *Western Economic Warefare 1947–1967*, Uppsala, Almqvist & Wiksell A. B., 1968.

Albinowski, Stanislow, *Commercial Policy of the E. E. C.*, Warsaw, Western Press Agency, 1965.

Aronowitz, Stanley, "Does the United States Have a New Working Class?" in George Fischer (ed.), *The Revival of American Socialism*, New York, Oxford University Press, 1971.

Arrighi, Giovanni, "International Corporations, Labor Aristocracies, and Economic Development in Tropical Africa", in R. I. Rhodes (ed.), *Imperialism and Underdevelopment*, New York, Monthly Review Press, 1970.

Bailey, P., "The Great Psychiatric Revolution", in Stanley Rachman (ed.), *Critical Essays on Psychoanalysis*, New York, Pergamon Press, 1963.

Bain, George Sayers, *The Growth of White Collar Unionism*, London, Ozford University Press, 1970.

Baran, Paul A., *The Longer View*, New York, Monthly Review Press 1970.

Baran, Paul A., *The Political Economy of Growth*, New York, Monthly Review Press, 1957.

Baran, Paul A. and Paul M. Sweezy, *Monopoly Capital*, New York, Monthly Review Press, 1966.

Beckford, George L., *Persistent Poverty*, London, Oxford University Press, 1972.

Bell, Daniel, *Work and Its Discontents*, Boston, Beacon Press, 1956.

Berger, Peter L. and Thomas Luckmann, *The Social Construction of Reality*, New York, Doubleday & Co., 1966.

Berle, A. A. and Means, *The Modern Corporation and Private Property*, New York, 1932.

Bluestone, Barry, "Capitalism and Poverty in America: A Discussion", *Monthly Review*, Vol. 24 (1972), pp. 65–71.

Boggs, Grace Lee, "Education: The Great Obsession", *Monthly Review*, Vol. 22 (1970), pp. 18–39.

Bottomore, T. B., *Classes in Modern Society*, London, George Allen & Unwin Ltd., 1965.

Bright, James A., *Automation and Management*, New York, Plimten Press, 1958.

Bright, James A., "Does Automation Raise Skill Requirements?", *Harvard Business Review*, July–August 1958.

Bright, James A., *Research, Development and Technological Innovation*, Homewood (Illinois), R. D. Irwin Inc., 1964.

Bright, James A., "Skill Requirements and Wage Aspects of Automation", paper delivered at the U.S. Labor Relations Council Conference, Washington, D.C., November 8, 1960.

Brown, J. A. C., *Freud and the Post-Freudians*, Harmondsworth, Penguin Books, 1961.

Childe, V. G., *Society and Knowledge*, London, George Allen & Unwin, 1958.

Confédération des Syndicats Nationaux (Confederation of National Trade Unions), "It's Up to Us: C. S. N. Manifesto", Daniel Drache (ed.), *Quebec—Only the Beginning*, Toronto, New Press, 1972.

Cooper, David (ed.), *The Dialectics of Liberation,* Harmondsworth, Penguin Books, 1968.

Corporation des enseignants du Québec (Quebec Teachers Corporation), "Phase One: C. E. Q. Manifesto", in Daniel Drache (ed.), *Quebec—Only the Beginning,* Toronto, New Press, 1972.

Dobb, Maurice, *Capitalism Yesterday and Today,* London, Lawrence & Wishart, 1958.

Dobb, Maurice, *Economic Growth and Underdeveloped Countries,* London, Lawrence & Wishart, 1963.

Domhoff, G. William, *Who Rules America?,* Englewood Cliffs (N.J.), Prentice-Hall, 1967.

Drache, Daniel, *Quebec—Only the Beginning,* Toronto, New Press, 1972.

Duboff, Richard, "Trade War Exercises", *Canadian Dimension,* Vol. 9, No. 6 –July 1973), pp. 37–44.

Eakins, David W., "Business Planners and America's Postwar Expansion", in David Horowitz (ed.), *Corporations and the Cold War,* New York, Monthly Review Press, 1969.

Ellis, A. E., "An Introduction to the Principles of Scientific Psychoanalysis", in Stanley Rachman (ed.), *Critical Essays on Psychoanalysis,* New York, Pergamon Press, 1963.

Emmanuel, Arghiri, *Unequal Exchange,* New York, Monthly Review Press, 1972.

Eysenck, H. J., "Psychoanalysis—Myth or Science?", in Stanley Rachman (ed.), *Critical Essays on Psychoanalysis,* New York, Pergamon Press, 1963.

Fine, Reuben, *Freud: A Critical Re-evaluation of His Theoreis,* New York, Van Rees Press, 1962.

Fischer, George (ed.), *The Revival of American Socialism,* New York, Oxford University Press, 1971.

Fletcher, Ronald, *Instinct in Man,* London, George Allen & Unwin, 1957.

Foster, W. T. and W. Catchings, *Money,* Boston, Houghton & Mifflin, 1925.

Frank, Andre Gunder, *Latin America: Underdevelopment or Revolution,* New York, Monthly Review Press, 1969.

Freud, S., *Beyond the Pleasure Principle,* New York, Liveright, 1950.

Freud, S., *Civilization and Its Discontents,* New York, W. W. Norton and Co., 1961.

Fromm, Erich, *Marx's Concept of Man,* New York, Frederick Ungar Publ. Co., 1961.

Geltmann, Emanuel and Stanley Plastrik, "Labor's Decade—Maybe", *Dissent,* August 1971, pp. 365–375.

Gerassi, John, "Imperialism and Revolution in America", in David Cooper (ed.), *The Dialectics of Liberation,* Harmondsworth, Penguin Books, 1968.

Goldfinger, M., "Capitalist Planning and the State", *Dissent,* April 1971.

Goldmann, L., *The Human Sciences and Philosophy,* London, Cape, 1969.

Gordon, David M., "American Poverty: Functions, Mechanisms, and Contradictions", *Monthly Review,* Vol. 24 (1972) pp. 72–79.

Gorz, Andre, *Strategy for Labor,* Boston, Beacon Press, 1964.

Guevara, Che, *The Diary of Che Guevara,* New York, Bantam, 1968.

Halliday, Jon, "Washington v. Tokyo: Wall Street v. Maranouchi", *New Left Review,* May–June 1971, pp. 39–46.

Halliday, Jon and Gavan McCormack, "Japan and America: Antagonistic Allies", *New Left Review,* January–February 1973, pp. 59–76.

Halliday, Jon and Gavan McCormack, *Japanese Imperialism Today,* New York, Monthly Review Press, 1973.

Hamilton, Richard F., *Class and Politics in the United States,* New York, John Wiley & Sons, 1972.

Hamilton, Richard F., "Class and Race in the United States", in George Fischer (ed.), *The Revival of American Socialism,* New York, Oxford University Press, 1971.

Harris, Marvid, *The Rise of Anthropological Theory,* New York, Thomas Y. Crowell Co., 1968.

Henderson, Leslie, "On Mental Energy", *The British Journal of Psychology,* Vol. 63, Part 1 (February 1972), pp. 1–7.

Himmelstrand, Ulf and Jon Lindhagen, *The Rejected Status-Seeker in Mass Politics: Fact and Fiction,* Public Opinion Quarterly 1970.

Horowitz, David (ed.), *Containment and Revolution,* Boston, Beacon Press 1967.

Horowitz, David (ed.), *Corporation and the Cold War,* New York, Monthly Review Press, 1969.

Horowitz, David, *Imperialism and Revolution,* London, Allen Lane, 1969.

Horowitz, David (ed.), *Marx and Modern Economics,* New York, Monthly Review Press, 1968.

Jallée, Pierre, *The Pillage of the Third World,* New York, Monthly Review Press, 1968.

Jallée, Pierre, *The Third World in World Economy,* New York, Monthly Review Press, 1969.

Kaysen, Carl, "The Social Significance of the Modern Corporation", *American Economic Review,* April 6, 1960.

Kemp, Tom, *Theories of Imperialism,* London, Dobson Books, 1967.

Kidron, Michael, *Western Capitalism Since the War,* London, Weidenfeld & Nicolson, 1967.

Kindelberger, Charles, *Europés Postwar Growth,* Cambridge, Harvard University Press, 1967.

Kohák, Erazim, "Being Young in Post-Industrial Society", *Dissent,* February 1971, pp. 30–41.

Kolko, Gabriel, *The Roots of American Foreign Policy,* Boston, Beacon Press, 1970.

Lange, Oscar, "Marxian Economics and Modern Economic Theory", in David Horowitz (ed.), *Marx and Modern Economics,* New York, Monthly Review Press, 1968.

Lasch, Christopher, "From Politics to Culture", in George Fischer (ed.), *The Revival of American Socialism,* New York, Oxford University Press 1971.

Lefebvre, Henri, *The Explosion,* New York, Monthly Review Press, 1969.

Lefebvre, Henri, *The Sociology of Marx,* New York, Vintage, 1969.

Leggett, John C., *Class, Race, and Labor,* New York, Oxbord University Press, 1968.

Levinson, Charles, *Capital, Inflation and the Multinationals,* London, George Allen & Unwin, 1971.

Lipset, S. M., *Rebellion in the University,* Boston, Little Brown & Co., 1972.

Lipset, S. M. and S. S. Wolin, *The Berkley Student Revolt,* Garden City, N. Y. Anchor Books, 1965.

Lockhart, Alexander, "Graduate Unemployment and the Myth of Human Capital", in D. I. Davies and Kathleen Herman (eds.), *Social Space: Canadian Perspectives,* Toronto, New Press, 1971, pp. 251–254.

Lockhart, Alexander, *The Effect of Recent Techno-Economic Changes on the Mobility Patterns and Opportunities of the American Middle Class with Particular Emphasis on Emergent Contradictions Between Occupational and Educational Factors,* unpublished M.A. thesis, Simon Fraser University, Burnaby, B. C., Canada, August 1970.

Lockhart, Alexander, "Future Failure: The Unanticipated Consequences of Educational Planning", in F. Pike and E. Zurick (eds.), *Socialization: Canadian Perspectives,* Toronto, New Press, 1973.

Magdoff, H., *The Age of Imperialism,* New York, Monthly Review Press, 1969.

181

Magdoff, H., "The American Empire and the U.S. Economy", in Robert I. Rhodes (ed.), *Imperialism and Underdevelopment*, New York, Monthly Review Press, 1970.

Magdoff, H., "The Economic Aspects of Imperialism", in George Fischer (ed.), *The Revival of American Socialism*, New York, Oxford University Press, 1971.

Magdoff, H., "Is Imperialism Really Necessary?", *Monthly Review*, Vol. 22, No. 5, (1970) pp. 1–14.

Magdoff, H., "Is Imperialism Really Necessary?, *Monthly Review*, Vol. 22, No. 6, (1970) pp. 1–13.

Magdoff, H. and Paul M. Sweezy, *The Dynamics of U.S. Capitalism*, New York, Monthly Review Press, 1972.

Magodoff, H. and Paul M. Sweezy, "Economic Stagnation and the Stagnation of Economics", *Monthly Review*, Vol. 22, No. 11, (1971), pp. 1–11.

Magdoff, H. and Paul M. Sweezi, "The Long-Run Decline in Liquidity", *Monthly Review*, Vol. 22, No. 4, (1970), pp. 1–17.

Magdoff, H. and Paul M. Sweezy, "The Mind of the Ruling Class", *Monthly Review*, Vol. 24, No. 2, (1972), pp. 1–15.

Magdoff, H. and Paul M. Sweezy, "War and Crisis", *Monthly Review*, Vol. 22, No. 2, (1970), pp. 1–12.

Mandel, Ernest, *Decline of the Dollar*, New York, Monad Press, 1972.

Mandel, Ernest, *Decline of the Dollar*, New York, Monthly Review Press, 1970.

Mandel, Ernst, *An Introduction to Marxist Economic Theory*, New York, Young Socialist Alliance, 1967.

Mandel, Ernest, *Marxist Economic Theory*, Vols. I & II, London, Merlin Press, 1968.

Mandel, Ernest, "Where is America Going?", *New Left Review*, No. 54, (March–April 1969).

Mandel, Ernest, "Workers and Permanent Revolution", in George Fischer (ed.), *The Revival of American Socialism*, New York, Oxford University Press, 1971.

Mandel, Ernest and George Novack, *On the Revolutionary Potential of the Working Class*, New York, Merit Publishers, 1969.

Marcuse, Herbert, "Art as Form of Reality", *New Left Review*, No. 74, (July–August 1972), pp. 51–59.

Marcuse, Herbert, "The Complete Text of a Talk Given at the 20th Anniversary Program of the Guardian", taped by Radio Free People and transcribed by Liberation News Service, 1969.

Marcuse, Herbert, "The Containment of Social Change in Industrial Society", unpublished text of Herbert Marcuse's Tuesday Evening Lecture on May 4, 1965, Fred Goff, Box 2123, Stanford, California, U.S.A.

Marcuse, Herbert, *Counter-Revolution and Revolt*, Boston, Beacon Press, 1972.

Marcuse, Herbert, *Eros and Civilization*, New York, Vintage Books, 1962.

Marcuse, Herbert, *An Essay on Liberation*, Boston, Beacon Press, 1969.

Marcuse, Herbert, *Five Lectures*, Boston, Beacon Press, 1970.

Marcuse, Herbert, "Liberation from the Affluent Society", 1970.

Marcuse, Herbert, "Liberation from the Affluent Society", in David Cooper (ed.), *The Dialectics of Liberation*, Harmondsworth, Penguin Books, 1968.

Marcuse, Herbert, "Liberation in Advanced Industrial Societies", a talk given at Simon Fraser University, Burnaby, B. C., Canada, and taped by the Department of Political Science, Sociology and Anthropology, 1969.

Marcuse, Herbert, *Negations*, Boston, Beacon Press, 1968.

Marcuse, Herbert, *One-Dimensional Man*, Boston, Beacon Press, 1964.

Marcuse, Herbert, *Reason and Revolution*, Boston, Beacon Press, 1960.

Marcuse, Herbert, "Re-examination of the Concept of Revolution", in *Marx and Contemporary Scientific Thought*,

Marcuse, Herbert, "Repressive Tolerance", in Wolf, R. P., Moore, Barrington, Jr., and Marcuse, H. (eds.), *A Critique of Pure Tolerance*, Boston, Beacon Press, 1965.

Marcuse, Herbert, "Sartre's Existentialism", in G. Novack (ed.), *Existentialism vs. Marxism*, New York, Dell, 1966.

Marcuse, Herbert, *Soviet Marxism*, New York, Vintage Books, 1961.

Marcuse, Herbert, *Studies in Critical Philosophy*, Boston, Beacon Press, 1972.

Montagu, Ashley, *Life Before Birth*, New York, Signet, 1965.

Miller, Herman P., "The Dimensions of Poverty", in Ben B. Seligman (ed.), *Poverty as a Public Issue*, New York, Free Press, 1965.

Mills, C. Wright, *Power, Politics and People*, New York, Oxford University Press, 1963.

Morril, Richard C. and Ernst H. Wohlenberg, *The Geography of Poverty in the United States*, New York, McGraw-Hill, 1971.

Nathanson, Charles F., "The Militarization of the American Economy" in David Horowitz (ed.), *Corporation and the Cold War*, New York, Monthly Review Press, 1969.

Nicolaus, Martin, "The Crisis of Late Capitalism", in George Fischer (ed.), *The Revival of American Socialism*, New York, Oxford University Press, 1971.

Novack, George, *Existentialism versus Marxism: Conflicting views on Humanism*, New York, Dell, 1966.

O'Connor, James R., "Merging Thought With Feeling", in George Fischer (ed.), *The Revival of American Socialism*, New York, Oxford University Press, 1971.

O'Connor, James R., "The Meaning of Economic Imperialism", in Robert I. Rhodes (ed.), *Imperialism and Underdevelopment*, New York, Monthly Review Press, 1970.

Phillips, Joseph D., "Economic Effects of the Cold War", in David Horowitz (ed.), *Corporations and the Cold War*, New York, Monthly Review Press, 1969.

Pike, F. and E. Zurick, (eds.), *Socialism: Canadian Perspectives*, Toronto, New Press, 1973.

Pitts, Jesse, "The Counter Culture: Tranquilizer or Revolutionary Ideology?", *Dissent*, June 1971, pp. 216–229.

Rachman, Stanley (ed.), *Critical Essays on Psychoanalysis*, London, Pergamon Press, 1963.

Rhodes, Robert I. (ed.), *Imperialism and Underdevelopment*, New York, Monthly Review Press, 1970.

Robinson, Paul A., *The Freudian Left*, New York, Harper & Row, 1969.

Roszak, Theodore, *The Marking of A Counter Culture*, New York, Doubleday, 1969.

Rowthorn, Bob, "Imperialism in the Seventies—Unity of Rivalry?", *New Left Review*, No. 69 (September–October 1971), pp. 31–54.

Salter, Andrew, *The Case Against Psychoanalysis*, New York, Capricorn Books, 1949.

Schon, D. A., "Beyond the Stable State", New York, Random House, 1971.

Sears, Robert R., *Survey of Objective Studies of Psychoanalytic Concepts*, New York, Social Science Research Council, 1942.

Seligman, Ben B., *Economics of Dissent*, Chicago, Quadrangle, 1968.

Seligman, Ben B., *Most Notorious Victory*, New York, Free Press, 1966.

Seligman, Ben B. (ed.), *Poverty as a Public Issue*, New York, Free Press, 1965.

Shakow, David and David Rapaport, *The Influence of Freud on American Psychology*, New York, Meredian, 1968.

Sheppart, Harrold L., "Poverty of Aging", in Ben B. Seligman (ed.), *Poverty as a Public Issue*, New York, Free Press, 1965.

Sherwood, Michael, *The Logic of Explanation in Psychoanalysis*, New York, Academic Press, 1969.

Sutcliffe, R. B., *Industry and Underdevelopment*, London, Addison-Wesley, 1971.

Sutcliffe, R. B. and Andrew Glyn, *British Capitalism, Workers and the Profit Squeeze*, Harmondsworth, Penguin Books, 1972.

Sweezy, Paul M., "The Future of Capitalism", in David Cooper (ed.), *The Dialectics of Liberation*, Harmondworth, Penguin Books, 1968.

Sweezy, Paul M., *Modern Capitalism and Other Essays*, New York, Monthly Review Press, 1972.

Sweezy, Paul M., *The Theory of Capitalist Development*, New York, Monthly Review Press, 1968.

Sweezy, Paul M., "Workers and the Third World", in George Fischer (ed.), *The Revival of American Socialism*, New York, Oxford University Press, 1971.

Szentes, Tamas, *The Political Economy of Underdevelopment*, Budapest, 1970.

U.S. Government Printing Office, *Measures of Productive Capacity*, Hearings before the Subcommittee on Economic Statistics of the Joint Economic Committee", Washington, D.C., 1962.

Varga, Y., *Politico-Economic Problems of Capitalism*, Moscow, Progress Publishers, 1968.

Varga, Y., *20th Century Capitalism*, London, Lawrence & Wishart, 1963.

Wachtel, Howard M., "Capitalism and Poverty in America: Paradox or Contradiction?: *Montly Review*, Vol. 24, No. 2 (1972), pp. 55–61.

Warren, Bill, "Capitalist Planning and the State", *New Left Review*, No. 72 (March–April 1972), pp. 3–30.

Warren, Bill, "Imperialism and Capitalist Industrialization", *New Left Review*, No. 81 (September–October 1973).

Wells, Harry K., *The Failure of Psychoanalysis*, New York, International Publishers, 1963.

Wells, Harry K., *Ivan Pavlov*, New York, International Publishers, 1956.

Wells, Harry K., *Sigmund Freud*, New York, International Publishers, 1960.

Whistler, L. T., *The Impact of Computers on Organizations*.

Williams, William Appleman, "The Large Corporation and American Foreign Policy", in David Horowitz (ed.), *Corporations and the Cold War*, New York, Monthly Review Press, 1969.